A Year with Martin Buber

JPS Daily Inspiration Series

University of Nebraska Press
Lincoln

A Year with Martin Buber

Wisdom on the Weekly Torah Portion

RABBI DENNIS S. ROSS

The Jewish Publication Society
Philadelphia

Passages and reflections by Rabbi Chaim Stern
used with permission from Lea Lane.

Acknowledgments for the use of copyrighted
material appear on pages 275–77, which constitute
an extension of the copyright page.

Library of Congress Cataloging-in-Publication Data
Names: Ross, Dennis S. (Dennis Sidney), 1953– author.
Title: A year with Martin Buber: wisdom on the weekly
Torah portion / Rabbi Dennis S. Ross.
Description: Lincoln: University of Nebraska Press,
2021. | Series: JPS Daily Inspiration | Includes
bibliographical references.
Identifiers: LCCN 2021007572
ISBN 9780827614659 (paperback)
ISBN 9780827618848 (epub)
ISBN 9780827618855 (pdf)
Subjects: LCSH: Bible. Pentateuch—Commentaries. |
Buber, Martin, 1878–1965—Teachings. |
Buber, Martin, 1878–1965.
Classification: LCC BS1225.53 .R6767 2021 |
DDC 222/.107—dc23
LC record available at https://lccn.loc.gov/2021007572

Set in Merope Basic by Mikala R. Kolander.

To Debbie and our loving family,
Joshua and Sam, Adam, Eliya and Libi,
and Miriam, and my mother, Sara,
and Debbie's mother, Rita.

Contents

II. EXODUS (SHEMOT)

III. LEVITICUS (VA-YIKRA')

IV. NUMBERS (BE-MIDBAR)

V. DEUTERONOMY (DEVARIM)

Acknowledgments

I thank my colleagues Rabbi Tom Alpert, Rabbi Stuart Geller, Rabbi Earl Grollman, and Rabbi Dan Ornstein for their continuing and caring involvement as well as my teachers of blessed memory: Rabbi Eugene Borowitz, Rabbi A. Stanley Dreyfus, and Rabbi Chaim Stern, whose wisdom continues to enrich my life and work. I also acknowledge the members of my interim congregations, Temple Emanuel Sinai, Worcester, Massachusetts; Congregation Beth Emeth, Albany, New York; East End Temple, Manhattan; Monroe Temple, Monroe, New York; Temple Sinai, Summit, New Jersey; West End Temple, Neponsit, New York; and Temple Am Echad, Lynbrook, New York, for our studying together and learning from one another. I thank my colleagues at Planned Parenthood Empire State Acts: Robin Chappelle Golston, Georgana Hanson, M. Tracey Brooks, JoAnn M. Smith, Carol Blowers, and Rev. Tom Davis, for leadership toward social justice by values and integrity. At The Jewish Publication Society, I thank director Rabbi Barry Schwartz for the concept and support that sparked and sustained this work, and managing editor Joy Weinberg, whose careful attention and patient direction opened depth and insight. I thank the University of Nebraska Press staff, for co-publishing this book. And most of all I thank my family, whose loving support makes it all possible.

Introduction

Years before anyone ever imagined walking into a Starbucks, a coffee shop with the clever name I and Thou opened in the trendy Haight-Ashbury neighborhood of San Francisco. I suspect the owners of I and Thou chose that name to say that theirs was a destination for great coffee *and* great conversation.

So, let's you and I imagine getting a cup at I and Thou. We meet at the door, order, grab a table, and are so excited to see each other that the talking starts before the coats come off. We speak honestly, listen carefully, and respond fully, agreeing on some things, disagreeing on others, paying no attention to the coming and going around us. A lull in the conversation brings a glance at a watch and a "Hey! I didn't realize we were carrying on *that long!*" We continue talking until our time together ends—as it eventually must. And, if Martin Buber were watching us from the next table, he'd likely say that we—along with the owners of this café—took a page from his best-known book, *I and Thou* (1923).

This classic work explains Jewish spirituality by examining two kinds of relationships, I-Thou and I-It. I-Thou, illustrated above, doesn't have to go on for two hours like we do at the café. For example, see yourself there, returning to the counter for a refill, and you notice something reassuring in the barista's smile, an unspoken promise to care for you—if only for as long as it takes to top off your cup. Rising above the low behavioral expectations for customer and server, the two of you make a human connection. The exchange contributes a little extra lift to your "Thank you!" and you add a decent tip. This brief interaction is I-Thou, too.

The second relationship is I-It. Take as an example an imagined café across town named I and It. Their coffee is fine; maybe it's even better. The problem is the service—so indifferent and impersonal that a customer wonders whether anyone cares you are there. Even so, I-It isn't necessarily bad; sometimes I-It is all a person needs. I-It can be businesslike and brusque, superficial and impersonal, perfect when you're in a hurry and just want a quick cup—"No sugar, a little milk" and done. I-It gets you through the morning drill en route to work—picking up coffee, paying for the paper at the newsstand—eyes on the headlines, neither glancing at the cashier as you put down the bills nor looking up at the commuter train conductor who checks your ticket while talking to another rider.

While I-It can be necessary and constructive, it can also be one-sided, commercial, detached, even manipulative or dominating. I-It becomes harmful, for instance, when someone disparages or degrades another human being as an "It": when there's excessive overgeneralization, inflexible pre-judgment or discrimination over race, religion, age, gender, sexual orientation, and so on—but I-It comes in degrees, so let's not be entirely dismissive. After all, most of us need the I-It that surrounds our getting food, shelter, clothing, and more. I want the I-It of a reliable auto mechanic and a good dry cleaner, the sanitation worker who picks up my trash and the letter carrier who comes to my front door six days a week, because these things help me live my life. Yet, where I need I-It to survive, I must have I-Thou to thrive, to be made whole and fulfilled. Only I-Thou does that.

Another thing. Buber teaches that there's more to I-Thou than just the two of us off in a corner talking over coffee: I-Thou is the foundation of Buber's vision of an ideal community.

I-Thou is both building block and mortar of Buber's vision for the ideal social order. Imagine a world where everyone acts the way we do at that café, where community after community fills with people who treat each other as Thou. That's what Buber sometimes speaks of as Hebrew Humanism: a utopian dream of a collaborative and fully inclusive society built one I-Thou at a time. And Buber gives us even more: an overarching spiritual dimension he calls Eternal Thou. Each I-Thou meets God in Eternal Thou, where every single I-Thou abides with God, forever. We can't see Eternal Thou, nor can we prove God exists, but as a matter of faith, when you and I speak as I-Thou, each of us fulfills our individual destinies on earth by bringing God into our relationship through the Eternal Thou. In I-Thou, earth meets heaven.

Buber has much to teach us about Jewish spiritual living, relationships, the Bible, psychotherapy, politics, and more. But first, let's look at his life story.

Who Was Martin Buber?

Martin Buber (1878–1965) defies labels as much as he disliked them. To call Buber a philosopher, writer, Jewish existentialist, sociologist, or theologian — or to consider him a philosophical anthropologist, as he sometimes allowed himself to be called — is to overlook much of his sweeping legacy as a scholar, teacher, author, poet, mentor, and activist. His intellect and work spanned an array of fields: world religions, spirituality, mysticism, education, psychology, language, politics, culture, psychotherapy, sociology, and social activism. His editions of Hasidic stories brought overlooked teachings to light and opened new conversations on Judaism. His widely praised German translation of the Hebrew Bible — started in collaboration with Franz Rosenzweig and completed on his own after Rosenzweig's death — was hailed and is still relied upon by many. Buber was a pillar of the Lehrhaus, an adult community for serious Jewish learning in Germany, and he was an outspoken activist later in his life in Israel. All this earned Buber nominations for Nobel Prizes from author Hermann Hesse and UN secretary-general Dag Hammarskjöld, in a story that begins when Buber was just three years old.

Martin Buber was the sole child of a very ordinary middle-class household in Vienna. The family apartment of his earliest years overlooked the Danube River, and its gently flowing waters gave Martin an early grounding of stability and security — until tragedy struck.

His parents separated when he was three, and a year later his mother suddenly disappeared, without warning or explanation.

Martin went to live on his grandparents' estate in Lviv, Ukraine. His grandmother, Adele Buber, ran the successful family farming and mining business and household, and provided Martin with homeschooling focused on European languages. His grandfather, Solomon Buber, edited and published more than a dozen volumes of painstakingly annotated midrash—classic Rabbinic commentary on the Torah. Both grandparents greatly influenced Martin's emerging spirit.

From time to time in those years, Martin's grandfather brought him to Hasidic synagogue services nearby. Even at that early age, Martin was taken by the rapture, joy, and fervor of the worship; the excitement of embracing, reading, and dancing with the Torah; and the warm, close relationships among the faithful and with the tzaddik, the community's religious leader who was deeply involved in the personal lives of the Hasidim.

Buber's interest in Judaism waned through high school and his university years in Vienna, Leipzig, Zurich, and Berlin, until the early Zionist movement rekindled an involvement that quickly grew to his leadership as editor of its newspaper, *Die Welt*. He used his position to champion what would become his lifelong vision for a Jewish state unlike any other state, based on Jewish values—what he later called Hebrew Humanism. Meanwhile, others in the Zionist movement paid much less attention to Jewish ideals, emphasizing instead the pressing need for a haven for persecuted European Jews and the economic and political development of a Jewish homeland. These disagreements over concept and direction grew heated and personal, and after a falling out with other leaders, Buber left the movement.

Soon thereafter, Buber withdrew from communal involvement and turned inward for Jewish spiritual exploration, study, and writing. He emerged from that isolation to teach, write, and speak in Germany. Even as the Nazis rose to power, he continued lecturing and writing, to the point of endangering himself and his family, as when Nazi police troopers repeatedly searched his home and personal library. As the social and political situation in Germany deteriorated, Buber secured a faculty appointment at the Hebrew University in Jerusalem. In 1938 the whole family formally relocated to Israel.

The move presented challenges as well as opportunities that ultimately led to more than two decades of teaching, study, writing, raising disciples, and activism. Buber's vision of community based on I-Thou, which included economic justice and equality, brought him to champion Israel's socialist kibbutz movement and Jewish-Arab reconciliation and partnership—all this and more until his death in 1965.

Buber's Jewish Legacy

For all that Buber accomplished, his work still doesn't get all the recognition it deserves.

First, among many reasons, Buber often wrote with artistic flourish. In *I and Thou*, for example, his voice is cryptic, poetic, wandering, and rapturous, all at once. Some say he enjoyed going out of his way to make simple ideas sound complicated. According to legend, when asked if he would write in Hebrew after moving to Israel, Buber joked that he didn't know the language well enough to obscure his thinking in it. To be sure, Buber makes for difficult reading, even in the best translations from the original German.

What's more, Buber did not always cite his Jewish sources, an absence that has allowed readers to challenge and dismiss the scholarship and Jewish authenticity of his work. For all the Jewishness of *I and Thou*, the book never mentions Jewish texts or teachers to support his arguments, thereby opening it to criticism that Buber pulled all of its "Jewish ideas" out of the air.

The reality is that *I and Thou* is a genuine Jewish book drawn from Buber's strong Jewish background. For example, he was so familiar with Hebrew, the Hebrew Bible, and the Rabbinic commentaries that when his grandfather, a midrash scholar, was puzzled by an occasional reference to medieval French in the Hebrew writings of the famous Torah commentator Rashi, Martin helped his grandfather make sense of both languages in the context of interpreting Torah.[1]

Buber, like many of his day, chose the Hebrew Bible over the Talmud. Where so many studied and lived by the fine points of Jewish law (as in the Talmud), Buber drew from the Bible's concepts, imagery, poetry, ethics, language, and social vision to create an ideal of Jewish living that would serve as the political, cultural, and spiritual foundation for life in a renewed Jewish land. Two of his other books, *Moses* and *The Prophetic Faith*, exemplify his rich understanding and fluid ability to explain the Hebrew Bible from a Jewish perspective.

In truth, for all of Buber's Jewish academic abilities and devotion, he frequently and intentionally downplayed his Jewish roots in order to appeal to a broader audience. As a champion for Judaism and for the acceptance of Jews in the larger society at a time and place in which Jews found themselves at the margins in their communities, Buber sought to increase the understanding and appeal of Judaism to outsiders. By writing without referencing Jewish texts, the Rabbis, or Jewish rituals, he hoped to present Jewish beliefs as universal. Indeed, his books did—and continue to—have an audience far beyond the Jewish community.

Ultimately, the spirit of I-Thou underlies Buber's nuanced and considered approach to halakhah. He calls on each of us to embrace those rituals that speak to us in our particular situation. To the disappointment and frustration of some, he rejects the expectation that everyone perform specified religious acts in certain ways at set times. He encourages us to embrace Torah through the entryway of I-Thou: in essence, to perform mitzvot that address us here and now, in relationship.

Buber's Core Jewish Teaching

Buber's interhuman Judaism is reflected in the teachings of one of the most respected and influential of the Rabbis, the Mishnah's Rabbi Hillel.

Rabbi Hillel summed up the essence of Judaism by expanding on the Torah's Golden Rule, "Love your fellow as yourself" (Lev. 19:18), explaining, "What is hateful to you do not do to another person. That's the whole Torah, and the rest interprets it" (Shabbat 31a). In the spirit of Leviticus and Rabbi Hillel, Buber's *I and Thou* teaches, "All real living is meeting."[2]

For Buber, a true "meeting" with others involves what he calls "inclusion"—that is, seeing both sides of a relationship, yours and mine, simultaneously. Being aware of each other as we are aware of ourselves and acting out of respect for another person's needs as well as our own require openness to someone else and appreciation of how that person thinks and lives. Such a practice encourages each of us to really "love your fellow as yourself."

Furthermore, to Buber, inclusion through I-Thou is the first step toward building community. Many trusting, interdependent, and simultaneous relationships radiate out into a larger community and ultimately resonate with God. As we encounter each other in I-Thou, we encounter God in what Buber calls the "Eternal Thou."

So, if you tell Buber that you are looking for God, he advises you to build a relationship. What is more, God needs our love, just as our neighbors do. Buber assures us that God draws strength from each and every I-Thou through the Eternal Thou.

This I-Thou moment of divine revelation is the foundation of Buber's examined Jewish living, the basis of his utopian social vision, and his key to all that is spiritual and everlasting. We meet each other, love each other, and love God, all at the same time.

Why We Need Buber Now

It is as if Buber foresaw the challenges of the Information Age. In 1923 he wrote in *I and Thou*: "The world of objects in every culture is more expansive than that of its predecessor." And, "They indicate a progressive augmentation of the world of *It*."[3] A century ago he observed that technological inventions were becoming increasingly prevalent and popular at the expense of our relationships. It would not surprise him to hear things like, "My kid never puts down her smartphone!"; "My boss just flamed me in an email!"; "Our son spends more time on video games than he does on doing homework, talking with us, and playing with friends, combined"; and "I hit 'Reply All' instead of 'Delete.' Now the whole world knows."

As our interactions with our creations and the world of *It* continue to expand, we need Buber, right now, to instruct us on how to recapture the spiritual side of life by identifying, entering, building, and preserving holiness in our daily routines.

I-Thou is very close at hand, with us and around us for all the times it passes unnoticed. It hides in plain sight. We "hallow the everyday" (a term coined by the late Professor Maurice Friedman, Buber's primary translator and interpreter) by creating holiness in simple and ordinary actions. Learning from Buber opens the door to richer and fuller living.

This book lifts away the veneer of daily living to reveal an otherwise hidden or ignored life-enhancing and Jewish spiritual practice; it identifies and clarifies Buber's Jewish insights and foundation so that we can better bring his ways into how we live. On the surface, it looks like there's nothing at all religious about a kind word with the guy who shows up at your front door to deliver your still-warm pizza or a spirited "Good morning!" to the stranger who boards a high-rise office elevator with you. Yet Buber shows us how this little bit of banter can also be a faith-filled exchange. A few seconds between strangers can "hallow the everyday," demonstrating the Divine Presence in life.

About This Book

A Year with Martin Buber is a contribution to The Jewish Publication Society's Daily Inspiration Series. Like other books in the series, it explores the Shabbat and festival Torah portions through the eyes of a Jewish figure (or figures) and includes personal examples from the life of the author. It offers three-part commentaries to each Torah portion, as assigned according to Shabbatot and Jewish holidays. The first part of the commentary, called "*P'shat*: Explanation," introduces and expands on the "plain," or "simple," meaning of the Torah text. It opens with a citation from a Torah portion, summarizes the narrative and background, and identifies and explores a Jewish theme. Often, the section enriches our understanding of the Torah by including material from the Rabbis of the Midrash, Talmud, and other Jewish sources, all preparing us for the second section, "*D'rash*," in this case, "Buber's Insight." *D'rash* in Hebrew means "interpretation," signifying an interpretation of Buber's work in light of the Torah portion's teaching. This second section greatly benefits from the work of the late Professor Maurice Friedman, Buber's primary translator and interpreter.

Buber teaches that Jewish spirituality is as much about what we do as it is about how we think, so we best approach Buber by appreciating how he lived his life. Buber once said that he doesn't talk "about" God; rather, he speaks "to" God, and it is in the act of speaking—in his and our actions—that we witness Buber's vision come to life.[4] This second section discusses Buber's abandonment by his mother, marriage to Paula Winkler, activism in the early twentieth-century Zionist movement, standing firm for Jewish life in Germany as the Nazis assumed power, relocation to Israel in his sixties, and exchanges with other trailblazers such as Abraham Joshua Heschel, Franz Rosenzweig, Carl Rogers, Mahatma Gandhi, Albert Einstein, and Dag Hammarskjöld. Another source for exploring Buber's outlook on living is Buber's anthologizing of stories about the early Hasidim. From Buber's editions of Hasidic tales, we draw lessons from legends of those masters. By illustrating Buber's *thinking* with examples from Buber's *living* and his writings about how the Hasidic masters lived, we honor Buber's commitment to illustrating Jewish ideals alongside Jewish life.

Unlike other books in the Daily Inspiration Series, *A Year with Martin Buber* also takes quotes from Buber's correspondence and conversation, out of a recognition that Buber's beliefs are more about how we live than what we think—Buber lived out his ideals, making his daily life a source for examples of his wisdom.

The third section of each commentary, "*D'rash*: A Personal Reflection," provides a personal illustration of the commentary's theme. Buber teaches that the spiritual life is lived on a "narrow ridge" of uncertainty, which brings me to reveal my own struggles as I grew from a child to become the person, husband, father, and rabbi I am.

Buber and Gender

Two women—Buber's grandmother, Adele Buber, and his wife, Paula Winkler Buber—were Buber's primary influencers. At the same time, along with his father and grandfather, his outside-the-home mentors, colleagues, interpreters, and disciples were all male; his Jewish and secular written sources were authored by men; and his Hasidic stories, thousands of them, tell of male rabbis, their male disciples and colleagues, with only occasional references to a rabbi's wife or townswomen as supporting characters. Without knowing his personal history, a student of Buber could come away with the impression that women were secondary to Buber's life and work.

This contribution to the Daily Inspiration Series is mindful that Buber taught, wrote, and reflected the gender outlook of his day. Yet it also seeks to demonstrate that Buber was more gender-balanced than might be otherwise assumed.

This book draws Torah translation from *The Contemporary Torah* (CJPS), a 2006 gender-sensitive adaptation of the first part of *The JPS Tanakh* (NJPS), which is cited when translating from the Hebrew Bible's later books. All other Hebrew-to-English translations are the author's and seek to be attentive to gender matters.

What Brings Me to Buber

My path to Martin Buber began when I was no more than twelve, with the excitement my grandmother brought home from adult continuing-education psychology classes, her bubbling with the instructor's words about the human mind as explained by Sigmund Freud, Carl

Jung, Alfred Adler, and others. I don't remember the specifics, but her enthusiasm left its mark on me: Examining our thoughts and actions, and putting what we learn into practice, makes for a better life—an insight that resonated with my then yeshiva and later Reform Jewish education. Even as a child, I was convinced that faith, intertwined with the science of human behavior, promises us that each person is important; each life makes a difference. Each one of us is part of something much bigger and more enduring than ourselves, and how we spend our lives matters.

In my later teens and through college, as I became active in youth groups and taught religious school, I benefited from the richness of Jewish communal living and tried to make my contribution. And in my college study of psychology and, later, in graduate social work, as if taking my grandmother's lead, I turned to the hopefulness of humanistic psychology, and the transformational possibilities of small groups and deeper conversations. Rabbinical school extended and strengthened my appreciation for the emotional and spiritual wisdom of the Torah and the Rabbis.

All these experiences came together through my studies of Martin Buber. His promise of divine wonder in the routine of daily life brought me to write this book to teach us all.

A Year with Martin Buber

1

Genesis (Bere'shit)

Bere'shit

Standing Over Against

GENESIS 1:1–6:8

*It is not good for the human to be alone. I will
make a fitting counterpart for him.*
—Genesis 2:18

P'shat: Explanation

God brings Adam into the world and immediately recognizes that
Adam needs a partner. God takes a rib from Adam and brings Eve to
life. Creation is now complete, and the Torah opens a conversation
on the fundamentals of human relationships.

Bere'shit calls Eve *ezer k'negdo*, which typically translates as a "fitting counterpart for him," yet the precise meaning of *ezer k'negdo* is
unclear. We can also read *ezer k'negdo* as "a helper *opposite* him," as if
Eve is Adam's colleague and opponent, all at the same time. How can
she be both? Adam and Eve's relationship stands as a paradigm for all
intimate relations. But exactly what is this paradigm?

The term *ezer k'negdo* appears just twice in the whole Bible, both
times in this chapter, so we have not further context. Fortunately,
though, the Rabbis offer ample insight.

The Rabbis carefully weigh each of the Torah's words through
extended conversations—sermons really—called midrash. They also
give us line-by-line commentaries that, together with the midrash,
contribute to our understanding of the Torah and Judaism.

So, when it comes to *ezer k'negdo*, do Adam and Eve cooperate or
clash? Rashi (Rabbi Shlomo ben Yitzhak, France, eleventh century),
the most widely known Jewish commentator, tells us that Eve will be

a helper "if he [Adam] merits." But, "if he does not merit, they will fight." Thus, Rashi sees Adam and Eve's relationship as conditional: emotion-filled, fragile, and in flux—they can be each other's "helper" or "opponent" depending on how they decide to relate. More broadly, Rashi implies, we are shapers of our intimate lives, and by extension, the larger social environment. How we build relations relies on our free will. It is up to us.

In another interpretation—for the Rabbis often disagree, and their conflicting opinions are preserved—commentator, philosopher, and physician Sforno (Ovadiah ben Ya'akov, Italy, fifteenth–sixteenth centuries) draws an analogy to a "balance scale." Partners stand on either side of the scale and, ideally, balance out one another. However different, they nevertheless carry the same weight and worth. Sforno sees Eve and Adam as on the same level, one for the other as a "fitting counterpart."

Resting on Rashi's emphasis on free will and Sforno's sense of balance, we turn to Buber and his concept of "Over Against."

D'rash: Buber's Insight

To be man means to be the being that is over against.

Buber was nearly eighty when he summed up this fundamental belief of "Over Against." Over Against asserts that a person becomes fully human through the I-Thou relationship. You and I are different, as becomes increasingly obvious when I see something about you or your situation that you don't see in yourself, just as you see something in me that I don't recognize. Candidly, yet lovingly, we offer one another perceptions that confirm or dispute these impressions in a conversation that takes its own course, spontaneously, without foreknowledge of our words or the outcome of our time together. Standing Over Against each other in I-Thou, we may alter a perspective or behavior, or hold ground. We do not become one person. In I-Thou, we remain distinct. And we are free to decide whether to accept or reject the opportunity to enter I-Thou from the very outset.

Here, *ezer k'negdo*, understood as "helper opposite," speaks positively about tension in relationships. A conversation that explores the difference and friction between people provides an opportunity to become fully human.

D'rash: A Personal Reflection

PARENTING OVER AGAINST

We speak of our children as if they are "ours," but they really belong to themselves. That our children are destined, God willing, to grow into their own as adults became obvious to me when, in the very first moments of life, our firstborn stood—or should I say "squirmed"—Over Against.

Adults awaiting a birth are called "expecting parents," even though most parents will tell you that they have no idea what to expect. So, we did the best we could to prepare. We weighed names, talked about furniture, thought about birth rituals, and the like. To be sure, Debbie had a much better understanding of what we were in for than I did.

Within minutes of Joshua's birth, the nurse put this swaddled baby into my arms, only after first checking that I knew how to support his head with the inside of my elbow (which I managed to figure out on my own, as if by instinct). Debbie took pride in those initial moments of father-son bonding, as I took on the wonder and exhilaration of a handheld reality that immediately gave birth to real-time worry.

I suddenly realized that something as simple as changing a diaper would demand untested skills. As the "full charge" dad I wanted to be, I'd have to remove that tightly wrapped swaddle blanket, deal with diapers—dirty and clean—and replace everything, perfectly. I started to get anxious and, in my desire for avoidance, imagined just leaving him in that tightly swaddled blanket, 24/7, forever . . .

But that was only the beginning of my sudden panic. How much food would he need? What if I gave him too much or not enough? What if he cried and I couldn't figure out why? All these fears started to overtake my mind . . . until something unexpected happened—he squirmed. His whole tiny body squiggled in my arms.

What's the big deal about a squirm?

I didn't expect it. No one warned me about it. It came without notice. It caught me off guard. And though it wasn't a big squirm, and I held onto him through it without even flinching, that squirm encapsulated my realization that children have minds of their own. Each child has free will that works outside their parents' control.

Babies squirm when they want, and they cry when they are hungry or need a new diaper, no matter what their parents say. Children sneeze when they catch cold, laugh when they think something is funny, and get upset when something is wrong. As they get older, they busy themselves with toys as they see fit, do their homework when they decide to, play with friends they choose, and all of this regardless of what their elders think they should want to do. Oh, we parents have some influence, but not as much as we might assume.

The independence I witnessed holding this swaddled baby carries on through life. A father-son bond isn't about two individuals becoming one. The parent-child relationship begins and grows Over Against, a little from the start, and more and more each day as, God willing, our children turn into adults and stand Over Against as our equals.

Noaḥ

Learning to Be Present

GENESIS 6:9–11:32

Noah was a righteous personage; He was blameless
in his age. Noah walked with God.
—Genesis 6:9

P'shat: Explanation

The earth has grown so corrupt and lawless that God decides to send a great flood to destroy everything, except for Noah, his family, and a selection of animals. Noah builds a life-saving ark. Rain follows, the earth floods, and the downpour ends after forty days. The waters subside, humanity gets a second chance, and we are left with many questions, including, "Why did God spare Noah?" In responding to that question, the Rabbis weigh Noah's merit.

We read that "Noah was a righteous personage; He was blameless in his age. Noah walked with God," which brings the Rabbis to question why the Torah qualifies Noah's righteousness with the words "in his age." What if Noah lived in an "age" when people were better behaved? Would the Torah speak so enthusiastically of his righteousness? The Rabbis explore this fine point to offer an important lesson on responsibility.

Noah receives praise, as well as criticism, among the Rabbis. Rashi sums it up with, "Some of our Rabbis explain it to his credit: he was righteous even in his generation; it follows that had he lived in a generation of righteous people he would have been even more righteous owing to the force of good example. Others, however, explain it to his discredit: in comparison with his own generation he was accounted righteous, but had he lived in the generation of Abraham he would have been accounted as of no importance" (on Gen. 6.9).

The conclusion? Noah's moral limits are evident when he shows no concern or sadness for the flood victims. He comes across as indifferent to the plight of the rest of humanity. By contrast, Abraham, who with Sarah covenanted with God, confronts God on a matter of justice when the cities and residents of Sodom and Gomorrah are to be destroyed for their sins. Abraham, concerned that the blameless will suffer the same fate as the perpetrators, expresses moral alarm when he challenges God: "Will You sweep away the innocent with the guilty? ... Far be it from You! Shall not the Judge of all the earth deal justly?" (Gen. 19:23, 19:25). Abraham was outspoken on behalf of any innocents, while Noah remained speechless. True, Noah "walked with God," but only because, in a world of tragic failure, Noah's moral mediocrity was the best God could find.

D'rash: Buber's Insight

I had a visit from a young man without being there in spirit.

A dramatic incident transformed Buber from a Noah into an Abraham.

In early adulthood, Buber spent many hours in private meditation. One such afternoon, a young stranger, Mehe, unexpectedly showed up at his home and interrupted Buber's session. While Buber let the visitor in for a conversation, he was preoccupied by the afterglow of his meditation. He listened to Mehe but withheld curiosity and responded with indifference and superficially. Mehe left with his concerns unaddressed.

Months later, another visitor brought Buber news of Mehe's death. Some said Mehe died in battle in World War I; others said suicide. Shocked, Buber told this second visitor that he felt personally responsible. Had he only asked Mehe a few questions, he might have saved his life.

The visitor responded that he knew that Mehe greatly appreciated the time with Buber. And while Buber understood that he had not caused Mehe's death, he knew that he had failed Mehe by withholding himself. Mehe had turned to Buber with hope, only to receive a less than wholehearted response.

Moreover, Buber saw his indifference as an affront to God. Even then, several years before releasing *I and Thou*, Buber believed that earthly deeds impact God in heaven, what he came to call Eternal Thou. By brushing off Mehe, Buber had squandered a spiritual opportunity.

This tragedy was a turning point for Buber. He made a firm commitment to be as attentive, actively curious, and responsive as he could when talking to someone—to be in a relationship he would later articulate as I-Thou.[1]

D'rash: A Personal Reflection

THE ADULT WHO DIDN'T KNOW HOW TO ASK

Sometimes being present comes naturally, and other times it's a struggle, as I witnessed in my early days as a student rabbi serving as a hospital chaplain.

We student chaplains entered each hospital room assigned to us without any information about that person's medical condition, history, family, occupation, or nationality. We were asked only to walk in, introduce ourselves, and listen.

On one of my first visits, a patient responded to my introduction with a sigh and said, "Oh, how I wish I felt better so I could talk with you!" I took his words as a sign that he wasn't up to speaking, so I told him I hoped he would feel better soon, and I would look for him my next time at the hospital. Then I left and went on to another room, but that experience left me feeling troubled the rest of the day into the night. I thought I could have done better with him, though I didn't know how. I felt like "The Child Who Doesn't Know How to Ask," one of the four children at the Passover table who sees something going on but can't find the right words to frame the question. I only asked myself, "What else could I have done?"

My next time at the hospital, I learned that the man was no longer a patient. Then I stopped by the section social worker for advice on how to handle this kind of situation in the future. "You could say, 'If you felt better, what would you tell me?'" she suggested. Great idea, I thought. Maybe putting a hypothetical situation into the conversation would bring us into deeper, more personal dialogue.

When I later shared this story with my supervising chaplain, however, she said I had done the right thing in the first place. "You can do what the social worker suggested next time, if you want, Dennis. But you also know I respect people and respect what they say to me. If they say they are not up to talking, I take them at their word and leave."

I thought about being in that kind of situation in the following months and years, and as you can see, I still think about it. While no one ever again spoke those exact words, "Oh, how I so wish I felt better so I could talk with you!" I have become more comfortable putting my uncertainty into words by saying something like, "I can come back in an hour and hopefully you'll be up to talking." By respectfully putting more of myself into the situation, I feel I am being more present.

In my work as a rabbi, I often find that the challenge is less about figuring out what to say and more to do with paying wholehearted attention, and not falling into myself as Buber did with Mehe. Sometimes, when talking with someone, I find it hard to listen because I am distracted by upsetting personal or work events. Or my attention lapses when I'm pressed for time or just tired. I know it's wrong to gloss over people when they talk, so I find, in these moments, it's important to reach for my curiosity and ask my conversation partner a clarifying question—that helps me stay on track. I try to rise to the moment with the hope that I am more than an indifferent Noah.

Lekh Lekha

Eternal Thou

GENESIS 12:1–17:27

And he built an altar there to Adonai who appeared to him.
—Genesis 12:7

P'shat: Explanation

What would you do if you heard God speak? We know what Abram and Sarai do. When God asks, they get up and go, and their devotion offers insight into how much God needs us.

God calls Abram and Sarai to leave their homeland for Canaan, where their descendants will grow into a large, thriving, and blessed nation. Sarai, Abram, and their household offer what amounts to a permanent farewell to relatives and friends, embark on a life-threatening journey, and start anew in an unknown place that could barely be imagined, all on the word of an invisible God. What trust! They reach the land, Abram builds an altar to sacrifice to God, then he travels on and builds another altar (Gen. 12:1–8).

Many admire Abram and Sarai's faith and courage, while others question why God asks anything of them in the first place. After all, an all-powerful, all-knowing, and all-capable God already has everything and has no need for Sarai, Abram, or altar sacrifices. Yet some Jewish teachers maintain that God is incomplete without the first Hebrews and the Covenant—God needs them and the people of Israel in order to become a full God. Rabbi Henry Slonimsky, of blessed memory, dean emeritus of the New York School of the Hebrew Union College–Jewish Institute of Religion, draws from Jewish sources to teach that God's stature—success or failure—literally depends on what human beings do. Rabbi Slonimsky recognizes that this bold theological suggestion is not a majority position in Judaism, but it nevertheless reflects Jewish teaching.[2]

In the Midrash, for example, Rabbi Yehudah, the son of Rabbi Simon, said, "When Israel does God's will, they add to the power of God on high, as it is said, 'With God we shall triumph' (Ps. 60:14). When Israel does not do God's will, the people diminish the great power of God on high, as is written (Deut. 32:18), 'you neglected the Rock who begot you'" (Lamentations Rabbah 1:33). In other words, God grows each time we do a mitzvah, as if our actions are our version of Abraham's altar offering to God. God's well-being rests in our hands. In another example, Rabbi Shimon, the son of Yochai, interprets, "'So you are my witnesses,' declares Adonai" (Isa. 43:12), as if to teach, "'When you are My witnesses, I am God, and when you are not My witnesses, I am not God,' in a manner of speaking" (*Sifrei Devarim* 346). From this perspective, God needs us. God created the world, called Abram and Sarai to service, and needs the Jewish people to serve God's purposes. God's being rests on our conduct.

To be sure, many folks see God as complete without us, regardless what we do. What's more, we cannot prove any of these claims. But for Buber, God needs us as we need God.

D'rash: Buber's Insight

Every particular Thou is a glimpse through to the eternal Thou.

What we do on earth has everything to do with God, for, as Buber teaches, each time we meet in I-Thou, we simultaneously encounter God in the Eternal Thou, where every I-Thou abides with God, forever. Just as Abram builds an altar and presents God an offering, our words and deeds are an offering to the permanent ingathering of Eternal Thou.

Buber relates a story of Rabbi Abraham Yaakov of Sadagora, who taught that we learn something from each thing, whether created by God or by a person. When the rabbi's disciple questioned what we might possibly learn from a telephone, Rabbi Abraham Yaakov offered a response that speaks to us in two ways—physical and spiritual. On the physical level, the telephone demonstrates that words spoken right here can be heard elsewhere, in another faraway place. As for the spiritual, I believe that Rabbi Abraham Yaakov teaches that our earthly words accumulate in another, invisible place, as part of the spiritual ingathering of Eternal Thou.

We can prove none of this, of course. Yet Rabbi Abraham Yaakov, as described by Buber, opens the possibility that our earthly speech has a heavenly influence.[3]

D'rash: A Personal Reflection

SETTING THE SPIRITUAL COMPASS

As happens with many people, my view of God has changed over time, from my childhood views to the beliefs that I—most of the time—hold today. And it is Buber, more than any other, who provides me with spiritual focus and direction through the Eternal Thou.

Even today, I sometimes see God as that enthroned heavenly figure who judges us by weighing our good and evil deeds on that scale on high. Or, when I lead the Mi she-Berakh prayer for comfort and healing, I sometimes imagine that God in heaven pays attention to each word of the prayer and sends goodness to each person we name. And then, from time to time, I think about the legend behind the Kaddish prayer, that a deceased loved one gets a little closer to God each time those ancient words are recited. At other times I really do believe the God of Israel inflicted ten plagues on Egypt and then split the Sea of Reeds to save us from Pharaoh in hot pursuit. And when these long-taught legends don't stir my spirits, as happens often too, I turn to Buber's Eternal Thou and an awareness that began during my social work internships.

When I was in social work school, I learned to use the word "process" to describe that "something in the air" in the back-and-forth, give-and-take of the counseling conversation. Even early on in my training, it didn't take more than a session or two with "clients" for me to start noticing the "magic" aloft. What is more, I found that, as one person's fingerprint differs from the next, each person that came in to see me evoked a different constellation of emotions in me, a set of feelings unique to them and to our time together. And then I began to notice that wonderful presence in conversations with family members and friends. Something bigger than our exchange of ideas and emotions—a miracle—was in the air between us. There was more to our conversations than met the eye, activity just beyond the border of our awareness. Our dialogue inserted us into a theological chain of events that could be imagined but not seen. And as my social work studies advanced and my respect for "process" became more pronounced, Buber and Eternal Thou clicked. . . . The Eternal Thou made perfect sense—I-Thou opens to Eternal Thou. My time spent with others was making a permanent, but invisible, contribution to the growing good.

Va-yera'

Many Forms of Candor

GENESIS 18:1–22:24

Shall not the Judge of all do justly?
—Genesis 18:25

P'shat: Explanation

Abraham's insight and courage come forward in Va-yera' as he brings us a lesson on the nature of candor.

God learns of the magnitude of Sodom and Gomorrah's sins and decides that the cities must be destroyed. God gives advance word to Abraham, who believes there must be righteous souls in those cities and that they deserve to be spared. Unlike Noah, who shows no concern for the victims of the great flood, Abraham's sense of justice drives him to call God to account. Troubled by the unfairness of collective punishment, Abraham declares: "Far be it from You to do such a thing, to bring death upon the innocent as well as the guilty, so that innocent and guilty fare alike. Far be it from You! Shall not the Judge of all the earth do justly?" (Gen. 18:25).

The Rabbis question why God, who answers to no one, decides to forewarn Abraham in the first place. Rashi has God mull, "It is improper for Me to do a thing like this without Abraham knowing. I gave him this land, and these five cities therefore are his. . . . I called him Abraham, the spiritual ancestor of a multitude of nations. How can I destroy the children without informing the parent? He loves me!" God recognizes and honors Abraham's responsibility for Canaan and those who live in it.

Acknowledging Abraham's moral argument, God offers to spare the cities entirely if ten innocents can be found within, but ten there are not. Destruction follows, and we come away knowing that as much as God demands justice, God will also consider a heartfelt plea for mercy. We also recognize Abraham's courage before God, and, in his candor, a call to us to reach into the soul and respectfully speak the words that live there.

D'rash: Buber's Insight

You did not read my Foreword.

In an (admittedly less dramatic) exchange that could nevertheless be compared to Abraham's reproof of God, Buber made himself equally clear to the noted Protestant theologian, teacher, and religious activist Reinhold Niebuhr by reproving him, "You did not read my Foreword."

By way of background, Buber had collaborated on many works with his primary translator and interpreter, Maurice Friedman. In one project, Friedman took the lead in compiling essays for an anthology, *Pointing the Way*. Buber was pleased with Friedman's selections, except for one essay that no longer spoke to him the way it once did. Still, they decided to include the essay, and Buber explained their decision in the book's foreword.

In spring 1958, Niebuhr reviewed the newly released book for the *New York Times*. Within the complimentary review, though, he raised some questions about this particular essay. By coincidence, Buber was then in the United States and scheduled to have breakfast at the Niebuhrs' Manhattan apartment the very morning the review appeared in the paper. As Niebuhr's wife, Ursula, would later fondly tell the story, Buber walked into the Niebuhrs' home with the review in hand, approached Reinhold—who must have been a foot taller than he was (Buber stood at just over five feet), pointed at Reinhold's stomach, and bluntly said, "You did not read my Foreword." And in an equally candid reaction, Niebuhr admitted he hadn't.

Whereas Abraham confronts God on a question of justice, life and death, Buber confronted a dear colleague to set the record straight. Both of these very different confrontations came with candor from the heart. Here, and at other times, Buber was known to speak his mind, to the point of being abrasive. Yet, his bluntness, alongside his demonstration of respect for others, served as a portal to I-Thou.

D'rash: A Personal Reflection

CANDID SPEECH IN A MOMENT OF CRISIS

After all the funeral details were in place, the wife of the deceased called once more to tell me how distressed she was to have inadvertently scheduled her late husband's funeral on their son's birthday. Immediately after realizing the uncomfortable coincidence, she called her son to express heartache about her oversight. He insisted that she ignore his birthday and carry on with the service as planned. But she wasn't at all at peace, and she called me to get my thoughts.

I didn't know what to say, let alone how best to be candid in an uncomfortable situation I had never encountered or imagined facing. I found myself pausing to think longer than I ordinarily would have before speaking. After all, funeral planning is enough of a challenge for families, and something or someone almost always gets overlooked, so we need to be understanding of ourselves and each other in that difficult situation.

Given her son's reaction—which, knowing the family, I thought we should take at face value—on top of the fact that details about the date and time had already been sent out to the family and community, it seemed best to proceed as planned.

The wife of the deceased and I agreed that I would contact the son to confirm that he wanted to let the funeral go ahead on his birthday. I would speak candidly (though I wasn't sure what I would say) and gauge his response.

"I just spoke to your mom," I told him. "As you know she is terribly distressed about the scheduling of the funeral. What do you think?"

"There's no reason to be upset. If anything, it's a comfort to know that forty-seven years ago, to the day, my dad became a father for the first time. It shows that life carries on."

What his mother and I had found disconcerting, the son had interpreted as a comfort. From being candid in a challenging situation, I learned something about finding the positive in the most trying moments.

Ḥayyei Sarah

Rising from Grief

GENESIS 23:1–25:18

Abraham proceeded to mourn for Sarah and to bewail her.
Then Abraham rose from beside his dead, and spoke to the
Hittites saying, "I am a resident alien among you; sell me a
burial site among you, that I may remove my dead for burial."
—Genesis 23:2–4

P'shat: Explanation

As Ḥayyei Sarah teaches, there are times to put emotions aside and attend to what needs to be done.

Sarah dies and Abraham immediately turns from mourning to buy a burial place. The Rabbis, often troubled by appearances, question how Abraham abruptly jumps from grieving to the business-like negotiation of a land purchase, as if he is uncaring or disrespectful of his recently departed wife. Here, the philosopher and grammarian Radak (Rabbi David Kimhi, France, twelfth–thirteenth centuries) stands up for Abraham, saying that the bereft patriarch models proper behavior by putting aside immediate and strong feelings to "attend to the funeral arrangements," thereby fulfilling the important mitzvah of *kavod ha-met*, honoring the dead.

According to Kimhi, Abraham summons the spiritual wherewithal to place grief on hold in order to honor the mitzvah of caring for the deceased. In that vein, when there is a death today, the Jewish tradition excuses immediate family members from performing other positive mitzvot, such as prayer and *tzedakah*, so that they can focus full attention on the funeral and shivah. As our portion opens, Abraham does not yet have a burial place for Sarah and thus prioritizes the details of funeral planning over expressing grief.

D'rash: Buber's Insight

*The world of It that is to be experienced and used . . . compare
it with objects, establish it in its order among classes of
objects, describe and analyze it objectively. . . . It is left as It,
experienced and used as It, appropriated for the undertaking
to "find one's bearings" in the world, and then to "conquer" it.*

Buber recognizes the complicated and quickly shifting nature of human emotions, as he explores the necessity and value of I-It.

Though Buber devotes much of *I and Thou* to the spirituality of the I-Thou relationship, he also presents the I-It relationship as essential and important, even when I-Thou must defer to I-It. Here we might think of I-Thou as emotional and spiritual connection with others, and I-It as the "business" side of life.

As Buber teaches, we need people and things in order to live. Think of buying a car or computer, or picking a college, or looking for a new place to live. You will "compare" one with the other, and "order," "describe," and "analyze" your options. You may well see the salesperson, college representative, or realtor as little more than a tool for getting what you need. There's nothing wrong with any of this, what Buber describes as I-It. Abraham too has to engage in I-It interactions to secure a burial place for Sarah.

To be sure, where I-Thou involves everything about a person, I-It includes only a small part. For instance, you go to a doctor who is also a friend. Your office visit opens with personal conversation about the family and then you start talking about your numbers—blood pressure and body temperature—"vital signs" that are truly vital, yet provide only a partial understanding of your personhood. If medication is in order, your doctor will ask if you are willing to

take it, but in the end, assuming you agree to follow the recommen-
dation, your feelings do not matter much. You get a prescription
from a pharmacist you never meet, while, back at the doctor's office,
someone files an insurance form to (hopefully) cover the visit. The
episode addresses a fraction of your identity—your health—and
then only a small part of that.

Of course, I-It is positive here. We need the I-It of good health.
What's more, when I am very sick or badly hurt, I don't want I-Thou
with a nurse or doctor. Treat me like an It, right now! Make me better right away, please!

Similarly, we also need the I-It of the daily routine in shopping, working, and eating. There's plenty of I-It in that weekly trip
to the supermarket: in politely but impersonally asking the shelf
stocker to check in the back if there might be extra boxes of your
sold-out favorite cereal, in looking at your phone while waiting
your turn at the register, or asking the bagger to be careful with
the eggs. And there's the I-It of office teamwork, in carrying out
the boss's instructions to the letter and on time, maybe even in
getting the job done better and faster. But after the work is in, and
you sit down with the "team" over lunch to celebrate, put business
aside, and share a few moments of I-Thou. Later, during the evening commute, there's I-It again: you may race ahead of other bus
riders to grab an open seat and unexpectedly wind up sitting next
to a neighbor. The two of you get talking, and where you were in
I-It a moment ago, you are now in I-Thou. We alternate between
I-Thou and I-It through the day, even during a conversation, often
without noticing.

Much of the time, there is nothing terribly wrong with I-It.
What's more, I-It often offers an opportunity to partake of something wanted or even cherished. Once the basic and enhanced
needs of life are met, the sacred becomes even more accessible
through I-Thou.

D'rash: A Personal Reflection

EMOTIONAL WHIPLASH

I took that quick pivot from emotion to funeral arrangement not long ago when my stepbrother died, and many responsibilities fell to me.

Arranging the funeral service itself was straightforward. Thankfully, Bob had preplanned everything, and one call to the funeral director got the service in place. But I had to scramble to call family and friends with the news of his death and the time of the funeral, all the while making sure his house and his dog were in good hands. Just as Abraham discovered, I quickly turned from emotion to business, especially when it came time to deal with the estate.

A photographer, Bob had a literal houseful of photos, boxes and boxes. What were we to do with all those photos, along with all the other remnants of his active life? It was hard to admit that things that were important to him had little meaning for me or anyone else in the family. We wound up giving away a good amount and, as for the photos, we displayed many at the funeral home and invited guests to pick out what they wanted to take as keepsakes.

He kept that tiny house very full. Ten times, at least, I filled up my car and trunk with clothing, household goods, yard equipment, and more to donate to my temple's tag sale. Of what remained, much was old, broken, or badly worn. We didn't want those things, and we didn't imagine anyone else using them. Eventually we came to admit the sad reality that only a dumpster in the driveway could serve the need.

People sometimes think that clergy, health professionals, and counselors have it easier when it comes to death because we deal with it so often. Yet, the reality is that we clergy grieve like anyone else, and in fact it becomes more complicated when we tell ourselves that having experience with death should expedite our ability to cope with it. To the contrary, and what's worse, when we take undue credit for professional expertise, what was one problem becomes two: having to manage both grief *and* its denial.

For me, the biggest challenge was the quick "flip-flop"—that is, the rapid shift between dealing with feelings and dealing with "stuff." Just as I-Thou quickly yields to I-It, and back again almost immediately, being alive guarantees that one's spirit bears a rigorous and unpredictable course of death and life. Here, I found that the presence of family and friends and such gestures as the kind words I didn't expect or ask for from a temple member, a handwritten sympathy note from someone I hadn't heard from in years offered great comfort.

Toledot

How Conflict Begins

GENESIS 25:19–28:9

Two nations are in your womb,
Two separate peoples shall issue from your body;
One people shall be mightier than the other,
And the older shall serve the younger.
— Genesis 25:23

P'shat: Explanation

Why do nations fight so much? How does the fighting begin? Toledot offers one perspective, suggesting that international conflict has deep roots — with origins in intense and long-standing sibling rivalry.

Rebecca is pregnant, and in much pain and distress over the mighty struggling within. She asks, "What good is life if I have to suffer like this?" and she learns, "Two nations are in your womb, two separate peoples shall issue from your body; One people shall be mightier than the other, and the older shall serve the younger" (Gen. 25:23). No wonder it hurts so much — a war is brewing within. As Rashi underscores the sense of the verse, the rivalry is inborn and a matter of spiritual destiny: He interprets the text to say that Rebecca hears, "From the time they leave your body, they will be distinguished — one to his evil and the other to his plainness" (on Gen. 25:23).

Esau emerges, then Jacob does, holding tightly to Esau's heel, the two fighting, foot-in-hand, through birth. The twins are fraternal, not identical — Esau is hairy, Jacob smooth-skinned — and Sforno interprets this physical difference to foretell the eventual divergence in their destinies: "They will also be politically apart" (on Gen. 25:23).

As predicted, the competition continues through young adulthood and beyond. Each son grows to found a people—Esau's descendants become Edom, and Jacob's become Israel, and these two nations vie fiercely through the generations. For Toledot, personal rivalry becomes group conflict, which for many stands as a paradigm for conflict today.

D'rash: Buber's Insight

*Appearing to be only where I was, I nonetheless
found myself there, too, where I found the tree.*

When conflict is so deeply ingrained that it appears to begin at birth, if not earlier, Buber's teachings about personal relationship offer a conceptual way to reconciliation. Buber bids us to begin to make peace through "Inclusion." That is, we hold our feelings in mind, yet in check—however strong these feelings may be—as we try to get an honest picture of an antagonist's reality. "Inclusion" describes how we see others as they are and envision ourselves standing in their place, without diminishing or disparaging our own perceptions. "Inclusion" is about imagining ourselves in two places at once.

Buber offers an analogy in the preface to his book *Daniel*, which appeared in 1913, a decade before *I and Thou*. (*Daniel* is often seen as a precursor to *I and Thou*.) He describes an experience hiking: He stops, presses the tip of his walking stick against the trunk of an oak tree, feels the stick in his hand, and simultaneously imagines the point where the stick touches the bark. He is trying to find himself at both ends of the stick at the same time. "Appearing to be only where I was," he writes, "I nonetheless found myself there, too, where I found the tree."

In a somewhat similar way, I affirm you and I affirm me in I-Thou, and you do the same—we each seek to enter both ends of the conversation in that precise moment. When we are committed to reconciliation and peacemaking, we can take the first steps toward peace in this very personal way: Both you and I, who differ in opinion, can try to intuit both sides of the conversation—one another's desires, needs, and vision.[4]

Further, Buber upholds that person-to-person conversation reduces the distrust and rhetoric that leads to armed conflict, an approach that resembles that of his friend, Swedish diplomat, economist, and author Dag Hammarskjöld, who served as UN secretary-general from 1953 to 1961.[5]

Hammarskjöld's commitment to in-person diplomacy predated his relationship with Buber. Three years before meeting Buber, when asked what he would gain from a personal visit to China, Hammarskjöld replied, "The risk of mistakes and false initiatives may be reduced. The possibility of saying the right word in the right moment may be increased."[6] So committed was Hammarskjöld to acting on his vision of making peace in person, he traveled the world, from war zone to war zone, to sit face-to-face with his negotiating partners. He said, "You can only hope to find a lasting solution to a conflict if you have learned to see the other objectively, but at the same time to experience his difficulties subjectively."[7]

The friendship with Buber began in 1958, during Hammarskjöld's second term as UN secretary-general. Deeply moved by reading Buber's *Pointing the Way*, Hammarskjöld contacted Buber and asked to meet. Learning that Buber was then in the United States, he invited Buber to visit at the United Nations, and Buber accepted.

When Buber reached the UN, Hammarskjöld put aside pressing business so they could have two uninterrupted hours of discussion about conflict and reconciliation. They met twice more in Jerusalem and, soon after, Hammarskjöld nominated Buber for a Nobel Prize in Literature.

Buber and Hammarskjöld believed that too many politicians were more concerned with the interests of third parties, such as constituencies and colleagues, who were not in the room, than in speaking honestly among themselves in person. Instead of prioritizing relationship building or safeguarding the truthfulness of their words, they were grandstanding to folks back home through propaganda and political spin—at the expense of having an honest conversation with the person standing right in front of them.[8]

Buber used the term "Crossfront" to describe his ideal first step. We reach that Crossfront when speaking honestly, without reservation, to identify areas of agreement and difference. Then, we get specific about the details of disagreement, instead of overlooking, politicizing, or demonizing.[9]

At the core, peacemaking starts at the grassroots and builds up. It begins with face-to-face, honest conversation that grows into trusting relationships that expand and interconnect, person-by-person, into sound communities, and then to a spiritually thriving nation and world.[10]

At one point in their relationship, Buber suggested that Hammarskjöld translate *I and Thou* from German into the diplomat's birth language, Swedish. Hammarskjöld, already an author, contacted his publisher and began work. In 1961, Hammarskjöld set off to the Congo on a peace mission, only to die en route, in a plane crash. An hour after learning of the tragedy by radio, Buber received his last letter from Hammarskjöld, which described his excitement and his publisher's enthusiasm for the translation in progress.

The charred remains of the partial translation—twelve pages—were later found in the plane wreckage. It appeared that Hammarskjöld was working on the manuscript while in flight and thinking about Buber until the very end, dying while laboring toward his dream of advancing on the road to peace, one person at a time.[11]

D'rash: A Personal Reflection

CAN CONFLICT END?

I was a kid when Hammarskjöld died. Like Buber, I learned of his death from the radio and felt sad. I had already been to the United Nations and knew what Hammarskjöld was trying to do well.

Family and school visits to the United Nations left an impression on me. I knew there was war in the world, and there was the potential for more. I was convinced that all these world leaders meeting together in one place could talk through their differences and make peace.

My last visit to the United Nations was as a leader of a Confirmation class trip. Our UN guide was unexpectedly critical of Israel; she took unfair aim and I told her so. To be sure, Israel, like any nation, confronts significant internal and external challenges, and I'm deeply upset by some of the things its leaders and people say and do. But in a world where no nation is perfect, and leaders of other nations do far worse, Israel is often wrongly singled out for criticism while the wrongdoing of others is ignored. I'm also disturbed when people put all the blame on one side, as if either the Arabs or the Jews are the sole originators and perpetrators of the conflict. The reality calls for a more nuanced understanding, which few at the United Nations are expressing these days.

I haven't gone back to the UN since, but I still have hope.

Va-yetse'

When Time and Space Become Secondary

GENESIS 28:10–32:3

So Jacob served seven years for Rachel, and they
seemed like a few days because of his love for her.
—Genesis 29:20

P'shat: Explanation

Jacob and Rachel were right for each other from the start. And as they get from that start to where they want to be, we gain insight into the complicated relationship of time, space, and matters of the spirit.

This love story begins on an angry note, when an infuriated Esau threatens to murder Jacob for stealing their father's end-of-life blessing. Jacob flees their home in Canaan for family in Haran. On arrival, Jacob meets Rachel, and it is love at first sight.

Jacob works fourteen years to earn marriage to Rachel. At the outset, Jacob thinks it will be seven years, but when those years pass, he is tricked into marrying Rachel's sister, Leah. He must work yet another seven years to marry Rachel as well, the woman he really loves. Yet the years "seemed like a few days because of his love for her."

The Rabbis marvel at Jacob's patience over those fourteen years. They attribute his fortitude to a miraculous ability to make space shrink and time fly. Previously, when Jacob fled home in Canaan for safety in Haran, the Talmud notes the trip went quickly because "the ground in front of him contracted" (*Sanhedrin* 95b). In other words, when Jacob wants to get somewhere in a hurry, heaven and earth move things apace. It seems that something similar happens to the waiting time when Jacob works to marry Rachel.

For Jacob, time and space became secondary to love and will; attention to the interpersonal, emotional, and spiritual prevails over the awareness of time and space.

D'rash: Buber's Insight

The world of It is set in the context of space and time. The world of Thou is not set in the context of either of these.

Just as space and time contract for Jacob, Buber explains that we lose track of time and space in I-Thou. Mindfulness of passing time collapses during the encounter, and our location, as well as what happens in the surrounding space, where we came from or where we expect to go afterward, fade to irrelevance.

To illustrate, Buber relates how Rabbi Shmuel told of his teacher Rabbi Rafael (d. 1816), who lived and taught in Bershad, Ukraine. One day, Rabbi Shmuel was walking down the road, when Rabbi Rafael called out to him to ride in his carriage. Rabbi Shmuel declined—he didn't want to crowd his teacher on the small carriage bench. Rabbi Rafael replied that the two should love each other even more than they already did and, as an outcome, they would feel like they had plenty of room.[12]

Underlying the parable is the recognition that good conversation draws the attention away from things that aren't perfectly right—we are so caught up with each other in I-Thou that a concern about seating space doesn't matter anymore.

When it came to questions of time, Buber, like Jacob, was well acquainted with the angst of waiting. For instance, it took ten stress-filled years of up-and-down negotiations to get his faculty appointment at the Hebrew University in Israel, and there were moments when it seemed that the job would never materialize. What's more, after he received and accepted the invitation, he worried that he would not succeed for lack of the very advanced and specialized Hebrew skills required for this unfamiliar academic setting. Yet there must have been something of I-Thou in his daily life during that painful decade in which the Nazis rose to power — relationships with students, mentees, family, and colleagues — to draw his attention away from all that waiting and worry, build his confidence, and endure the waiting time.

The loss of awareness of time and space fades in I-Thou, just as consciousness of cause — what brings us together — abates. The reason for our meeting becomes secondary to being in each other's active presence. In the same light, the expected outcome of our meeting — what we do next, where we go afterward — moves out of awareness while I-Thou happens. In I-Thou, all that matters is you and me, here and now.

D'rash: A Personal Reflection

I-THOU ON THE FLY

Has this happened to you?

You are flying home alone after a brief time away. You're at the gate, sitting in the lounge, reading, munching on something, planning on getting back early enough to take your time to unpack and get ready for work the next day. And it will be good to sleep in your own bed. Then you get a little bit of bad news: The flight is delayed for twenty minutes because of stormy weather. You don't think much of it, because what's twenty minutes? But shortly after, the airline adds another twenty minutes, and then twenty more, all because of weather. Of course, you recognize the importance of putting safety first, but you start getting annoyed, and progressively more annoyed, with the added delays.

Suddenly, without warning, the person sitting next to you says something, you start to talk, the two of you enter I-Thou . . . and the magic of time and space come into play. Now that you are caught up in conversation, your perception of time (how late you are) and space (you're a long way from home) disappear. You forget about what you need to do to return to the office tomorrow. The only thing that matters is the conversation with this stranger, right now.

Eventually, they call your flight and you say goodbye to this brief friendship. And your mood has changed. You are no longer upset, because you realize that the delay and lost time were secondary to the opportunity to be graced by I-Thou.

Va-yishlaḥ

Holy Insecurity

GENESIS 32:4–36:43

Jacob was greatly frightened.
—Genesis 32:7

P'shat: Explanation

Jacob bests Esau, his twin, by usurping their family mantle. A humiliated and enraged Esau threatens to kill Jacob, who flees home for his life. Va-yishlaḥ opens more than fourteen years later, when the brothers are to meet for the first time since the estrangement.

Jacob gets advance word that Esau is accompanied by an armada of four hundred, and, as the Torah says, "Jacob was greatly frightened." He implements a survival strategy. First, he divides his household into two, thinking, "If Esau comes to the one camp and attacks it, the other camp may yet escape" (Gen. 32:9). Then he dispatches gift-bearing envoys to Esau, thinking, "If I propitiate him with presents in advance, and then face him, perhaps he will show me favor" (Gen. 32:21). He also sends a deferential message that refers to Esau as "my lord" (Gen. 32:19) and speaks of himself as "your servant" (Gen. 32:21), hoping this too will placate his brother.

Some Rabbis are troubled by Jacob's subordination to Esau. After all, Jacob has a strong spiritual foundation, including a family birthright, a father's blessing, and God's promise of protection. Thus, Jacob's lack of self-confidence must be an indicator of a lack of faith. Midrash Rabbah carefully examines Jacob's language and has God call out to him in anger: "You subordinated yourself and called your brother, 'My Master' eight times! By your life!" (Genesis Rabbah 75:11). That is to say, the Rabbis expected Jacob would trust God deeply, put his destiny in God's hands, and unflinchingly stand up to his brother. Instead, Jacob acts as if he is faithless and doomed.

The night before the brothers reunite, a mysterious half-person, half-angel confronts and wrestles Jacob by the river in the dark. Jacob takes on the fight without hesitation or question, as if entering the next round of a lifelong wrestling match that began in utero. He competes fiercely and holds his own through sunrise, when this unknown figure must leave. Jacob walks away from the encounter with a hip injury and a limp, yet he has prevailed and receives a new name, *Yisrael*, "He wrestles with God" (Gen. 32:33). The brothers meet, and reconcile, that very day.

D'rash: Buber's Insight

You must descend ever anew into the transforming abyss, risk
your soul ever anew, ever anew vowed to the holy insecurity.

Accepting and embracing fear and worry of the likes that Jacob faces is a first step in building faith, Buber teaches, as he gives us the term "Holy Insecurity." Holy Insecurity takes insecurity as a given. It teaches that it is fruitless to fight off worry or avoid it. Once we admit that everything is at risk, in each moment, we are ready to enter I-Thou and encounter the sacred. I-Thou makes a demand: "You must descend ever anew into the transforming abyss" as you jump into the unknown, again and again. A person can be hopeful, but there is no way to anticipate what the future holds. There's Holy Insecurity in each I-Thou.

I-Thou demands putting everything on the line while passing through an unpredictable course of events. It means entering a relationship without any expectation or precondition and being open to the possibility of having or wanting to make personal change. We may be uneasy or reluctant when entering I-Thou, like Jacob as he prepares to confront his brother and his past. It's a natural reaction to avoid something frightening instead of welcoming it. But by taking the uncertainty into account when building faith, that faith becomes extraordinarily strong, strong enough to confront the unpredictable and frightening. Holy Insecurity is the price we pay for the possibility of transcending our challenges and worries.

Buber would come to welcome and confront his doubts and self-doubts over the unknown and unexpected. Yet these ideas about Holy Insecurity did not come easily for him. As World War I opened, Buber found himself among the many intellectuals swept up in supporting an almost messianic vision of the international armed conflict. Along with others, even in the Jewish community, he was taken by the spirit of German nationalism, determination, and unity, and championed Jewish war involvement as a contribution to German strength and spirit. Never mind the horrors of war, the deep reluctance of soldiers—Jewish and not—to fight, and the tragic deaths of soldiers and civilians. Drawing from the historic example of the Maccabees, who triumphed over the Seleucid Greeks to regain the Great Jerusalem Temple and rebuild the Land of Israel and the Jewish spirit, Buber argued, in public lectures and published writing, that war strengthens and binds souls.

Buber's militaristic position nearly ruptured his relationship with his mentor and friend Gustav Landauer, who was horrified by what he called this "war Buber." Landauer saw Buber's nationalism as a personal betrayal, and a betrayal of Jews who had no choice but to put their livelihood and families aside, and their lives on the line. He accused Buber of fantasy thinking and withdrew from a journal project with Buber, who became greatly upset. The two met at Landauer's home shortly after.

Perhaps Jacob's example of fright and self-doubt gives insight into how Buber and Landauer felt as their meeting approached, each intellectual so passionately and publicly invested in their differing positions. Yet, after several days of apparently deep and sustained conversation, Buber yielded. He underwent a radical reversal from a full-hearted endorsement of the military campaign to public condemnation of war and what he saw as empty nationalism. The Buber-

Landauer encounter mimicked Jacob's wrestling with that night demon as surely as Buber, like Jacob, emerged from the meeting to begin a new day as a changed person.

There's Holy Insecurity at work here for Buber, for what must have been trepidation in anticipation of a difficult meeting. Yet he put personal spirit and public persona on the line, sat down with Landauer, and came away from the confrontation to shrug off public perception and embarrassment to self-correct in front of his community. This spiritual transformation was a critical step in Buber's redefining the foundation of social gathering as spiritual rather than national. Buber's entering Holy Insecurity sparked important insight that would lead to the formulation of *I and Thou*.[13]

As much as you or I may dream of challenge-free living instead of being forced to wrestle with angels, Buber teaches that durable peace of mind begins by recognizing that comfort and certainty are never guaranteed, not for Jacob, Buber, you, or me. Buber wants us to embrace the fight. Holy Insecurity can open the way to personal growth and spiritual renewal.

D'rash: A Personal Reflection

INSECURITY BRINGS LEARNING

I sure was frightened when, as a rabbinical student, I began working as a hospital chaplain. My classmates and I were told that in order to be effective at supporting and helping people in a life-altering or life-threatening medical setting, we had to put everything on the line and trust in ourselves. "You are entering a new chapter in your personal and professional life. Go with your gut," I heard. "Rely on your instincts. Reach inside yourself and you'll know what to do. Most of your missteps will be small, but you will recover from them. The worst that will happen is you will learn something." That was easy to say but hard to believe or act on.

Early on, I poked my head into a hospital room and introduced myself as I entered. The man greeted me with, "Don't walk into a room, head first, looking like you are afraid, Rabbi. You belong in here. Come in with your whole body at once."

I was taken aback, though I tried not to show it. I was there to comfort him, at least in theory, and as our conversation carried on, maybe I did do something for him beyond extending him an opportunity to teach me something. To be sure, all my feelings were "out there."

The Talmud (*Ta'anit* 7a) offers, through Rabbi Ḥanina, "I have learned much from my teachers and even more from my friends, but from my students I have learned more than from all of them." So it was for me with that hospital patient, who taught me how my body speaks the unspoken of what's inside.

Holy Insecurity may mean entering a conversation—or a hospital room—having no idea what lies ahead, and with all my years as a pastoral counselor to people in medical need or at a turning point in life, I still have some of that unease in me when entering a novel situation. Perhaps my conversation partners see it as well, maybe not. Holy Insecurity, though, is more about identifying my unease and accepting it. It means realizing that, whether it looks it or not, I am always outside my "comfort zone" and at risk of getting knocked off center. Yet these times have been, and continue to be, "ever anew," as opportunities for spiritual growth.

Va-yeshev

On the Narrow Ridge

GENESIS 37:1–40:23

Now Israel loved Joseph best of all his sons — he was his child of his old age; and he had made him an ornamented tunic.
— Genesis 37:3

P'shat: Explanation

Following years of conflict and uncertainty, it looks like life will finally settle down for Jacob. After all, the name of this Torah portion is Va-yeshev, "And he settled." But peace and calm are not to be. More turmoil is in store for Jacob, and we take another lesson from the importance of managing uncertainty.

Considering the word "settled," Rashi draws an analogy to foreshadow the unsettling challenges ahead: "A flax dealer brought his camels, laden with flax, to a town. A blacksmith was startled: 'What will happen with all that flax?' A wise guy commented, 'One spark from your bellows will burn it all'" (Rashi on Gen. 37:1). Jacob's life is the flax and one mistake sparks a colossal flare-up, notwithstanding his stature as a patriarch.

Jacob (here known to us as Israel) "loved Joseph best of all his sons — he was his child of his old age; and he had made him an ornamented tunic" (Gen. 37:3). According to the Talmud, Jacob spent more money on this one coat than he did to clothe all the other brothers combined. Extracting a cautionary lesson for parents — playing favorites inflames sibling rivalry — the Rabbis underscore how Jacob's misstep led to the catastrophic enslavement of the people of Israel in Egypt (*Shabbat* 10b).

D'rash: Buber's Insight

I do not rest on the broad upland of a system that includes
a series of sure statements about the absolutes, but on
a narrow, rocky ridge between the gulfs where there
is no sureness of expressible knowledge but [only] the
certainty of meeting what remains, undisclosed.

Buber's life was more of a journey on "a narrow rocky ridge between the gulfs" than a "rest on the broad upland." To be sure, he often chose the more acrobatic and challenging route, as when assuming leadership in the early Zionist movement. Buber quickly rose to prominence, only to resign after terrible and public disagreements over vision and principle.[14]

For us, as for Buber, the wild ups and downs of life will, time and again, foist and strand a person atop that "narrow ridge." There is no direction up there, "no sureness of expressible knowledge," only "the certainty of meeting what remains, undisclosed." Uncertainty is the only certainty we have.

As if questioning whether anyone will ever be truly "settled," Buber points to Rabbi Moshe Leib of Sassov (1745–1807), who teaches that each person walks the edge of a knife blade, struggling to maintain balance and avoid falling one way or the other and landing in the abyss.[15] And, Buber would add, for times of upset, imbalance, worry, and falling, there is the support and strength of I-Thou.

Buber recalls an incident between Rabbi Hanokh of Alexander, who lived by the faith that heaven and earth, though estranged, will reconcile through human action, and Rabbi Hanokh's teacher Rabbi Simcha Bunam of Pzhysha (d. 1827).[16] Rabbi Hanokh approached Rabbi Simcha with a question that had been burning in him for a year before he found the strength of will to raise it. Rabbi Hanokh's face ran with tears when he asked why God put him, a mortal human being, on the face of this earth. Rabbi Simcha responded that he, too, was profoundly troubled by this existential question, and invited his disciple to join him for a meal and deeper conversation that would bring an opportunity for sharing concerns and offering mutual support, thereby drawing the two questioning teachers even closer.[17]

Soulful coming together can fortify the person on that narrow ridge.

D'rash: A Personal Reflection

LEARNING TO BALANCE

"People invite their clergy into their lives," said my friend and mentor Rabbi Earl Grollman. Being invited into someone else's life is a privilege. For congregants, it means trusting their clergy to stand with them through ups and downs. For those of us who are clergy, it means we encounter a range of routine and intense human experience, all in one day—a preschool reception, a conversation with an adult child about an upcoming unveiling ceremony for a parent, lunch with a local minister friend, a conversation with a temple leader about a new congregational project, several b'nai mitzvah lessons—and that's all before afternoon religious school. Being a rabbi demands being there for people. Clergy don't have all the answers, but we are privileged to be invited to walk with others on their Narrow Ridge.

I took the Narrow Ridge when I began as a hospital chaplain. I was told:

Start with plenty of watching and listening. Begin by trying to get a conversation going. Walk into a room and ask, "How are you doing today?" with emphasis on the word *today*, in this moment, here and now. And if you or someone you love has the same or a similar medical problem as the person you are talking to, don't bring it up—you're not there to tell them your story. But keep in mind that there is no perfect formula that works for everyone in all situations. In case something unexpected and unsettling happens, and it will, just be yourself. Don't be afraid to admit you don't know the answers.

That advice served me very well. Sometimes I'd be with a person who turned the conversation back on to me, my schooling and my plans for life. I let them know a little about myself before bringing the conversation back to them. When people spoke negatively about Judaism or their birth faith, or were angry at the hospital, the doctors, or God, I knew I wasn't there to defend my beliefs or anything or anyone else. I was there to listen to their concerns.

And then it happened, the anger that demonstrated I was on the Narrow Ridge.

"How are you doing today?" I asked a man I had never met before.

"How the hell should I be doing? I'm in the hospital. What do you expect?"

Well, truth be told, having seen a good number of hospitalized people by then, I knew that some people are not upset. Some are relieved to be in good hands and getting the care they need. Some have made their peace with a life-threatening condition. Some are grateful for my visit. Nevertheless, I felt terrible. While I had hoped to contribute to putting this person at ease, instead I only added to his distress. I felt like I'd fallen off that Narrow Ridge and landed flat on my face into that abyss. Trying to keep my balance, I apologized and quickly made my exit.

Afterward, I reviewed the situation with my supervisor. He acknowledged that "this happens" and encouraged me to go back there the next week. I didn't want to go back, but I knew he was right. After all, becoming a rabbi means learning how to deal with the Holy Insecurity of these challenging situations so I can hang in with people through the highs and lows. When people are forced to live through agonizing moments not of their choosing, it is an important part of the clergy's calling to accompany them on that unplanned and unwanted journey.

So, I took my supervisor's advice. The next time I was on that hospital floor, as soon as I walked into the room, before I could finish saying hello, the man apologized for what he'd said to me. He was on the edge of tears as he explained his situation. He was worried, and not just about his health but his family, over how they would manage without him, emotionally and financially. And my apprehension immediately turned to wanting to have a relationship with him. After all, for an entire week, with more important and personal things to worry about, this man harbored deep remorse for what he'd said to me.

In serious and informal situations, we walk this Narrow Ridge each day, with the hope that we maintain our balance and never lose footing. And when we do stumble, we hope to muster our own capacity — and the support of mentors, friends, and loved ones — to rise again.

Mikkets

Trapped in a Dream

GENESIS 41:1-44:17

And Pharaoh said to Joseph, "I have had a dream, but no one can interpret it. Now I have heard it said of you that for you to hear a dream is to tell its meaning."
—Genesis 41:15

P'shat: Explanation

Dreams play an important role in the Bible, from Jacob's nighttime vision of angels dancing on a ladder to this scene, in Mikkets, as Joseph, imprisoned for a crime he did not commit, correctly interprets the dreams of his cellmates, the royal cupbearer and the royal baker. Just as Joseph foretells, the baker is executed and the cupbearer returns to his post in Pharaoh's palace. As the cupbearer leaves prison, Joseph asks that he mention him to Pharaoh, but the cupbearer forgets.

Time passes, and Pharaoh wakens from troubling dreams that neither he nor any of his advisors can interpret to his satisfaction. Amid the palace upset, the cupbearer remembers and mentions Joseph's remarkable dream interpretation abilities to the king. Joseph suddenly finds himself before Pharaoh to hear, "I have had a dream, but no one can interpret it. Now I have heard it said of you that for you to hear a dream is to tell its meaning" (Gen. 41:15). With God's help, Joseph discerns the future hidden in Pharaoh's dream. The king frees Joseph from prison and appoints him as senior palace assistant.

D'rash: Buber's Insight

Dreams are not I-Thou relationships at all, but hint at them.

In the Torah, dreams predict the future. By contrast, Buber sees in dreams a window to the spirit.

You awaken from sleep and recall a dream just ended—something that happened is over. Buber, interested in the here and now between people, points out that dreams are inside people, and not between them. Dreams lack interpersonal dimension. Taking these insights further, Buber says that dreams provide the basis for a conversation in the present—between people, and here and now.

By comparison to Buber, Sigmund Freud, the founder of psychoanalysis as the basis for modern psychology, psychotherapy, and psychiatry, took dreams as fodder for analysis. Buber saw such an approach, which traps a person inside someone else's interpretation, to reflect I-It. Buber refused to analyze or impose a specific interpretation on a dream. Instead, he asked the dreamer to explain what that dream meant in that particular moment and in the presence of another person. This approach reflects I-Thou and brings us to a historic story about what to make of dreams.

Months before his "I Have a Dream" speech, the Reverend Dr. Martin Luther King Jr. referenced Buber in his "Letter from a Birmingham Jail." Reverend King was in Birmingham, Alabama, leading the campaign to integrate water fountains, lunch counters, and restrooms when Birmingham authorities locked him up for violating Alabama law prohibiting mass public demonstrations.

King took two books with him to prison—Albert Camus's *The Rebel* and Buber's *Between Man and Man*. Meanwhile, eight white local clergy members placed an ad in the *Birmingham News* labeling King an outside agitator and extremist. Infuriated, King sat down and, in the sunlight falling between the jail cell bars, wrote what became known as the "Letter from a Birmingham Jail."

The "Letter" cited Socrates, Thomas Jefferson, St. Augustine, and Martin Buber. King described the political, economic, and social wrongs of segregation, and he referenced Buber to speak to the moral and theological failings of segregation. King wrote that dividing people by race treats the next person as *It* rather than *Thou*.[18]

D'rash: A Personal Reflection

DEFENDING DREAMS

I took away a lesson about approaching and interpreting dreams as a social work intern at a university student-counseling center.

We were in group supervision. The several campus social work interns would present their experiences to the team, which included a psychiatrist, a psychologist, and other social workers. One of the interns described a student counselee with a passion for social justice, to the point of revolution, over a range of issues—race, poverty, and more—that she believed needed urgent attention. A team psychiatrist smiled, as if joking, even though he was serious, as he said that each of the student's dreams of social justice could be traced to an internal psychic dynamic.

I knew there was something deeply wrong with what the psychiatrist said. In his eyes, the dream of social justice was of clinical value, a symptom rather than an inspiration. Dreams of a better world reflected emotional turmoil and not much else. I just couldn't accept an interpretation that struck me as more cynical than clinical. Back then, though, I couldn't put my thoughts into words quickly enough, so I went through the rest of the semester with my concerns unaddressed.

I carried those memories with me when, for my synagogue teens, I led a "Civil Rights Journey" through the Southeast United States. Our itinerary included the King Center in Atlanta, Georgia, and the Rosa Parks Museum in Montgomery, Alabama. We marched, as Reverend King and others had, across the Edmund Pettus Bridge in Selma, and we learned about Leo Frank and Emmett Till, who were falsely accused and brutally murdered. And we met people who had lived through this history. A woman who had joined King on the fifty-mile march from Selma to Montgomery described how her mother couldn't get a transfusion from a local hospital because they had no "Black blood," the only blood she was allowed to receive, because a white person's blood was forbidden to her. A retired Birmingham minister described how he had been beaten. And the teens, who dream of a better world, began to see that this dream for justice and equality, and the struggle to achieve it, is also theirs.

Va-yiggash

Learning to Put Feelings into Words

GENESIS 44:18–47:27

Then Judah went up to him and said . . .
—Genesis 44:18

P'shat: Explanation

Years have passed since Joseph last saw his brothers: when they abandoned him to die in an empty desert pit. Unbeknownst to them, a merchant caravan pulled Joseph out and sold him into slavery; eventually he rose to become second-in-command to Pharaoh. Meanwhile, drought and famine have struck Canaan, forcing the brothers to travel to Egypt for food, where plenty grows along the moist and fertile Nile Delta.

All the brothers have matured in the interim. Earlier on, Joseph tattled and bragged, and the brothers reacted by bullying and attacking him. Here, in Va-yiggash, Judah finds a way to put complicated feelings into thoughtful words that heal the family and shape the direction of Jewish history.

The brothers reach Egypt. Joseph, who oversees food distribution, immediately recognizes them, but the brothers don't recognize him, with his dress and appearance so changed, and Joseph exploits the situation. He tests whether his brothers' ways have matured by hiding his identity from them, accusing them of spying, and framing their youngest brother, Benjamin, with the crime of theft. As Va-yiggash opens, Judah, who now views Joseph as a cruel trickster, puts his life on the line to demand an end to the antics: "Then Judah went up to him and said, 'Please, my lord, let your servant appeal to my lord, and do not be impatient with your servant, you who are the equal of Pharaoh'" (Gen. 44:18). Judah's honest speaking and heartfelt tone break Joseph's cold veneer and set the foundation for restored family relationships.

Despite the positive ending, some Rabbis are critical of Judah. Rashi accuses him of snarkiness, as he confronts Joseph with, "May my words enter your ears" (on Gen. 44:8). Rabbi Judah says of his namesake, Judah, "He went up to him to pick a fight" (*Bereshit Rabbah* 93:6). In contrast, Rabbi Nehemiah defends Judah: "He went up to him to make peace" (*Bereshit Rabbah* 93:6), in keeping with Buber's recognition that speaking person-to-person has the potential to end conflict and bring reconciliation.

In the plain sense of the text, the brothers mature to speak with respect, candor, and dignity.

D'rash: Buber's Insight

And I was too timid to ask.

Whereas Joseph was traumatized at the hands of his brothers, Buber's mother fled home to elope with a Russian officer without even saying goodbye, and left him with significant emotional scarring. Much later in life, Buber recalled his three-year-old self rushing to the window and out to the balcony of the family's Vienna apartment, urgently trying to capture his mother's attention, but she never turned around. In the aftermath, the deeply confused and hurt boy was sent to live with his grandparents, in what is Lviv, Ukraine, today, hundreds of miles from Vienna. Time passed, and Buber's angst only deepened as no one broached the topic (in that time and culture, people didn't discuss personal matters).

Looking back on his silence some eight decades later, he reflected, as if he were one of the Passover seder's Four Children, "And I was too timid to ask."

D'rash: A Personal Reflection

GROWING INTO CANDOR

Assertiveness did not come naturally to me, either personally or professionally. The big change came in social work school, as I learned to better recognize my thoughts and feelings and put them into words.

I began social work school after college and rabbinic ordination. I was already working full-time as a congregational rabbi when I found a social work program that would let me go part-time, and little by little, I got the degree. In social work school, I learned how to pay better attention to what people say and do, recognize the significance of what I was witnessing, and put my thoughts into words. Until then, I might have noticed a conversation partner's body language or someone's tone of voice in a group meeting, but I didn't attach much meaning or importance to any of what I saw or heard. Then came social work field practice, where I'd have a conversation with a client in a counseling session—someone recently divorced, a new parent, for instance, any person seeking help when facing a life situation. After each session, I'd do a handwritten "verbatim" summary of our conversation. In writing a verbatim, we students would divide a sheet of paper in half and put a recollection of the verbatim conversation on the left and "comments" on the right. Comments could include a note on the significance of the client's movement or posture, such as a clenched jaw as a sign of anger, words spoken more softly as an indication of upset, or leaning back and slumping as a reflection of resignation. We also wrote down our reactions to the process, such as uncertainty about how to respond or what we were thinking when we spoke to the client. To be sure, while verbatims were not a totally accurate record, they provided our sense of what went on, or what we thought or wished went on, which took us to the next step and the real learning.

We'd review verbatims in several ways—privately with a supervisor, in group meetings during case review, or in class at school—and each one of these reviews brought insight and learning. Comments from teachers, supervisors, and classmates helped me identify and better explain what I thought and felt as others spoke, and how to react with greater sensitivity to others in the moment. More than anything else, I learned how to stay on topic and go deeper in the conversation. These lessons stayed with me, as evidence that we can learn to communicate more effectively and connectedly.

Va-yeḥi

The Importance of Supportive Relationship

GENESIS 47:28–50:26

Dan shall be a serpent by the road,
A viper by the path,
That bites the horse's heels
So that his rider is thrown backward.
—Genesis 49:17

P'shat: Explanation

Jacob realizes his life will soon end and turns to bless his children and grandchildren, thereby offering us a lesson on the need for relationship.

Jacob first blesses Ephraim and Manasseh, his grandsons by Joseph, and predicts that they will be a source of blessing through the generations. Next, Jacob blesses his twelve sons individually with poetic words and puzzling metaphors. What's more, some of the blessings are uncomplimentary. For instance, Jacob compares Dan to a serpent and snake.

When it comes to serpents, the Torah and the Rabbis elsewhere speak harshly. For instance, they criticize the serpent of the Garden of Eden, whose cunning leads Adam and Eve to sin by eating the forbidden fruit of the Tree of Knowledge of Good and Evil. Rashi, for one, highlights how the serpent brings on its own undoing. On one hand, the serpent is the "shrewdest all the wild beasts" and speaks smoothly (Gen. 3:1). Yet, "His strength was his downfall." The serpent's carefully crafted words lead to the sin of eating from the forbidden tree, and the serpent's negative influence is punished with the loss of its legs. It is destined to crawl on its belly and live by eating dirt (on Gen. 3:1).

Thus, we are left puzzled by a father's end-of-life blessing, while Buber turns to the serpent for a lesson on the limits of self-sufficiency.

D'rash: Buber's Insight

That tender surface of personal life which longs for contact
with other life is progressively deadened or desensitized.

Buber teaches that companionship is the foundation of meaningful living through a novel interpretation of the classic Garden of Eden story. He recalls Rabbi Simha Bunam of Pzhysha being asked about the serpent's punishment, which at first glance might appear to be more of a reward than a curse. After all, "dirt shall you eat all the days of your life" (Gen. 3:15) means that food is always there, worry free, leaving the serpent entirely self-sufficient, without having to work for anything. Yet Rabbi Simha replies that having all you need is more of a curse than a blessing. It means never having to rely on God—or anyone else. On the contrary, he wants us to need each other, and to know that we need one another, in relationship.

Buber underscores Rabbi Simha Bunam's approach when he speaks of "that tender surface of personal life which longs for contact with other life." Yet Buber worries that the challenges and pressures of life will cause a person to lose interest in the opportunity for that "contact"; these critical relationships are at risk of being destroyed, frayed, "deadened or desensitized." In this regard, self-sufficiency can be more of a punishment than a blessing. While a person (or a snake) may well be able to survive alone, the soul risks becoming "deadened or desensitized," isolated and estranged, left to "long for contact" and in need of relationships. It is with others that we thrive.

D'rash: A Personal Reflection

A GREAT IDEA UNTIL IT IS NOT

Through my work as a religious advocate, I traveled to Washington DC to join a team meeting with a congressperson who had a history of opposing government funding of health care for the poor. In his view, people should stand on their own and not rely on others for help, regardless of the hand that life deals them.

The other advocates in the room spoke first, talking about the positive community impact of federal health care programs. When it came my turn to talk, I told a personal story: "My mom was a single mom, who raised me to be who I am along with my brother, a doctor. She did this, in part, with the support of the government. My family and I have more than repaid the government for its investment in us, and I hope that others have the same opportunity."

The congressperson smirked, and I don't think I changed his mind. But I do give him credit for taking the time to meet with us when other like-minded policy makers brush off folks like me.

In the days that followed, I thought about that time in my early life. I remembered the deep, but unspecific, uncertainty that no one really put into words. I was only ten, my brother, five, and we kids had no idea what was involved with money, a mortgage, life insurance, or any of those things the adults spent so much time talking about. But I do remember plenty of praise for Social Security and veterans' benefits, which gave my family the financial support we needed to help us move forward.

I have benefited from the social safety net. So, I listen carefully, and with some skepticism, when there's talk of self-made people who've succeeded on their own, or rugged individuals who need no outside support or help. In my experience, those social narratives don't stand up to examination. The reality is that too many people never get the basics they deserve to begin with, be it quality education, adequate health care, clean water, and safety in their homes and neighborhoods.

On top of this, no one is entirely "self-made" by personal vision and hard work alone. What about the teachers, nurses, doctors, sports coaches, relatives, friends, colleagues, and hosts of others whose support and mentoring have enabled those of us who have been fortunate enough to succeed to be who we are? Self-sufficiency is a great idea, but only until it's not.

To be sure, the Torah teaches self-reliance, and the Rabbis underscore the importance of taking personal responsibility. For example, according to Maimonides the highest level of charity is to provide a gift or loan, enter into a business partnership, or find work for people in need, so they can stand on their own and not ask others for help (*Mishnah Torah, Gifts to the Poor*, 10:7). This go-it-on-one's-own attitude stands alongside the acknowledgment in Judaism, through the lens of *tzedakah*, that anyone's life can take a bad turn at any point. It is our responsibility to support one another.

II

Exodus (Shemot)

Shemot

Get Off the Road

*I must turn aside to look at this marvelous
sight; why doesn't the bush burn up?*
—Exodus 3:3

P'shat: Explanation

Now that Israel has suffered for four hundred years under Pharaoh, Moses happens upon a flame of hope. Having taken refuge in Midian (after killing a taskmaster for beating a Hebrew slave), where he works as a shepherd for his father-in-law, Jethro. Moses is out with the flock when "an angel of Adonai appeared to him in a blazing fire out of a bush. He gazed, and there was a bush all aflame, yet the bush was not consumed." Moses does a double take: "I must turn aside to look at this marvelous sight; why doesn't the bush burn up?" Startled, he hears God describe Israel's impending redemption and learns that *he* will lead the people to freedom.

Moses's response to the fire, "I must *turn* aside to *look*," brings Rashi to highlight the physical and spiritual dimensions of the text. Moses first takes a physical "turn" of the body and then follows with a deeper, spiritual "look." Where the "turn" is external and visible, the "look" is an internal pivot, a step up of the soul from small-time shepherd to leader of the people.

The incident at the burning bush marks a transformational moment for Moses as well as for Jewish history. A shepherd's presence of mind—pausing long enough to realize the fire burns without physical fuel—sets the stage for the Redemption from Egypt, the Revelation of Torah, and the development of the Jewish people. Mindfulness and a quick turn direct the destiny of Israel and the world.

D'rash: Buber's Insight

A deed of the everyday ... prepares for
the messianic completion.

For the soul that wanders the workday wilderness, the struggle is great, yet the potential for redemption hides in plain sight along the commuter's roadside: "Turn aside and look." Walk into the office building at the start of yet another workday and note that especially warm greeting from the security guard, the chance exchange with a stranger on the elevator, or the cheerful "Good morning!" from the ordinarily reserved receptionist. An otherwise ignored "deed of the everyday" brings a sense of peaceful wholeness here and now, what Buber calls "the messianic completion." All it takes is a good look, Moses style. Redemption from the routine depends on us. Redemption is at hand.

On the challenges of finding the time for encounter, Buber relates the reminiscences of Rabbi Menahem Mendel of Rymanov (1745–1815), who longed for the days before there were real roads, when a traveler had to pull over at nightfall to pass the evening in an inn. This overnight stop allowed time for prayerful reflection, reading, or sharing a good conversation with another traveler. Nowadays, a person travels the roads 24/7, nonstop, and bypasses the spiritual opportunities that were one time at hand.[1] Rabbi Menahem Mendel, undone by the ever-increasing speed of early nineteenth-century life, yearned for a more livable pace.

Buber was a perpetual road warrior of sorts. Always working, hard-driving, and getting things done—a "workaholic," predating the label—Buber was driven to complete a monumental Bible translation from Hebrew to German, the first in centuries, begun in collaboration with his colleague and friend the Jewish thinker Franz Rosenzweig. Even on a mountain hike with family, Buber carried a

Hebrew Bible, a Hebrew-German dictionary, and a notebook to follow up on translation ideas in real time.

And yet, Buber always set work aside when someone showed up at
his study to talk. He would sit the visitor down and hear the person
out, take the words to heart, and offer a fullhearted response. I imagine that these moments provided Buber with a good reason to step off
the busy road of work to talk and listen. In the spirit of Rabbi Menahem Mendel and the Torah's Moses, he would leave the highway of
doing for a conversation. That is, he would pause to take in the sight
of a burning bush unconsumed, setting the way for the "messianic
completion" in I-Thou.

D'rash: A Personal Reflection

HIDING IN PLAIN SIGHT

We were with friends at a restaurant at the end of a very busy workday, having a relaxed dinner in one of those cozy places with oversized chairs and large tables that encourage people to take their time
to talk and eat. Our table was alongside a fireplace, and every now
and then, I'd stare into the flames and wonder when someone would
be coming over to throw on another log, but no one came, and the
fire, nevertheless, burned on. I eventually figured it out: This fireplace burning "unconsumed" was gas fueled, and the logs were not
wood but fireproof cement. And, I realized, human inventiveness had
replicated the Torah's miracle, and I, like Moses, had to look twice to
realize something unusual was happening in very plain sight, and all
the while a meandering conversation about the kids, the weather, and
work assumed "messianic" proportions for the moments of reprieve
in I-Thou.

I bet Moses foresaw us at that restaurant fireside. When he studied
the burning bush, I think he glimpsed into each spiritual encounter
in Eternal Thou through all time. Our dinner conversation contained
an echo of his call from the Divine.

Va-'era'

Reification

EXODUS 6:2–9:35

*Pharaoh's heart stiffened, and he did not
heed them, as Adonai had said.*
—Exodus 7:13

P'shat: Explanation

Va-'era' raises difficult and complicated questions about divine justice, as God appears to unfairly punish people for behavior beyond their control.

Moses tells Pharaoh to release the Hebrew slaves. Pharaoh refuses, but the decision to refuse is not his—it comes from God. As we read earlier, God has already relayed to Moses that God will not allow Pharaoh to heed Moses and Aaron's call for freedom—"I, however, will stiffen his heart, so that he will not let the people go" (Exod. 4:21)—and that's just what happens. When Moses and Aaron confront Pharaoh, "Pharaoh's heart stiffened, and he did not heed them, as Adonai had said" (Exod. 7:13), and Egypt suffers through ten devastating plagues as a consequence. Pharaoh cannot let the Hebrews go, even if he wants to. God takes away his freedom to decide, and he and his nation have no choice but to suffer.

So, here's the question: How can a caring and fair God punish wrongdoing when doing the wrong thing is the only, divinely ordained, option? How could God call an entire nation to task in such a way? The Rabbis are deeply troubled by this appearance of God's injustice.

Ḥizkuni (France, thirteenth century) proposes that this stubbornness isn't about human free will or divine trampling over it. Rather, the issue is one of God's providing Pharaoh with fortitude. God gives Pharaoh the superhuman resolve to withstand ten monumental plagues and not die of fear. Why would God do such a thing? To some of our Rabbis, God hardens Pharaoh's heart for pedagogical reasons: to impress upcoming generations about the miracles of the Exodus, and leave them awestruck by God's capacities: "It was with a mighty hand that Adonai brought us out from Egypt, the house of bondage" (Exod. 13:14). That is to say, the "hardening" provides a "teachable moment" to demonstrate God's wondrous might.

The kabbalist, philosopher, poet, and physician Rabbi Moses ben Nahman (Spain and the Land of Israel, 1194–1270), known by his Hebrew acronym, Ramban, and, in English, Nahmanides, suggests a similar interpretation. By way of background, the then ruling Spanish authorities periodically forced Ramban to defend Jewish teachings during politically motivated, rigged public dialogues, or disputations. It is said that the Ramban was so adept at disproving the false accusations against the Jewish community that he intimidated the intolerant authorities, who would have put him to death had he not fled Spain for Israel.

Here (on Exod. 10:1), Ramban characteristically defends the Torah, arguing that future generations will be so astounded by God's mighty feats of nature that they will pass this story down in perpetuity and inspire their descendants to sustain the faith. To Ramban, keeping the faith for centuries to come is enough of a justification to deprive Pharaoh of free will.

Yet, for many of us, this response is inadequate and unsettling. We are still left questioning the fairness of holding Pharaoh accountable for behavior beyond his control.

D'rash: Buber's Insight

If a man lets it have the mastery, the continually growing world of It overruns him and robs him of the reality of his own.

The Hebrew Bible presents God as depriving Pharaoh of the ability to see clearly, analyze objectively, reach a logical decision, and/or act on it. But Buber does not accuse God of an injustice. Instead, Buber attributes the root cause to Pharaoh.

To Buber, Pharaoh suffers from a failure of self-control. The king creates his own situation by giving his emotions permission to overwhelm his moral judgment. Writing in *I and Thou*, Buber explains: "If a man lets it have the mastery, the continually growing world of *It* overruns him and robs him of the reality of his own." That is, Pharaoh welcomes It as a spiritual thief. He willfully lumps all Israel together as inferior to rationalize the enslavement. He permits I-It to rob him of the opportunity to see each member of Israel as Thou and, thereby, he misses the opportunity to meet God.

The word "reification" speaks to such a tragic expansion of It. Reification happens when one small part of a person—age, height, weight, gender, skin color, religion, ethnicity, sexual orientation, nationality, language, profession, political party, and so on—swells up to negatively define this entire human being and obscure any and all of this being's positive attributes. It expands into rudeness and disrespect, bigotry, discrimination, and sometimes persecution. Thus, as Pharaoh wills it, a reified image of Israel plunders his spirit, leaving him incapable of recognizing that a slave is really another human being, like himself, deserving of honor and respect.

To be sure, there are times when we characterize people as It, to the good. An orchestra conductor in a tux walks up to the podium and the audience knows the concert is about to begin. A uniform—on a restaurant server or a first responder in an ambulance or fire truck—defines this person's role as welcome and communicates what to expect. Categorizing people can be helpful; acting on that information can be a positive—unless it becomes reification.

Buber experienced the bigotry of reification many times. In 1933, days before the Nazi-declared boycott of Jewish stores, a storm trooper appeared at the Bubers' front door, gave the Nazi salute, and asked Buber to describe his line of work so that a proper sign—identifying the building as a Jewish business such as a law office or doctor's office—could be placed in the front window. Buber, who showed a defiant streak even when it put him at personal risk, said he didn't believe in labels and would leave it to the trooper to decide the sign. After entering the Buber home and seeing its extensive library, the soldier pulled out a sign that indicated a Jewish bookstore.[2] A reified Jew was someone the Nazis knew exactly how to hate.

D'rash: A Personal Reflection

DEFINING JEWS DOWN

There's a lesson on reification presented at the United States Holocaust Memorial Museum in Washington DC—an insight I reexperience each time I visit while leading a group of high school students.

The lesson begins as we approach the first museum exhibit on the top floor. After an elevator ride in a cage-like, dimly lit elevator car, apparently designed to resemble a gas chamber, the doors open to a large photograph of astonished American soldiers in a recently liberated concentration camp. The stunned soldiers stand over the remains of murdered Jews. A short walk down the hall leads to an exhibit on the Nazi pseudoscience of race—where the reification lives.

The exhibit documents how the Nazis proposed a so-called superior Aryan race and reified anyone, especially Jews, who didn't fit their imaginary ideal. The Nazis misappropriated medical tools to measure differences in hair color and bone structure in the fallacious attempt to uphold a baseless racial narrative and define Jews as inferior and deserving to suffer and die. Nazi reification, built upon centuries of social, cultural, and religious antisemitism, purported a so-called scientific, genetic justification for genocide.

In corrupting the science of human physiology, the Nazis asserted a stiff-hearted adherence to the blatantly false belief that hair a shade darker or a forehead a little broader demonstrates a human being's inferior essence and unworthiness of life.

Bo'

History as Strangers, Responsibility as Redeemers

EXODUS 10:1–13:16

A mixed multitude went up with them.
—Exodus 12:38

P'shat: Explanation

As the Hebrews leave a decimated Egypt, a self-invited "mixed multitude" joins them in flight. The Torah doesn't say much about the origins of these tagalongs, leaving it to the Rabbis to raise a spectrum of opinions about where the mixed multitude comes from and what they want.

To some of the Rabbis, the mixed multitude is a band of opportunistic Egyptian interlopers who flee their plague-ravaged homeland for what they believe will be better times with the Hebrews. In contrast, Rashi says they are an upstanding "aggregation of converts to Judaism from various peoples" (on Exod. 12:38). Regardless of their motives and character—trustworthy and faithful or not—the Hebrews let them in.

At this time in the Torah's narrative the Hebrews don't yet have to open themselves to strangers—and why should they, given their recent painful memories of being exploited as slaves because they were strangers in Egypt? It's understandable how, after the Hebrews' four-hundred-year-ordeal of bondage, they'd want nothing of this mixed multitude. They could rightfully send them back to Egypt, but the story does not go that way. To the Hebrews' credit, they put aside the very natural inclination to turn a cold shoulder and preemptively protect themselves from further harm, or put forward an imagined reason as a pretext to exact revenge. In a foreshadowing of the Torah's teaching to protect and care for the stranger, the Hebrews allow the mixed multitude to join them—and, as we get further into the Bible, they go on to extend a firm and clear measure of protection to the strangers among them.

The Torah safeguards the stranger as a member of a vulnerable social class. Later in Exodus we read, "You shall not oppress a stranger, for you know the feelings of the stranger, having yourselves been strangers in the land of Egypt" (23:9). Deuteronomy goes further, instructing us to "befriend the stranger, for you were strangers in the land of Egypt" (10:19). The stranger is fed (Lev. 19:9–10) and partakes of the Shabbat day of rest, just like all of Israel (Exod. 20:10). The Torah provides the stranger and the people of Israel with the very rights and protections Hebrews were denied in Egypt.

Ultimately the Torah draws on the memory of the Hebrew slave experience to underscore and reiterate this foundational mitzvah to care for the stranger, and repeats this mitzvah thirty-six times—more times than any other mitzvah in the Torah, including keeping Shabbat, the holidays, and the dietary laws. Moreover, the Torah includes the stranger in the same vulnerable social class as the widow and orphan. Having no natural human advocate, this class receives protection as an extension of God's caring and love. The history of Jews as strangers drives the theological foundation for Jewish responsibility to act as redeemers. Jews emulate the God who cared for them when they were needy by protecting and caring for those in need.

In our day we learn to care for the stranger through the Passover seder. The ritual reading of the Haggadah, "telling," recalls the slave experience in Egypt as the basis for teaching that no one else should have to suffer as the Hebrews did. The experience of being the stranger is a firewall against acting like the Egyptians, who took painful advantage of the Hebrews when they were strangers in their land.

D'rash: Buber's Insight

*God loves the sojourner. If I love God, in the course of
loving him, I come to love the one whom God loves, too.*

We love God when, for all our differences, we love one another,
an ideal that Buber upheld in relationship with his Israeli-Arab
neighbors.

The Buber family chose to live in the mixed Jewish-Arab Jerusalem neighborhood of Abu Tor. Buber appreciated the Arab style of
architecture—large rooms and high ceilings that provided ample
space for his 15,000-volume library. He also had personal relationships with the family's Arab neighbors.

During the dangerous and frightening days of Israel's 1948 War
of Independence, the Bubers evacuated their Abu Tor home for a
safer Jerusalem neighborhood. When Jewish properties in Abu Tor
were being plundered, Buber's Arab neighbors risked their lives to
protect the Buber house and contents. An Arab friend of the family and neighbor, Jussaf Wahab Dajani, stood guard when Iraqi soldiers searched the Buber home and tried to enter the library. Dajani
stopped the soldiers right at the library door, told them what was
inside, and insisted that they would have to kill him to get in. The
soldiers said that they respected learning and left Dajani and the
Buber home unharmed.[3]

Buber's personal commitment to improved Jewish-Arab relations
extended well beyond his neighborhood. He was a founder of the
group B'rit Shalom, "Covenant of Peace," devoted to deeper Arab-
Jewish understanding and creating Israel as a binational state. Seeing more than enough opportunity for both peoples to share the
land and the national economy, he affirmed that when one group
advances, everyone moves forward. While recognizing the challenges
in bridging the many significant Jewish-Arab grievances, he cherished a vision of collaborative living that reflects the Jewish value of
loving the stranger.[4]

D'rash: A Personal Reflection

THE STRANGERS AMONG US

The stranger enters and blesses our lives in many different ways.

When it comes to having dinner out, for example, you and I may trifle over where to eat and what to have — Japanese, Mexican, Indian, and the like — while immigrants, documented or not, work under challenging, even dangerous conditions. Behind swinging kitchen doors in restaurants across any town, immigrants chop, dice, and mix for diners who ask them to go light on the garlic or to steam instead of stir-fry.

Perhaps a cook suffers a burn from a wok and can't afford treatment because money is tight. Maybe a new hire who hasn't yet learned to slice vegetables safely cuts a finger and refuses medical assistance because a distant relative allegedly got deported after an emergency-room visit. Perhaps a waitress sends home that extra dollar we leave for a tip to pay for badly needed clothing for a grandchild. The immigrant who clears the restaurant table or washes dishes, who mows the lawns or paints the house, or who looks after our children or our elderly is entitled to protection and basic life services, including health care, a safe home, food, clothing, and an education for their children, too.

I take special note when, like any rabbi, I spend time with frail older adults, many receiving care from immigrants. I don't have any idea of their caregivers' legal status, but I see what immigrants do. When a person can't walk unaided, an immigrant steadies her arm and protects her from a fall. When someone is too weak to handle a spoon, an immigrant is there for hand feeding. Immigrants sit with our elderly in front of the TV, sharing in a soap opera, baseball game, or the midafternoon news. Immigrants provide comfort and support to individuals and families through illness and the end of life. When I meet these immigrants, I ask where they are from and what brought them to the United States. I ask about their families, here and in their homelands. I believe it is important and proper to demonstrate that immigrants matter to us and to acknowledge the conditions of their personal lives.

Be-shallaḥ

Daily Spiritual Practice

EXODUS 13:17–17:16

*And Adonai said to Moses, "I will rain down bread for
you from the sky, and the people shall go out and gather
each day from that day's portion—that I may test them
to see whether they will follow My instructions or not."*
—Exodus 16:4

P'shat: Explanation

The people of Israel fail a spiritual test, and in the process demonstrate the need for discipline in cultivating a recurring personal spiritual practice.

Food is scarce in the Sinai wilderness, so God provides manna to
sustain the people. White in color, resembling coriander seed, manna
that tastes like wafers in honey rains down each morning as a fine
frost that covers the earth. How did this miracle food get its name?
God tells Moses that the people, having never seen manna before, will
ask, "What's this?" (in Hebrew, "*Mi nah?*" corresponding to "manna"
in English). The name is in the question.

Manna comes with instructions. Fresh manna arrives six mornings a week. The people are to go out and gather only a day's worth
at a time, with the exception of the day before Shabbat, "when they
apportion what they have brought in, it shall prove to be double the
amount they gather each day" (Exod. 16:5)—ostensibly so the people
avoid the work of ingathering on the day of rest.

Rashi sees these instructions regarding "keep[ing] the commandments . . . [of not] leav[ing] any [manna] over and . . . [not] go[ing]

out on Shabbat to gather [it]" as a test of faith in God. Some community members fail the test by taking more manna than they need—
and the leftovers turn bad. Others fail by going go out to gather on
Shabbat, only to find none on the ground. The failures demonstrate
that they are not yet ready to enter Canaan. The peoples' spirits
are ruled by painful memories of Egypt; they are unable to follow
simple directions and live responsibly as free people. Out of this
story, we learn that the people need more time in the wilderness to
mature so that they can live on their own. And as we turn to Buber,
we draw from the experience with manna to learn about recurring
spiritual practice.

D'rash: Buber's Insight

*Through the meeting that which confronts me is fulfilled,
and enters the world of things, there to be endlessly
active, endlessly to become It, but also endlessly to
become Thou again, inspiring and blessing.*

When Buber, in *I and Thou*, spoke of I-Thou as "endlessly active,
endlessly to become *It*, but also endlessly to become *Thou*," he was
addressing the reality that we inevitably and continually flow from I-It
to I-Thou, in and out again, and calling on us to make the effort for
ongoing renewal. This means that we must work at getting to I-Thou
every day. Just as gathering manna was an ongoing spiritual discipline,
so do we engage in this recurring spiritual practice of seeking I-Thou.

Buber recalls Rabbi Kalman of Cracow, who told of Rabbi Zevi
Hirsh of Rymanov (d. 1846), who spoke in the name of Rabbi Menahem Mendel of Rymanov (d. 1815), who understood the story of the
manna as a lesson about recurrent physical and spiritual care. As surely
as the body needs manna, daily, the spirit requires ongoing feeding
too. An unrefreshed spirit withers as surely as stored manna decays,
and, Buber says, I-Thou inevitably reverts to I-It.

Since I-Thou will grow stale without ongoing nurturance, I-Thou needs to be renewed "endlessly," again and again. If we feed the spirit regularly, it will flourish, inspired and blessed.

There is a great example of renewable Jewish spiritual practice in Jewish prayer. The daily morning service includes the *Birkot ha-Shachar* (blessings of the morning) that call attention to the sacred character of what might otherwise appear to be very ordinary and unconsidered events. There's praise of God for the wondrous ability to waken and wipe sleep from our eyes, for having clothing to wear, for freedom, for being able to learn Torah, and more. Another morning prayer, *Yotzer* (Creator), considers the inexplicable workings of the universe and blesses God, who "fashions light and creates dark" and "renews the creation each day." And the nighttime *Ma'ariv Aravim* (Who makes the evenings pass) describes how "light rolls up before the dark" thanks to powers far beyond us. Each of these prayers, and their regular repetition, reflects the need for continuing attention.

Outside the regular prayer cycle, additional blessings recognize the sacred in our daily lives. There is a blessing to recite when hearing a clap of thunder that startles a soul from reverie or for marveling skyward at a comet tail's streak in the night. There is another blessing for the first time you put on a new coat and another one for surviving a life-threatening illness or accident. Each one of these prayers recategorizes a seemingly ordinary experience as a holy occasion and attunes the spirit to grace that which would otherwise pass unnoticed. Just as a daily portion of manna is a material gift and spiritual opportunity, regular prayer directs our attention to grace in the routine.

D'rash: A Personal Reflection

I CAN'T "SET AND FORGET"

When I'm up at the house in Western Massachusetts, most of my days begin at 6:00 a.m. or earlier. The alarm clock announces, "This is NPR," and within a few minutes, I'm out the door for a three-mile walk along a tree-lined country road. I take in the morning quiet, inevitably broken by calling crows or rustling fallen leaves stirred by a startled squirrel or chipmunk. A crescent of sun rises behind a nearby mountaintop.

I'll also walk mornings when I am in Manhattan, along the path that circles the Central Park reservoir. My walk often begins in the dark, as high-rise apartment and office lights glitter like jewels. The climbing sun casts an orange halo around rooftops, and blinding rays streak through crosstown streets, east to west, and into my eyes.

The mind races further and faster than the feet, from afterthoughts about a conversation I had the day before to what will happen at the morning's first office meeting. I'll wonder what's for breakfast or get an idea for a reflection like this. And sometimes I get distracted, almost in a trance, and I find myself asking, "Where did the time go? How did I get right here, right now?" This daily portion of physical exercise is a spiritual practice.

Perhaps you have what feels to you like a regular spiritual practice, be it prayer or study, or exercise, reading, making a kind of art, or having a conversation with a family member, friend, or stranger. The good fortune of being able to devote oneself to a daily practice is a gift from the skies. Many folks, forced by circumstances of life to work long days for little pay, are barely able to provide for themselves and their families, with little to no time to tend the spirit. Having time for a daily practice is itself a privilege that calls for an expression of appreciation.

People wonder whether I would be more productive if, instead of walking around, I put that time into work. Yet I don't feel at peace with myself without that daily morning exercise. When it comes to the spirit, I can't "set and forget." I need to renew myself each day.

Yitro

All of Us, Together at Sinai

EXODUS 18:1-20:23

God spoke all these words, saying, "I am Adonai your God."
—Exodus 20:1

P'shat: Explanation

Just three months after leaving Egypt, Israel reaches Sinai and experiences the event known as the Revelation.

Creation, Redemption, and Revelation are the Torah's centerpiece happenings. God creates the world, redeems Israel from Egypt, and now, in Yitro, reveals the Torah at Mount Sinai. The capstone of the Revelation, the Ten Commandments, open with, "God spoke all these words, saying, 'I am Adonai your God'" (Exod. 20:1-2).

The sum of Jewish teaching flows from this mountainside moment between God and Israel. As Rabbi Yitzhak says: "Whatever the prophets of the future prophesied, it was all received at Sinai" (Midrash *Tanhuma Yitro* 11). Moreover, the Rabbis maintain that the Revelation embraces everyone and everything—Israel, humanity, and the universe—through all time.

The Rabbis imagine that each generation of Israel—every Jew that ever lived or will live—stands together at Sinai (Midrash *Hagadol*, Deut. 29:12), thus underscoring the centrality of Revelation. The Revelation also resonates in the heavens. The Rabbis teach that, while the angels jealously hoped to keep the Torah for themselves and out of human hands, Moses defends God's decision to give the Torah to Israel, asking the angels, "Did you descend from Canaan to Egypt for Pharaoh to enslave you?" (*Shabbat* 88b). The Torah is worthy compensation for Israel's four centuries of bondage, an ordeal the heavenly angels avoided.

The Revelation also garners attention in all of earth's corners, affecting the natural order and all living things. In the name of Rabbi Yoḥanan, Rabbi Abahu teaches that, when the Torah was given, birds stopped chirping and flying and the sea's waves ceased: "The world went entirely silent when the Voice went out" (Exod. Rabbah 29:9). The Revelation impacts Israel, all people, and the entire world.

D'rash: Buber's Insight

What happened once happens now and always. And the fact of this happening to us is a guarantee of it having happened.

Buber brings a unique Jewish approach to this highlight moment in Jewish history. The Rabbis imagine that all Jews—past, present, and future—were there at Sinai. And Buber brings each of us to that mountainside that very day by teaching that whenever you and I speak as I-Thou, we speak with God, just as Israel did at Sinai.

Revelation is ongoing for Buber, even as he seems to contradict himself when he teaches that each encounter is unique.[5] So, the question becomes, "How can a one-of-a-kind event repeat itself?"

The resolution to this question has to do with Eternal Thou. On the one hand, each I-Thou is discrete, never to recur. On the other hand, each and every I-Thou brings us into God's presence in Eternal Thou. To be sure, the existence and workings of Eternal Thou are as unprovable for Buber as that moment of Sinai is for the Rabbis. Nevertheless, Buber sees both as "fact." Each one of our unique, kindred conversations is made of the same spiritual substance as our collective time with God at Sinai.

The Bible is filled with these kinds of self-contradictions and paradoxes, and Buber accepts all of them as "fact." He takes the Bible seriously, not literally. He doesn't fret over the specifics of the Sinai miracle—or over talking snakes, great floods, or any of the Bible's other wonders. He tells us that the people thought something remarkable happened. They turned from their rational side to their spiritual side and used the term "miracle" to describe what they saw.

In the Bible's era, in Buber's time, and in our day, we witness things that defy understanding and explanation. Sometimes, what actually happens is less important than what we make of it. On these occasions of astonishment, awe, or wonder, a person's rational inclination yields to their mystical inclination in the attempt to make sense of the inexplicable.

Similarly, the Hebrew Bible can be said to reflect the difference between Jewish history and Jewish memory. For those of us, including myself, who view it in such a way, the text has less to do with what actually happened and more to do with recollection: what we think and say about events.

Buber cherishes the Bible as a record of the conversation between Israel and God. He also affirms that we speak to God by speaking with each other, and the Revelation we gain from one another at any point in history is as truthful as the Revelation at Sinai.

D'rash: A Personal Reflection

THE TORAH PARADOX

To be Jewish is to embrace a paradox. It requires the summoning of all one's heart, soul, and strength to love and believe—without any basis in fact.

I unknowingly entered this paradox as a kid when I went to yeshiva, a school that was really two competing schools in one. In the morning we went to "Hebrew" school—as we called it—where rabbis described a real Garden of Eden and showed us what they believed to be the likely spot where it had been on a modern map. We learned that the earth is no more than six thousand years old, meaning natural wonders like the Grand Canyon came from Noah's flood, and that people aren't descended from monkeys—God made us as we are. Fossils?

God put them there to test your faith, to find out whether you believe in the truth of Torah or in scientists, who got it wrong. In the afternoon, after lunch, we had "English" school—science, math, history, and more, with teachers who could have taught in my neighborhood Brooklyn public school.

Rarely did anyone raise a question about how to reconcile it all, how a Jew could possibly balance the conflicting truths of Torah and science. In third grade, a classmate did ask the rebbe how we know the Torah is true. The Rebbe responded, "We know that the Torah is true because the Torah says it's true. The Torah tells us that there were 600,000 witnesses at Mount Sinai. How can 600,000 people be wrong?"

Even as kid, I knew it was more complicated than that.

As I got older and involved in Reform Judaism, my early childhood yeshiva learning stayed with me, Torah alongside evidence-based science. In rabbinic school, I learned about the "documentary hypothesis," which rose in popularity in Europe just before Buber's time and became more widely upheld over the years. Looking at documented history, culture, and archaeology to explain how people wrote and compiled the Hebrew Bible, various experts offered different theories culminating more or less in the conclusion that the Hebrew Bible was written by more than one author—more likely, several sources over several centuries—and the text was compiled, edited, and reedited until it reached the form we know today.

To me, there is something wonderfully liberating about the progressive approach to Judaism that recognizes the truth of Torah on one hand and the truth of lived human experience—science, history, philosophy, culture, relationships, and more—on the other, and doesn't obsess about how or why.

Religion is based on faith; it's not rational. No one should expect it to be provable, scientific, or logical. One can love both Torah and science at the same time, as I do, without worrying about being unable to reconcile the details and conflicts. Ultimately, the real question isn't one of how the Torah came to be. I want to know what the Torah, the Rabbis, and modern interpreters teach about how to live.

Mishpatim

Respecting Religious Difference

When two or more parties fight, and one of them pushes a
pregnant woman and a miscarriage results, but no other
damage ensues, the one responsible shall be fined according
as the woman's husband may exact, the payment to be based
on reckoning. But if other damage ensues, the penalty shall
be life for life, eye for eye, tooth for tooth, hand for hand, foot
for foot, burn for burn, wound for wound, bruise for bruise.
— Exodus 21:22–23

P'shat: Explanation

There is no singular or "right" way to interpret the Hebrew Bible, as
you've witnessed if you've ever joined a Shabbat morning Torah study
discussion, where one truthful reading of the text may well open the
door to another, conflicting truth. Even the Bible itself offers an array
of perspectives when it comes to understanding God, the soul, what
happens after we die, and more.

The reality that the Torah does not speak with one unified, clear
voice becomes especially apparent when discussing the morality of
abortion. Many Jews are surprised to learn that the word "abortion"
never appears in the Hebrew Bible. When it comes to intimacy and
children, the Bible candidly discusses intercourse, procreation, infer-
tility, stillbirth, and more, but on abortion, the text is silent.

Mishpatim comes close to discussing abortion when describing
the legal consequences for accidentally striking a pregnant woman.
If the woman is injured, the assailant is punished with the very same

wound she received: "eye for eye, tooth for tooth, hand for hand," and the like. Should the woman die of that injury, the perpetrator is put to death—"life for life." But if the woman miscarries, then the assailant merely pays a fine. In other words, the loss of a potential person, the fetus, incurs a smaller penalty than the death of a living person, the woman. A fetus has a moral standing, but the woman's moral standing is higher.

Of course, religious people have long disagreed over what the Bible says about abortion and much more. In a pluralistic democracy, I believe the wisest course of action begins by respecting these different interpretations. The greater good is best served by protecting each person's right and responsibility to read, interpret, and act on the Bible's teachings as directed by personal conscience.

D'rash: Buber's Insight

Their power to enter into relation is buried
under increasing objectification.

Buber recognizes and respects differences of faith. By contrast, he notes, some people are so deeply convinced that their way is the only way that they cannot relate to others who see a matter differently. For example, some religious purists freeze their Bible into an "object," which undermines "their power to enter into relation." Their own interpretation matters above anyone else's.

Buber showed his love for the Bible by applying his God-given mind to build a personal understanding of its teachings for his life. At the same time, he greatly respected religious approaches other than his own. He would engage with any Jew willing to talk to him. He also worked closely and warmly with Christian scholars and leaders on interfaith relations and wrote extensively about Christianity from a Jewish perspective. Additionally, earlier in his career he wrote and taught about his personal explorations of Taoism and produced a German translation of Taoist parables.

When it came to Taoism, Buber was especially taken by the concept of noninterfering action. Noninterference speaks to the delicate balance between interference and indifference. It considers the tension between overinvolvement and underreaction to events and people around us. It demands careful listening and observing, and thoughtful and considered action that respects one's own integrity and that of others. Noninterference means being in relation with another, as that person is, without seeking to analyze or dominate.

In a Taoist parable, "Silence," Buber relates how one sage yearns to meet another, and, after a long time, the first visits the second. The two exchange glances in silence, without speaking, and then part. Sometime later, the first sage describes that visit to a third sage and is questioned on the absence of speech. The first explains that wisdom came by simply being with this longed-for teacher—there was full attention and no need to talk. The appreciation of their moment together offered a lesson on noninterference.

This exploration of Taoism contributed to Buber's Jewish approach to human relations and I-Thou. Just as God appears attentive in dialogue with leaders in the Bible, Buber recognizes the importance of our being attentive in the presence of other human beings.[6] His journey of inquiry into Taoism, by extension, deepened his appreciation and respect for differing religious viewpoints.

In this light, we can see the Bible as an entryway to critical conversation in an ongoing dialogue among you, me, and God. And we honor the Bible text just as we honor alternate understandings of the text that emerge when you and I speak as I-Thou.

D'rash: A Personal Reflection

FAITH-BASED ADVOCACY

I've always seen myself as a synagogue rabbi, which I still am, and had never imagined becoming a religious advocate. But the opportunity presented itself, and I jumped at it. I've been working with

Planned Parenthood for the better part of two decades as an advocate for public policies that protect and advance access to contraception, keep abortion safe and legal, and provide sex education for teens. We've also promoted intersecting needs, such as marriage equality for same-gender couples, maternal health protections, and paid family leave.

My religious advocacy is all about church-state separation. This means that I'm not looking to impose my faith teachings about health care or the beginning of life on the law or on the private lives of others. Rather, my clergy colleagues and I work to make sure that existing laws protect people as they talk to their health-care providers, consider the teachings of their faith, and exercise their personal consciences.

Moreover, when it comes to talking with policy makers about prospective laws, I believe religious perspectives can properly inform—but not determine—how we set public policy. Freedom of speech means that each of us has a right—I would add, a civic responsibility—to make our opinions known to our representatives. Just as atheists have the right to be heard, voices of faith need to be included in the public conversation. Under the principle of church-state separation, however, religious voices are not supposed to have the final word.

Time and again, I see how much our policy makers want to hear from their constituents. Public officials want to do a good job of representing us, and they appreciate knowing what's important to us so they can focus on our priorities. They hear from religious people all the time about climate change, reproductive health care, gay rights, and more, but many of these people act as if they are the spokespersons for all faithful when they point to the Bible to make a case that contradicts my beliefs. So, I bring a positive countermessage to policy makers. I make sure they know I am a religious person, too. I make sure to point out that there is a diversity in religious belief and that others don't speak for me.

Above all, when I speak with a public official about reproductive rights, I take a lesson from Buber with me: God gives each of us the capacity to determine what is in our heart, act on our decision, and try to build a better world for ourselves and the generations to follow. And I also believe that when we speak with those who write the laws, we can best see them as God's agents for bringing the good to life.

Terumah

Not Within, Between

EXODUS 25:1–27:19

*And let them make Me a sanctuary that
I may dwell among them.*
—Exodus 25:8

P'shat: Explanation

Terumah is a sacred construction manual, a step-by-step guide for planning and building the Tabernacle (also called the Tent of Meeting), which served the Jewish people as a worship space during forty years of wandering through Sinai. God provides the rationale for creating this portable shrine, telling Moses, "And let them make Me a sanctuary that I may dwell among them." Israel builds the Tabernacle so that God abides with the people.

Israel gathers at the entrance of the Tabernacle to hear God's instructions, offer sacrifices, and come closer to God. The Tabernacle houses many ritual objects: a candelabrum, or menorah, for daily lighting; an altar for sacrifices; a table for holding breads to feed the priests; a gold-covered wooden Ark of the Covenant for safeguarding the stone tablets of the Ten Commandments. Cherubs, *k'ruvim*, adorn the Ark of the Covenant, as the biblical text prescribes: "The *k'ruvim* shall have their wings spread out above, shielding the Ark cover with their wings. They shall confront each other; the faces of the *k'ruvim* being turned toward the cover" (Exod. 25:20).

Terumah speaks of *k'ruvim* as if we should already know what they are—but we don't know as much as Terumah assumes. The *k'ruvim* might be understood as human-animal hybrids with wings and faces. Previously in Genesis, after God expels Adam and Eve from the Garden of Eden, *k'ruvim* armed with fire swords guard Eden's gates against Adam and Eve's return to paradise (Gen. 3:24). *K'ruvim* are mentioned elsewhere in the Hebrew Bible, yet here, in Exodus, one thing in particular about them stands out.

The *k'ruvim* "confront each other" above the Ark of the Covenant, which rests in the Holy of Holies. They look directly at one another, in the eye, as they stand aloft in that most sacred space in our Tabernacle. That's where we find God, in that holy place, between the *k'ruvim*, where the *k'ruvim* "confront" each other, face-to-face.

D'rash: Buber's Insight

Spirit is not in the I but between I and Thou. It is not like the blood that circulates in you, but like the air which you breathe.

As God dwells between the *k'ruvim*, Buber says God dwells between us as we "confront" each other through I-Thou. To Buber, God is not in us but between us—not in the I nor in the Thou, but as if in the dash, in the "confrontation," in the middle of the action between the parties. When I-Thou happens, the interpersonal outshines internal thoughts and emotions. Writes Buber in *I and Thou*: "It is not like the blood that circulates in you, but like the air which you breathe."[7] Something miraculous is in the air.

Buber's approach reflects a Jewish perspective about mitzvot that is less about faith (the internal) and more about action (the external). Judaism primarily accesses spirituality through deeds, such as reciting blessings before and after eating, when Shabbat begins, at a wedding, or while having a conversation. Judaism asserts values that come to life through relation to people and the world.

Buber's approach resembles that of the psychiatrist Viktor Frankl (1905–97). Frankl practiced in Austria until the Nazis arrested him in 1942. While incarcerated in Theresienstadt and Auschwitz, amid extreme deprivation, violence, and death, he refined his approach called logotherapy, which speaks to the importance of a person's discerning and living a meaningful life. Logotherapy, a term that comes from the Greek *logos*, "reason," focuses on ensuring that a person has a reason to live. In time, Frankl would publish what became a classic book on the subject, *Man's Search for Meaning: From Death Camp to Existentialism.*

Frankl taught that we make life meaningful by looking beyond ourselves to relationships and by fulfilling responsibility. Like Buber, he believed that accomplishing a purposeful task or responding to the words or needs of another human being could make life meaningful, even under great suffering and moral deprivation—and, as a by-product, create positive feelings. The internal is an outgrowth of the relational. As an analogy, the human eye works properly when it looks outward. When it sees itself, as when covered with a cataract, it does not perform its task. The eye must gaze beyond itself in order to advance the spirit.

As with the eye, as with mitzvot, as with relationships and responsibility: We enter the spiritual when we nobly focus beyond ourselves. Even though it can be nearly impossible to live out these beliefs under all circumstances, be they ordinary or extreme, nonetheless, we make life meaningful when life looks outward.

D'rash: Personal Insight

IN THE SANCTUARY, IN COMMUNITY

That spirituality between people lives in the synagogue. My spirituality comes from comfortable, personal bonds and easy conversation with members of my Jewish community.

Family and community can blend into one, as when our children received their Hebrew names in the sanctuary where we pray each week, and, years later, when they joined me at Junior Congregation and experienced the synagogue as a spiritual home too. I feel this way when my family joins me for services and also when I connect with congregants and colleagues. Some of those personal relationships, made long ago, continue to thrive today, decades later.

During the coronavirus outbreak, it became very clear that protecting health and safety meant we had to stop coming together for services and go to the second-best option, livestreaming. Our temple staff worked overtime to set up the electronics, and while I did not expect to get much out of remote praying, I was surprisingly taken by what popped up on the computer screen—dozens of little picture boxes with smiling faces of temple members happy to see each other, share greetings, and welcome Shabbat as a community. We lit candles from home, said prayers, chanted songs, and it was Shabbat together again. With all the upset around us, I felt relieved and uplifted. And there was more: People who were "stuck" out of town joined us online. Folks who recently stopped driving Zoomed to the conversation. A person recovering from life-threatening surgery dialed in from the hospital. Temple teens sat with their parents, joining as family in prayer. What I expected to be second best turned out to be better than that. For all we lost, we also gained.

Tetsavveh

The Sanctity of Decision Making

EXODUS 27:20–30:10

Inside the breastpiece of decision you shall place the Urim and Thummim, so that they are over Aaron's heart when he comes before Adonai. Thus Aaron shall carry the instrument of decision for the Israelites over his heart before Adonai at all times.
—Exodus 28:30

P'shat: Explanation

Tetsavveh describes the priests' special garment, a colorful holy work uniform that includes a headdress as well as a sash, tunic, and elaborate ephod, a curious ritual garment made of gold, purple, and crimson yarns and fine linens. Above the ephod rests a gold-adorned "breastpiece of decision" containing twelve precious stones, including emerald, turquoise, sapphire, and amethyst. God instructs Moses: "Inside the breastpiece of decision you shall place the Urim and Thummim, so that they are over Aaron's heart when he comes before Adonai. Thus Aaron shall carry the instrument of decision for the Israelites over his heart before Adonai at all times."

So, what are the Urim and Thummim, this "instrument of decision"? The answer isn't fully clear. The Torah doesn't describe how they looked or explain how they are used. Later in the Bible, it appears they were tossed like dice or coins to discern God's will for taking action. For instance, when the king of Israel wanted to know whether to go into battle, the priest turned to the Urim and Thummim to seek and receive God's guidance—a yes-or-no answer. Rabbenu Bahya ibn

Pakuda (Spain, eleventh century) suggests the purpose of the stones, or "letters," as he calls them. After the priest posed a question, the letters/jeweled stones on the breastpiece of decision lit up to spell out the direction for the nation. Bahya insists that the breastpiece addressed only matters of major concern, such as whether or not to go to war (on Exod. 28:30).

Today, it's tempting to dismiss the Urim and Thummim as primitive and outdated. Yet we moderns also invest time and energy in the hopes of foreseeing the future, be it the magnitude of an oncoming hurricane, the direction of the stock market, or the outcome of an election. Like our ancestors, we possess the very natural, intense, and longstanding human desire to discern the future and plan appropriately.

D'rash: Buber's Insight

I am only someone who has seen something
and who goes to a window and points.

You could say that Buber was a one-person Urim and Thummim because of how frequently people sought out his advice and he gave it. Some came from a great distance to show up at his front door without an appointment, and he'd drop whatever he was doing for a sit-down conversation. Hearing out his visitor, he'd then proceed to offer an on-the-spot reaction, speaking decisively about something as significant as a career choice or whether to marry. The strongly opinionated Buber often sounded like he was giving an order or command, though that was not his intention.

At an eightieth birthday celebration with American Friends of the Hebrew University in New York, Buber told the story of one such visit. After Buber listened and shared his thoughts, the visitor praised Buber in messianic terms, and Buber recoiled. He protested: "I am only someone who has seen something and who goes to a window and points."[8]

Buber saw himself as just pointing out a direction—the direction he believed to be best—for each person who solicited his counsel. He spoke with authority and sounded like he was commanding, even though from his perspective he was merely advising. His bold suggestions reflected the confidence that I-Thou gifted him to discern what was already in the person and empowered him to support his conversation partner in discovering a pre-existing inclination. That is, his advice made hidden wisdom more visible, understandable, and actionable for his advisee.

To be sure, Buber sounded self-important, even arrogant, when speaking so definitively about someone else's path after only one conversation, as if he were a human Urim and Thummim. His conviction came from his recognition of the transformational and sacred potential of I-Thou. Even a brief look into the soul, he trusted, could discern and set a person's life compass.

D'rash: A Personal Reflection

WHEN THERE IS NO GOOD OPTION

Sometimes, extreme and tragic life situations call for personal decisions that even an Urim and Thummim cannot resolve. Many years ago, my teacher in philosophy of religion at Queens College, Professor Ernest Schwarcz, relayed one such situation.

A Holocaust survivor born and raised in Hungary, Professor Schwarcz was a sweet, gentle man, devoted to his wife, his students, and his career. Our class topic was Danish philosopher Søren Kierkegaard's understanding of the Binding of Isaac, how Abraham had approached God's baffling request of to offer up his son Isaac, as portrayed in Kierkegaard's book, *Fear and Trembling*. We saw the situation as a "double bind"—that is, Abraham facing conflicting and irreconcilable options, with any outcome unwanted. He could either sacrifice his son, a heartbreaking act that would risk the destiny of the Jewish people, or he could leave Isaac unharmed and thereby defy God's request. It was an upsetting, no-win situation. To illustrate the depth of such a dilemma that challenges the human capacity to decide, Professor Schwarcz told us a story from the Holocaust.

He was living in Budapest under an incremental Nazi extermination protocol. The Nazis would gather Jews in small groups to be escorted to the banks of the Danube River to be shot, so many each day that the river turned red. Meanwhile, the Hungarian resistance created an elaborate scheme to help Jews escape. They secured a Nazi commander's uniform and motorcycle. The fighter would hop on the cycle, find a group of Jews under death escort, and order the guarding soldier to release the Jews into his custody. The "Nazi commander" then took the Jews to a nearby alley, where he distributed forged documents and counterfeit money, and sent the Jews off on their own.

One day, however, something terrible happened. The mother of the imposter officer turned up in one of the groups about to die. She saw her son and could not contain herself, creating such a scene that real Nazis came over and figured out what was going on. Then the Nazis gave the resistance fighter an option: Either he would shoot everyone in the group, including his mother, or the Nazis would shoot him along with everyone else. There was no promise to the imposter beyond that and, even if there was one, there were no assurances the Nazis would honor their word. In other words, they might kill him either way. Or maybe they would keep him alive and torture him for more details about his resistance group. What should he do?

Professor Schwarcz told us this story with his warm voice and gentle smile. Believe it or not, I was so dumbfounded by the story that I don't remember what he said the resistance fighter did. But I do remember how my teacher, of blessed memory, used this story to illustrate that there are times in life when there is no viable option. And to this day, I wonder whether he was the fellow on the motorcycle.

Ki Tissa'

Eclipse of God

EXODUS 30:11–34:35

*As soon as Moses came near the camp and saw the calf and the
dancing, he became enraged; and he hurled the tablets from
his hands and shattered them at the foot of the mountain.*
—Exodus 32:19

P'shat: Explanation

Sometimes God seems distant, if not entirely absent.

As Ki Tissa' opens, Moses is on Mount Sinai and the people are growing increasingly anxious. He's been gone from the community now
more than a month, without a word from him or God. Will he ever
return? Will God ever speak again? Are the people of Israel doomed,
abandoned in the wilderness, without a leader or direction? Some of
the people brazenly defy the second of the Ten Commandments by
building a golden calf for idol worship.

When, at last, Moses returns from the mountaintop, "as soon as
[he] came near the camp and saw the calf and the dancing, he became
enraged; and he hurled the tablets from his hands and shattered
them at the foot of the mountain" (Exod. 32:19). God threatens to
destroy the entire nation until Moses convinces God to punish only
those who sinned.

The prolonged absence of God and Moses sparks this sad story,
in a foreshadowing of a theological theme that carries through the
Torah and the rest of the Hebrew Bible: as the Bible moves forward,
God becomes less and less prominent, to the point of seeming totally
absent. Whereas God is the main personality in the earlier biblical

books—God creates the universe, brings a great flood, calls Abram and Sarai to leave home for Canaan, and much more—as we get further along in the Bible, God gets less and less mention. By the book of Esther, for example, God doesn't speak, isn't spoken to, and isn't even named! Meanwhile, human beings rise to become the Bible's primary focus. In effect, God steps back as the people step up.

Elsewhere, God's distance is a response to Israel's unfaithfulness: "I will hide My countenance from them and see how they fare in the end, for they are a treacherous breed, children with no loyalty in them" (Deut. 32:20). This usage of "hide My countenance," *hester panim*, or "face hiding," speaks to God's intentional withholding of the Divine Presence and protection as a punishment for human misconduct. This, in turn, opens the opportunity to look at Buber's concept of the Eclipse of God.

D'rash: Buber's Insight

Eclipse of the light of heaven, eclipse of God—
such indeed is the character of the historic hour
through which the world is passing.

To explain God's absence, Buber brings us the idea of the "Eclipse of God" as he describes it in a 1952 book by the same name. Buber likens the Eclipse of God to an eclipse of the sun. In a solar eclipse, the moon passes between the earth and sun and the world grows dark and gray. During an Eclipse of God, as during the Holocaust, for instance, people behave in ways that make it hard, if not impossible, for God to be seen. But God is present. God is not dead, but eclipsed—alive, yet inaccessible and invisible to human eyes. Life grows dark.

A solar eclipse does not happen in the sun or inside the earth but in between. It occurs when something—the moon—gets in the way and obscures the light. In the same line of thought, the Eclipse of God is not within the person, but between humanity and the Divine. People get in the way of God and the earth, and God's light cannot be seen.

I-It swells up and rules. Human behavior obscures the sight of a God who very much wants to be apprehended. And, as for us, how unfortunate it is that God seems absent just when we need God the most.

In 1951, during another time of eclipse, the Cold War with its threat of nuclear annihilation, Buber spoke of that turning-point moment as "the historic hour through which this world is passing." Yet surely each generation faces urgent challenges, and every hour carries transformational danger alongside potential. Buber offers us the reassurance that we have the capacity to end the eclipse and encounter God's light once again.[9]

D'rash: A Personal Reflection

A SIGN OF GOD IN WONDER

It's one thing to say that God is dead, another thing to say God is in eclipse, and yet another to say there never was a God to begin with.

Some time ago, I went through a phase of reading book after book about atheism. A look at my bookshelf might lead a person to wonder why a rabbi who believes in God has so many books written by people who don't. And, if you'd asked me why while I was in that atheism-reading phrase, I would have simply said that I thought there'd be something to learn, even there.

But, to my surprise, I didn't learn much. Maybe I was reading the wrong writers, but nothing in those books spoke to me. If anything, I was badly put off by repeated over-the-top attacks on the beliefs, practices, and principles I hold sacred.

The memory of all that reading returned when I saw a recent Pew Research Center report called "10 Facts about Atheists."[10] Of the ten facts, there were no surprises in nine. I already knew that the number of American atheists has been growing, nearly doubling, from 1.6 to 3.1 percent, over the last decade or so. I'd already guessed correctly that the typical atheist is likely to be a man, identify as a politically liberal Democrat, and look to science—not faith—for life guidance.

And it didn't surprise me that a majority of Americans would vote for a person of faith over an atheist. But one finding stood out: Atheists are a tiny bit more likely than American Christians to say they experience "a deep sense of wonder about the universe" at least once a week.

Here I would have guessed that only religious people experience a "sense of wonder," be it weekly or ever. I was surprised to learn that atheism and wonder go together, let alone that many atheists experience wonder "deeply." Until then, when I thought of wonder, my thoughts immediately turned to God, the very thing atheists reject.

I could be wrong, but I suspect that this finding may have less to do with atheism and more to do with those who identify as religious. At least in my experience, many religious folks don't often give wonder the spiritual recognition it deserves. For instance, when Jews think of prayer, their thoughts typically turn to petitionary prayer: petitioning God to bring important or urgent things like peace, health, or success. People rarely tell me they pray to cultivate their sense of wonder, even with all the prayers of thanksgiving and appreciation for food, clothing, good health, and more in our tradition.

And so, I love the title of one of many books by Buber's friend and colleague Rabbi Abraham Joshua Heschel: *I Asked for Wonder*. Wonder is certainly worth asking for. What would life be without it? To marvel in something mysterious and unexpected, to experience curiosity, excitement, and awe in its presence: this is the spiritual uplift of wonder.

Bottom line: Many who believe in God have something to learn from those who don't.

Va-yak'hel

Shabbat as Cornerstone

EXODUS 35:1–38:20

On six days work may be done, but on the seventh
day you shall have a sabbath of complete rest.
—Exodus 35:2

P'shat: Explanation

From the days of the Hebrew Bible through our own, Shabbat holds a foundational position in Jewish life. In Genesis, Shabbat is the day of rest and refreshment for God and for us. Elsewhere in the Torah, we mark Shabbat by refraining from such work as gathering food and lighting fire. Later, the Rabbis of the Mishnah provide a more extensive definition of "work." Included among the prohibited activities, now sorted into thirty-nine categories, are writing and carrying items between public and private property.

Interestingly, the Torah offers two different reasons for keeping Shabbat, depending on which of the two different versions of the Ten Commandments you're reading. Exodus (chapter 20) and Deuteronomy (chapter 5) agree that Shabbat applies to the entire household, including servants and work animals—all living things. However, Exodus bases Shabbat rest on God's rest—just as God created the universe in six days and rested on Shabbat, we work six days and rest on the seventh. Deuteronomy, on the other hand, finds a rationale in the history of the Exodus from Egypt. God frees us from slavery, so each person needs to be free from labor one day each week.

The significance in the difference? By rooting Shabbat in Creation, Exodus makes Shabbat universal: Shabbat includes everyone and everything. In contrast, Deuteronomy speaks particularly to Jews, the only ones freed from Egypt. Where the Exodus Shabbat is based on the making of the universe, Deuteronomy rests on the making of the Jewish people. The two interpretations, taken together, are at the intersection of Jewish theological cornerstones: God, the Creation, and the Revelation.

D'rash: Buber's Insight

The older I become, and the more I realize the restlessness of my soul, the more I accept for myself the Day of Rest.

Buber has a negative reputation among some when it comes to keeping the mitzvot, Shabbat in particular. It is true that, as he entered adulthood, he rejected many religious practices (such as wrapping tefillin, which he did wear for a time after he became bar mitzvah), taking on only those that spoke to him in the moment.[11]

Shabbat came to speak more personally to him as the years went on. His grandchildren recalled regular Friday evening Shabbat dinner rituals in the Buber household. Their grandmother lit Shabbat candles, and their grandfather led *Kiddush* and read a story after the meal.[12] As Buber got older, he appears to have grown to appreciate Shabbat as a time to reflect, absorb, and figure out what all his varied and demanding life experiences meant. Shabbat was the moment to gather in the harvest of days.

It seems that Buber's earlier way of living reflected the character of an individual in a story about Rabbi Levi Yitzhak of Berditchev (d. 1809). Rabbi Levi Yitzhak once saw someone rushing down the street, in such a hurry that this person looked straight ahead and ignored everyone and everything around him. Rabbi Levi Yitzhak asked this individual about the reason for the hurry. The response? Worry over work and earning a livelihood. Rabbi Levi Yitzhak told him that sometimes life pursues us, and that all a person needs to do is stay still and life will catch up with us, right where we stand.[13] Shabbat, for Buber, is a time to stand still and catch up.

D'rash: A Personal Reflection

GATHERING THE FRUITS OF LABOR

It was a not-too-warm early summer day when I visited a friend at his home on a former farm in Western Massachusetts. As we stood on the porch, he pointed out the maple and oak and other trees, their differences something I as a city boy had never grown to appreciate. Turning to a lone tree in the front of the house—an apple tree—he remarked that, toward fall, he expected a bear to return as in past years, shake the tree, and eat the fallen fruit. He said he loved having a bear in the neighborhood.

Our house is in the town next to his, and our suburban neighborhood gets the same wildlife, including rabbits, deer, raccoons, foxes, and the occasional snake and bear—and, I have to admit, the last two scare me. I know of no one around us who was ever hurt by a snake or bear, but I don't want to be the first. Nevertheless, I got past my fears to try to see that bear from the bear's point of view. I came away thinking there wasn't much difference between that bear and me or anyone else in the workforce. During the week, we shake trees of life and gather what falls to sustain ourselves and our loved ones. And Shabbat provides a traditional Jewish framework to do yet another ingathering, looking back on the week and considering the fruits of harvest.

Shabbat, for me, means being at synagogue, joining in worship as a service leader or as a member of the congregation. I use that time to reflect on what I did during the preceding days, what I want to do, where I fell short, what happened in the world, how it impacts me, what if anything I can do in response to shape the larger direction. As I read and sing, those traditional prayers and music embrace me as I embrace them. Above all, Shabbat observance ensures that I am not a passive observer of my life or an object controlled by my world. Shabbat calls me to shape and pursue my destiny and support others in their life journeys.

Moreover, Shabbat is a time for entering relationships that get overlooked or forgotten during the week. It is a day to sustain and build bonds with friends and members of the community. The little chats — and sometimes more extended conversations — before and after a Shabbat service bring us closer, as, together, we look back on a week of work on the tree of life and reflect on the ingathered fruits.

Pekudei

There Is No Sin in Having Money

EXODUS 38:21–40:38

*These are the records of the Tabernacle, the Tabernacle
of the Pact, which were drawn up at Moses' bidding.*
—Exodus 38:21

P'shat: Explanation

Where some say that the material is the enemy of the spiritual, Judaism often takes a different and nuanced approach: We are to enjoy and benefit from what we own. At the same time, possessions impose responsibilities of stewardship and charity. It is no sin to be wealthy—individually, or communally—if those assets are managed and dispensed with integrity and compassion. Pekudei offers deeper insight.

The Jewish people responded generously when called on to contribute to the construction of the Tabernacle. Pekudei details donations of precious metals and stones, fine linens, and more. And once the coffers were full, Moses asked for a review of income, expenses, and assets—that is, a "financial audit." But why? Didn't he trust the people? And didn't the people trust him?

The Rabbis explain that with all the precious objects coming in, rumors of financial misconduct circulated. Rabbi Hama says people noticed Moses was gaining weight and assumed he skimmed off the top. "His friends said to him, 'A person who works in the Tabernacle, why shouldn't they be rich!' When Moses heard this, he said to them, 'By your lives! When the Tabernacle is complete, I will give you an accounting'" (Exodus Rabbah 51:6). Moses asks for an audit to stifle the rumors and clear his name.

The Rabbis recognize the power of temptation and maintain that the material and spiritual need and complement each other. Rabbi Elazar ben Azariah's saying, "If there is no flour, there is no Torah; if there is no Torah, there is no flour" (*Pirke Avot* 3:17) speaks to the circuitous relationship between means and faith. The material and spiritual go hand-in-hand in Pekudei, where the people generously support the Tabernacle and the assets are managed with integrity.

D'rash: Buber's Insight

Man's will to profit and (his will) to be powerful have
their natural and proper effect so long as they are
linked with and upheld by his will to enter relation.

Thanks to the family farming and mining businesses, Buber grew up in a materially comfortable household, received a sound education, and eventually inherited a sizable endowment from his grandparents and father—but the Nazis froze those assets. In 1938, Buber fled for Israel without hope of ever recovering the funds. He borrowed from friends to survive. A fear of being unable to repay the obligations weighed on him heavily, until he eventually rebuilt his financial base through writing.[14]

Buber maintains that wealth imposes a moral responsibility on its owner. He writes in *I and Thou*, "Man's will to profit and (his will) to be powerful have their natural and proper effect so long as they are linked with and upheld by his will to enter relation."[15] In other words, a person's wealth serves a moral purpose when it supports and advances the collective well-being. What is more, there is something wrong with depravation. Not only does it shirk the Jewish value of *oneg*, taking delight; habituation to abstinence also impairs one's ability to recognize and support those who are in true need.

Buber tells of Rabbi Israel of Koznitz, Poland (d. 1814), who received a visit from a person of great means. Rabbi Israel asked the visitor what he typically ate, and heard described a spartan diet, basically no more than bread or water. He urged the visitor to eat better, in keeping with his finances. Afterward, Rabbi Israel explained his response to his disciples: A rich person who eats with extreme frugality will believe the poor can survive on rocks.[16] Those who have should take enjoyment, all the while keeping in mind those who need.

D'rash: A Personal Reflection

MONEY ON MY MIND

Even as a kid I spent a good amount of time thinking about money. My mother would take me on errands that included a stop at a large bank where heavy metal front doors, a high ceiling, a uniformed guard, and somber tellers told me something very serious was going on in there. And I was so excited as a fourth grader to get a school savings account and watch my twenty-five-cent weekly deposits accumulate on bank "punch-card" statements, and thrilled to receive the occasional few pennies of quarterly interest that I saw as found money.

Through summers in high school, I worked in an accounting office, taking in deposits and payments for an ocean cruise company, and I figured out how to file income tax on my own. A year of college basic accounting classes once led me to consider going into financial planning. And, through the years, I have been drawn to reading books and articles on personal finance, without giving much thought about where this inclination came from, until I recently read about a woman with a similar passion.

She described her strong emotional connection to money, and her comfort and enthusiasm for managing her finances. She came to realize that, after her father died when she was young, turning her attention to money gave her a sense of security. She saw how money sustains her. It provides a sense of safety that advances the joy of living. As I read her story, I realized that as she described herself, she was describing me.

A person is fortunate to have a personal financial foundation that can provide both materially and spiritually in the present and hopefully be protective in the future.

III

Leviticus (Va-yikra')

Va-yikra'

Will and Grace

LEVITICUS 1:1–5:26

Adonai called to Moses and spoke to him.
—Leviticus 1:1

P'shat: Explanation

Va-yikra', the third book of the Torah, receives the English name of Leviticus because it includes instructions to the Levites about serving as priests in the Tent of Meeting. The very first word of Va-yikra' means literally that God "called," as in, "Adonai *called* to Moses and *spoke* to him."

But why does the text include both "called" and "spoke"? According to the Rabbis, God only has to say it once. It should have been enough that God "called" Moses; why does the Torah also say God "spoke" to him?

Rashi takes God's two-step summoning as an expression of God's bountiful love for Moses. Recognizing that it must be profoundly startling for any human, Moses included, to hear from God, Rashi proposes that God makes the first call so Moses can prepare himself to receive God's spoken instructions. The "call" is a "heads up" that will help Moses focus on what God has to say.

After all, the timing of the interaction is beyond Moses' control. God addresses Moses according to God's timetable, as an act of *grace*, which brings us a lesson from Buber on the nuanced nature of I-Thou.

D'rash: Buber's Insight

It can, however, also come about if I have both will and grace.

You can't make I-Thou happen. You can try to force I-Thou to occur, but don't be disappointed—your effort may not succeed. I-Thou happens by itself, but only sometimes, when we are open and willing. It can "come about if I have both will and grace."

If Moses is not paying attention, he will not hear what God has to say, because Moses' openness and attentiveness are acts of *will*. That is, when there's no "will" for I-Thou—we're tired, bored, indifferent, struggling, wanting to be left alone—then the "grace" of I-Thou will not occur. I-Thou demands "both will and grace."[1]

So we can't "will" I-Thou any more than Moses can will to hear God—both come by *grace*. I can control my will—I can tell myself, "I am open to I-Thou today"—but my openness obligates no one but me. I can't successfully impose on you so that you let me look into your soul when you don't want me in there; nor can you force yourself into mine when I'm unwilling. We have to sync, with the same intention and openness, with a simultaneous and similar will for the grace.

And when it comes to "both will and grace," I was surprised to learn that the name of the TV situation comedy *Will & Grace* took inspiration from Buber.[2] Chronicling the adventures and mishaps of Manhattan apartment dwellers Will, a gay lawyer; Grace, a straight interior designer; and their over-the-top neighbors Jack and Karen, *Will & Grace* portrays the strong, trusting, and candid relationships typically seen as I-Thou.

D'rash: A Personal Reflection

WITHOUT WILL OR GRACE

Imagine a family at dinner.

"How was school today?" a parent asks a teen.

"Fine."

"What happened?"

"Nothing."

An hour or so later, all of a sudden, the child wants to talk to the parent: "My friend did something funny today." But now that parent is racing out of the house to go to a meeting.

Or, sometimes you want to talk, but your housemate or relative isn't interested. Or your partner wants to talk, but you don't.

In all of these cases there is no conversation, because one party has no interest in talking in the present moment. That is, there is no grace when the will is not there.

There's mutuality at the heart of I-Thou, a need for two willing partners to simultaneously enter dialogue right then and there. It takes two to encounter.

There are times we hope for the grace of I-Thou, but it is not to be had. Sometimes there is no explaining why not. It can be frustrating, disappointing, even demoralizing when a potential conversation partner rebuffs an attempt to engage. A good friend stays out of touch, despite my overtures; I try to understand that life fills up quickly and now is not the time. I'm at the post office or the hardware store and a clerk or cashier responds gruffly to a simple question; I try to understand that life may be complicated for this person at this moment, just as it can be for you and me. At other times I've urgently wanted someone to hear me out as I describe a burden, and no one is to be found.

For the times I-Thou is wanted but not to be, all a person can do is to keep the faith that I-Thou will soon return. On these occasions, the lighter times and the heavier ones, my keeping faith depends on me: I have to keep trying to summon the will to seek the grace of I-Thou.

Tsav

The Afterglow

LEVITICUS 6:1–8:36

*The priest shall turn them into smoke on the altar as
an offering by fire to Adonai; it is a guilt offering.*
—Leviticus 7:5

P'shat: Explanation

The Tent of Meeting is open for sacred work. The walls are up, the altar is in place, the priests' garments are made and ready. Now, as God instructs the priests on the details of the ritual sacrifices, one sacrifice stands out for carrying a higher measure of sanctity: the guilt offering that atones for sin.

For all the times people say there is little to learn from Israel's experience with ritual sacrifices, the guilt offering offers an important lesson. The priest eats this offering inside the Holy of Holies, the most sacred area of the Tent of Meeting. Further, uneaten portions receive special care: "The priest shall turn them into smoke on the altar as an offering by fire to Adonai; it is a guilt offering" (Lev. 7:5). A total burning contributes to atonement—the sin literally goes up in smoke. As a result of the guilt offering and the full consumption by fire, the sin is no more, the relationship with God is mended, and life is good again.

Imagine walking into the Tent of Meeting feeling distressed over a sin and, thanks to the sin-offering ritual, the misdeed is consumed by fire and you walk away completely restored. With the transgression gone, upset yields to relief, even uplift. Once again you are at home in the world.

The word "Afterglow" speaks to the spiritual reset that follows such an intense, sacred experience. An Afterglow is a common, after-the-fact, response of the spirit. It is a residual, internal shift that says: *Thanks to what just happened, my self-perception or worldview has changed.*

I imagine a similar post-Flood Afterglow for Noah. The rain ends, the water recedes, and a rainbow spans the sky as evidence of renewed relationship with God. The era of sin and lawlessness has washed away; the human community begins anew.

There's another Afterglow in the Torah: one for Jacob, as he limps away from a night of angel wrestling. His hip is wrenched, but there's an Afterglow in the knowledge he confronted this night demon and prevailed. Jacob is renamed "Israel"—that is, the one who "struggles with God."

We, too, have an Afterglow, when we come away from I-Thou. We carry the Afterglow as spiritual evidence of a wholehearted encounter.

D'rash: Buber's Insight

A man does not pass, from the moment of the supreme meeting,
the same being as he entered into it . . . something happens.

When Buber writes in *I and Thou*, "A man does not pass, from the moment of the supreme meeting, the same being as he entered into it . . . something happens."[3] What is that "something" that "happens?"

You see it in the Afterglow, which demonstrates the person is changed. The time of togetherness has ended, but a lingering spiritual difference abides in the air around you. The encounter taught you something you never imagined existed or reminded you of something important you had forgotten. You entered the conversation with one set of emotions and walked away with different, perhaps unexpected, feelings. A new mood reigns.

We've spoken of Afterglow in positive terms, as when conversation starts with upset and ends with relief. But given the risk—the Holy Insecurity that marks the Narrow Ridge of I-Thou—an Afterglow can also be seen in a person's postencounter distress. We take a risk by walking into an encounter. No one can accurately anticipate the course of the conversation or the outcome. A person's sense of self is on the line with each I-Thou.

The late Professor Maurice Friedman, Buber's primary translator and interpreter, apparently left his first meeting with Buber carrying an Afterglow tinged by misgiving. Friedman had begun his academic career by devoting his research and writing to Buber's work, including a doctoral dissertation on Buber's approach to the problem of evil, without ever meeting Buber. In fact, Buber and Friedman had corresponded for six years without encountering one another face-to-face.

Friedman was living in the United States when his mother traveled to Israel to visit cousins living on a kibbutz when Buber was living in Jerusalem. She spent eight hours on buses riding between the Galilee in Israel's North and Jerusalem in Israel's center to personally deliver her son's letter to Buber. The two met and had a very full conversation — Friedman never found out what they discussed. Not long after, on Buber's visit to New York City, Friedman and Buber finally sat down to talk in Buber's Upper West Side hotel room.

Buber greeted Friedman with a deep eye-to-eye look that reassured Friedman he was warmly valued. Buber opened the conversation by saying that he knew Friedman recognized that, for all an author can research and write, we do not really know one another by what we read or put on paper. Rather, as Buber taught and Friedman understood, we learn about each other in person, when we meet.[4] Then Friedman mentioned a recent meeting between Buber and the controversial poet T. S. Eliot.

By way of background, Eliot had used unflattering language to speak of Jews, leading to reasonable accusations of antisemitism. Buber had just met Eliot, and Friedman asked about their meeting, pointing out that his curiosity came from knowing that Buber and Eliot had many differing opinions. Buber responded that when he meets someone, he is not really interested in opinions, but in the person. He argued that people are more than their ideas, and it is critically important to avoid prejudgment. We should strive to put opinions aside and be open to the person in the moment. Friedman later wrote that he felt reprimanded by Buber, but that he deserved to be corrected, given his understanding of Buber's ways.[5]

I know I would be embarrassed, if not mortified, had that been my first conversation with Buber. I would have felt I'd been called out on a fundamental by a person I most respected, and I suspect Friedman felt something like that, and his Afterglow would have included such mixed feelings. At the same time, Friedman also knew that Buber wouldn't hold that comment against him — Buber would let things like that "go up in smoke." Buber was comfortable speaking his mind in I-Thou, be it with Friedman, Eliot, or anyone else.

How hard it must have been for Friedman in those very first moments together, to look directly back into the eyes of someone he had greatly admired from a distance for so many years. At the end of the day, entering I-Thou means stepping into uncharted territory.

D'rash: A Personal Reflection

SPIRITUAL RESET

It's no rare occasion and no secret that clergy, rabbis included, disagree with members of their communities over any number of things. Many years ago a temple member and I stood on opposite sides over something to do with a child's bat mitzvah. I don't remember any of the details, but I do remember what happened not long after.

Learning that this woman just had serious surgery, I headed from the temple in northern Westchester to see her in a specialized hospital in Manhattan. Between the medical ordeal she was now going through and what had happened between us in that agitated conversation, I anticipated it would not be an easy visit. All I could feel was worry about what would happen. As much as I tried to calm myself by clearing my mind of expectation and prejudgment, I grew more and more anxious as I reached the hospital, took the elevator up to her floor, and walked down the hall to see her.

"I am so glad to see you!" she practically shouted.

Whatever happened between us was history, up in smoke. Between the time of our argument and her surgery, she let go of it, which helped me do the same. We talked for some time, and, when our conversation ended, I headed back to the temple with an Afterglow of relief. Thanks to our time together at the hospital, our relationship was restored and my spirit renewed. She was in the hospital to be healed, and, thanks to her grace, our time together had healed me.

It is so very hard to avoid anticipating, especially when we're expecting something negative to happen. But it is important to be willing to sideline negative memories, at least enough to be open to the possibility of I-Thou.

Shemini

Learning from Loss

LEVITICUS 9:1–11:47

And Aaron was silent.
—Leviticus 10:3

P'shat: Explanation

Tragedy strikes when Aaron's sons, priests, bring unauthorized fire and incense into the Holy of Holies: Nadab and Abihu die on the spot at the hand of God. Moses immediately explains to Aaron, "This is what the Eternal meant by saying, 'Through those near to Me I show Myself holy and gain glory before all the people'" (Lev. 10:3). Aaron's response? "And Aaron was silent."

The Rabbis struggle to comprehend God's unforgiving and harsh behavior toward Nadab and Abihu. Some Rabbis point to the magnitude of the sin, arguing that God's holiness and glory are on the line: the transgression is egregious, the brothers are responsible, and the punishment is just. As to the substance of the sin, the Rabbis disagree. Some point to a failure to follow God's instructions about fire and incense. Others say the brothers entered the Tent of Meeting drunk. At the end of their conversation, the Rabbis remain distraught over God's drastic act.

There is also concern surrounding Aaron's silence—as we read, literally, "And Aaron was silent." After all, you would expect a shocked and heartbroken parent to say *something* after the sudden death of *two* sons, or, at the very least, to show some sign of grief. Midrash *Tanhuma* defends Aaron, pointing to Moses' words as so wise and compassionate, they fully console Aaron and leave him speechless. In another opinion, Ramban says that Aaron first "cried and wailed and then fell silent" (on Lev. 10:3), as if an intense and profound emotional and spiritual outpouring leaves Aaron entirely drained.

Viewing this sorrowful incident through Buber's life experience, we find an example of how shock can leave a person speechless.

D'rash: Buber's Insight

No, she will never come back.

Buber, as a little boy, confronted an incomprehensible tragedy that birthed a profound silence.

Martin was born into a very typical middle-class Vienna household. The family apartment, overlooking the gently flowing Danube River waters, evoked feelings of protection and security—until his parents separated when he was three. His mother left Vienna a year later, without warning, explanation, or promise that he would ever see her again.

At a time and in a home where private feelings stayed that way, no one tried to explain his mother's disappearance or tell him when or whether she was expected to return. His world was upended. Little more than a toddler, he didn't know how to put feelings into words. He was handed a tragedy, and the response of his elders was silence.

The family had Martin move in with his paternal grandparents, Adele and Solomon Buber, who showered him with loving care and attention. Though he understandably longed for his mother, he never said anything about it. The silence continued. He assumed and dreamed he'd see his mother again, soon.

One day, when he was five, a twelve-year-old babysitter dashed his hopes, bluntly saying, "No, she will never come back." Martin was left speechless and deeply devastated.

As months and years moved on, the words "No, she will never come back" filled his mind and clung to his soul . . . and expanded in their significance as a lesson about his situation, every relationship, and the human condition. As much as we love others and want to be with them, each relationship, fragile and tenuous, must end, with warning or without.

Buber's abandonment created a pained and lifelong emptiness that he only occasionally mentioned. As an adult, Buber wrote his friend Franz Rosenzweig that he felt as though he was always seeking out his mother. At one point, Buber compared his emotional reaction to the rise of the Nazis and their attacks on democracy to the feelings of a child losing a mother and urgently seeking reassurance. While Martin's grandparents compensated for at least a portion of his loss, and he later told his beloved wife of sixty years, Paula, that her presence soothed his deep longing. Nevertheless, the emotional memory carried through his entire life.[6]

Perhaps young Martin's sitter, a child herself, thought she was doing Martin a favor by saying something no one else had the nerve to utter. Perhaps she just took it on herself to tell him the truth, as a bully, flaunting knowledge of the situation that she had gleaned from eavesdropping on a conversation among adults in the neighborhood. Regardless, the girl turned out to be wrong on that account. Buber's mother came back—and again there was silence.

He was in his thirties, married, and a parent when Buber next saw his mother. He wrote very little about this experience, and never publicly explained why she returned, what brought her to see him, or why she chose that specific time. However, he later recalled how he looked into the "stunning beauty" of her eyes, only to hear in his mind the word "mismeeting" to describe that he had nothing to say to her. Her presence apparently stirred within him a great emptiness and left him speechless. She was back, but it was as if she wasn't there.[7]

There are times when it seems silence is the only possible response.

D'rash: A Personal Reflection

WHEN DEATH IS SUDDEN

First there's silence, and then, with fortune, comes understanding.

My father died suddenly when I was ten, and, as time passed, the silence and shock grew to an understanding that continues to mature all these many years later. Recognizing the stark reality that my father would never come back has helped shape who I am and how I support others.

Not long ago, I was preparing to meet with synagogue leaders to discuss the possibility of my serving as their Intentional Interim Rabbi following the recent, sudden, and tragic death of their cherished rabbi. I had only met this rabbi once, but I'd been taken by his thoughtfulness and caring way he spoke about the congregation. Beyond that, I knew very little, and I wondered what to say to his community leaders.

We began with an interview at a temple leader's home. Before we started, I thought about my life experience with sudden death: the lessons I took from silences and the words that eventually followed. The first interview question addressed the point directly: "You know about our situation, Rabbi. What can you say to us?"

"My father died suddenly when I was ten," I said. "So I have spent the bulk of my life living in the framework you are describing, a sudden tragedy where someone very much loved suddenly is no longer there. Among the many things I know is that there is a time to mourn and a time to lead. And now, as we are meeting to discuss the congregation's future, this moment is the time to talk about leading."

First, I acknowledged their grief. Then we turned the conversation to what needed to be done for the community. This was one of those times I was fortunate to find words to speak to the moment. Through Buber's Inclusion, I acknowledged my awareness of each side of the meeting, speaking to both the leaders' grief and uncertainty about their future and my own wanting to support them in acknowledging the heartache and beginning to move forward. They heard me clearly.

As things turned out, the leaders and I decided to move in different directions, and I never became their rabbi. But as I reflect on that conversation, I realize how my life experience taught me how we must work to move ahead with life.

Tazria^c

Healing through Meeting

LEVITICUS 12:1–13:59

*But if the discoloration remains stationary, not
having spread, it is the scar of the inflammation;
the priest shall pronounce that person clean.*

—Leviticus 13:23

P'shat: Explanation

Meeting brings healing.

These chapters of Leviticus provide detailed instructions for the diagnosis and treatment of a variety of medical situations. Here, in Tazria^c, Moses brings God's word that a person with a skin condition is to meet with the priest at the Tent of Meeting. The priest examines the skin, figures out what, if anything, is wrong, and advises a care plan, all according to the Torah. For some problems, the priest recommends a process that begins by sending a person away from the camp until the inflammation heals. Healing flows from God, as underscored in Exodus, "I am Adonai, your Healer" (15:26). Here, in Tazria^c, God dispenses instructions for healing in a meeting with the priest, God's representative.

Protecting health is an important Jewish value. In this text, God's healing arrives when the priest meets with the people.

D'rash: Buber's Insight

I'm against individuals and for persons.

When it comes to healing through a meeting, spiritual well-being is also part of the equation.

Granting Buber an honorary doctorate in medicine in 1962 for a lifelong devotion to healing the human spirit through dialogue, the University of Münster in Germany deemed him a "Doctor of Souls."[8] Just four years earlier, Buber and another doctor of souls, the pioneer of humanistic psychology Carl Rogers, met for a historic ninety-minute public dialogue on "The Nature of Man as Revealed in the Inter-Personal Relationship." This dialogue, a meeting between two trailblazing thinkers and doers, clarified several similarities and differences in their thinking about psychotherapy, with particular attention to the counselor's approach to the client.

Rogers and Buber had much in common beyond a shared commitment to the transformational potential of human relationship. Each grew up in a strong religious household; Rogers entered ministerial studies before turning to mental health. And when it came to mental health, Rogers and Buber took a similar holistic approach. Both distanced themselves from the prevailing Freudian understandings. They rejected a pathology-focused view that broke a person down into classifications like id, ego, and superego. They refused to categorize behavior and diagnose psychological conditions, or chalk up human conduct to instincts or drives. They renounced pinning labels on people and instead affirmed the goodness, worth, and untapped potential of each conversation partner. Ultimately, just as the title of that evening's dialogue affirmed, they insisted we become fully human by relating to each other.[9]

For all that they agreed upon, their conversation brought a number of differences to light. Buber, a theologian, framed human conversation within theology; Rogers, a therapist, remained secular. Rogers championed self-learning that rises from open dialogue in a safe and affirming environment, but Buber wanted more.

As their dialogue came to a close, the moderator, Buber's primary biographer and interpreter, Maurice Friedman, referred to Rogers's then unpublished article, "What It Means to Become a Person." The article explained Rogers's revolutionary approach to "client-centered therapy," in which a therapist encouraged clients to tell their own stories as they saw fit, instead of the therapist's analyzing clients and providing a clinical diagnosis. Rather than presenting the therapist as the authority, Rogers saw clients as the expert in themselves. Through their self-expression in a safe, nonjudgmental setting, they would become more self-confident and empowered to act appropriately on their feelings and beliefs. The therapist was a supportive facilitator who ensured that each client's perspective came forward clearly and would be affirmed.

In contrast, Buber saw therapy as striving to be more of a conversation between equals in which the therapist was on the same level and a full respondent to the client. In what Buber's disciples came to call "Healing through Meeting," Buber refused to limit the therapist to reflecting, clarifying, or validating what the client said. As Friedman pointed out, instead of emphasizing the therapist's reaction to the client, Buber wanted the reciprocity of a genuine response. In saying to Rogers, "I'm against individuals and for persons," Buber was affirming his belief that each client becomes a "person" through mutual relationships with other "persons." Each individual would best be healed through a more reciprocal therapeutic relationship—a Healing through Meeting, where a "meeting" is a conversation between equals.

On the other hand, and in self-contradiction, Buber also saw the psychotherapy that Rogers (and many others) offered as predicated on an imbalanced relationship. While clients tended to be uncertain about their thoughts, feelings, and behavior, their counselors could see both sides of the relationship simultaneously—their own feelings, thoughts, and reactions as well as those of the counselees. To Buber, the counselor's greater capacity to look into the personality and soul created a power differential that spoke of I-It rather than I-Thou, an imbalance that the counselor had to address.

Ultimately, Rogers and Buber agreed that "the effective moment" in psychotherapy—evidence of healing—comes when the client and the therapist are involved in what Buber called Inclusion: when they simultaneously see both sides of the relationship. With Inclusion, the client and counselor are on the same emotional level and in the same spiritual lane. For both Buber and Rogers, what would later be called Healing through Meeting can arrive when an imbalanced I-It grows into a balanced I-Thou.

D'rash: A Personal Reflection

HEALING THROUGH LISTENING

I came to a better understanding of Buber's approach to psychotherapy in the final stages of writing my previous book, *God in Our Relationships: Spirituality between People from the Teachings of Martin Buber.* It happened when Maurice Friedman read and commented on the book draft and, among several very gracious comments, pointed to the importance of highlighting what occurs when the client sees both sides of the relationship—when therapy passes from I-It to I-Thou, from one-sided to two.

To be sure, much of psychotherapy is I-It. The counselor is paid to listen, may need to report to an insurance company, follows a code of ethics and legal requirements—and is restricted to a fifty-minute conversation. Measured, timed, and evaluated, this therapeutic conversation is I-It. But to Friedman's point, I-It does grow into I-Thou . . . a phenomenon I have seen firsthand.

As I went on to read more of Professor Friedman's writings, I was taken by his use of the term "Touchstones of Reality." As he explained it, people get a sense of what's real in their social environment through "touchstones"—interactions and conversations with family, time with friends, achievements at work, engagement with their religious community, and so on. Touchstones reassure us that we are loving and being loved, that we are productive members of society, that our efforts have positive and lasting impact. Touchstones ground us, become meaningful to us, and build us up. Spiritual healing arises from a growing appreciation of these touchstones in the therapeutic setting and in daily life experience.

As I contemplated Professor Friedman's thinking, I reflected on my own mental health training and saw myself as living out Rogers's teachings. Years ago, in a group social work supervision class in which we reviewed our fieldwork with clients, I had raised a concern about one of my counselees, a college student who lived with her parents and did very little talking at home. Her parents, her father especially, said it all. But when she came to me for counseling, she talked and talked. I just listened, occasionally repeated or paraphrased her words, or asked a clarifying question, rarely adding anything. I had no idea what our time together was accomplishing.

My instructor responded that this careful listening was doing my client great good. The counselee saw me as a wise authority. Someone she respected was paying active attention as she spoke. By my simply being present and attentive, I was validating her words and the underlying emotions. I wasn't supposed to give her a formula for living or impose a diagnosis on her. Supportive listening—that is, being "client-centered" with someone seeking help—can itself be a curative.

This young woman continued to take the lead in our time together; she owned it and filled it with her thoughts and words. She had my full attention, all of which I learned to hope would help her come into herself as an emerging adult. I realized that I followed Rogers's model—providing active, thoughtful, responsive listening, asking clarifying questions from time to time . . . and that seemed to make all the difference to her.

Metsora^c

Faith and Science Together

LEVITICUS 14:1–15:33

And the priest shall offer the burnt offering and the
meal offering on the altar, and the priest shall make
expiation for that person who shall then be pure.
—Leviticus 14:20

P'shat: Explanation

Like the previous Torah portion, Tazria^c, Metsora^c is something of a medical casebook that considers illness in spiritual terms.

For instance, for the treatment of one kind of skin condition, Metsora^c advises, "And the priest shall offer the burnt offering and the meal offering on the altar, and the priest shall make expiation for that person who shall then be pure" (Lev. 14:20). Skin problem? Bring it to the priest to heal the body and purify the spirit. In other words, in Metsora^c, both faith and medical science are aligned.

So, too, the Rabbis honor both science and miracles. Recognizing the set ways of nature, they give us daily prayers that praise God for each morning's orderly and predictable sunrise and for the moon and stars that appear, reliably, each evening. Simultaneously, the Rabbis hold close the Torah's miracles, such as a splitting sea and a talking snake. From time to time, they invent creative explanations that handily reconcile respect for a routinized, natural order with an unshakable commitment to the absolute, unquestionable truth of the Torah.

In one example, the Mishnah (*Pirke Avot* 5:6) teaches that God implants ten miracles at the end of the sixth day of Creation, just as the very first Shabbat begins: the rainbow that follows Noah's Flood, the manna eaten while wandering the desert, the tablets and letters of the Ten Commandments, the place where the earth opens to swallow the rebel Koraḥ and his followers, Balaam's talking ass, and more. God places each miracle on a heavenly timer, so to speak, set to launch precisely when needed.

Beyond this fanciful and resourceful explanation, Buber reiterates the natural human tendency to turn to spiritual language to explain things we don't understand.

D'rash: Buber's Insight

The meeting of a people with events so enormous that it cannot ascribe them to its own plans and their realization but must perceive them in deeds performed by heavenly powers.

In *Moses: Revelation and Covenant*, his book exploring the life, times, and history of Moses and the people of Israel, Buber considers the relationship of science and faith as he describes the miracle of Sinai: "The meeting of a people with events so enormous that it cannot ascribe them to its own plans and their realizations but must perceive them in deeds performed by heavenly powers."[10] When we lack words to explain an astounding event, our minds pivot from scientific and rational to personal and spiritual, and words like "miracle" come into play.

What can you possibly say when something so unimaginably miraculous literally leaves you at a loss for words, as when a very ill person given little time to live returns to full, robust health? Sometimes, too, something so unusual or astonishing, like the view from the Grand Canyon rim at sunset, upends our expectations and emotional balance. When the extraordinary arrives unexpectedly at just the right time and way, we're left voiceless with wonder.

No language can explain, nor any scientific theory clarify, the conditions that elevate emotions over intellect and evoke the sense of awe. On such occasions, as happened to Israel at Sinai, Buber sees the rational and scientific yield to the spiritual, bringing people to speak in terms of "deeds performed by heavenly powers."

D'rash: A Personal Reflection

"YOU ACCEPT SCIENCE?"

Passover was approaching when a newspaper reporter called my temple to get a rabbi's perspective on the upcoming holiday, which gave me an unexpected opportunity for a brief conversation on the complicated relationship of science and faith.

I told the reporter that Passover celebrates two things. First, there's the wonder and excitement of our freedom from slavery, which leads to our expression of the hope that all people will be free. In addition, Passover celebrates the arrival of spring, the goodness of the natural world, and our responsibility to protect the climate out of respect for God's creation and the trust God places in us.

"You mean you believe global warming is real?" she asked. "You accept science? I thought it must be either religion or science, one or the other. I didn't know religious people think science is true!"

"Yes, we accept science," I responded. "And we teach that you can believe in science and faith at the same time. And other religious groups think the same. Our national organizations of Reform Judaism belong to the National Religious Partnership for the Environment, and a good number of other religious organizations belong to it, too."

I used to get angry when people expected me to respond like some clergy who ferociously believe in the Bible and deny anything scientific that seems to conflict with their faith. Whenever a reporter would paint me with that old brush, I used to think, "You should know better than that." But, over the years, I've learned not to rush to judgment when people judge me. When religious leaders champion a literal reading of the Bible in which it really did rain nonstop for forty days on Noah's family-and-animal-filled ark and the sea really did split in two when Moses raised his walking stick, it's easy for people to fall into assuming every religious person looks at the world that way. I've learned to take this kind of moment as an opportunity to teach someone something, here to affirm my belief that science and faith are aligned . . . and to hope that those listening will take the understanding to heart.

'Aḥarei Mot

The Curtain Will Part

LEVITICUS 16:1–18:30

Adonai said to Moses, "Tell your brother Aaron that
he is not to come at will into the Shrine behind the
curtain, in front of the cover that is upon the ark, lest
he die; for I appear in the cloud over the cover."
—Leviticus 16:2

P'shat: Explanation

The portion 'Aḥarei Mot means "after the death"—that is, in the wake of the tragic death of Aaron's sons. As we saw in Shemini, after the young priests take fire pans, puts fire and incense on them, and offer God an "alien" fire, God responds with a burst of fire.

'Aḥarei Mot recalls that heartbreak when God instructs Moses, "Tell your brother Aaron that he is not to come at will into the Shrine behind the curtain, lest he die" (Lev. 16:2). While Aaron has unrestricted access to the Tabernacle's outer courtyard, permission to pass through the curtain leading into the shrine of the Holy of Holies is strictly limited to the Day of Atonement. Aaron may not enter the Holy of Holies just because he feels like it—to do so means death.

For Aaron, for Buber, as well as for us, the sacred, at times, is inaccessible. In those moments, it is important to avoid despairing and, instead, have faith that the curtain will again part.

D'rash: Buber's Insight

It vanishes but it comes back.

On the significance of the curtain that blocks admission to the sacred, Buber relates how Rabbi Eleazer of Koznitz teaches that when a window curtain is closed, there is nothing to see. But when a person draws open a curtain, a beloved can gaze in.[11] The physical and spiritual curtains of daily life allow or shut off access.

In the same way that Rabbi Eleazer's parted curtain extends an invitation, the privilege of I-Thou is also intermittent and operates independently of personal will. There's no "on-off switch." We can make ourselves available, and, if graced, we can enter or not, as we in that moment decide. For those times a soul yearns for I-Thou, yet is not given permission to enter, Buber encourages us to keep the faith. The renewed opportunity for I-Thou will return—"It vanishes but it comes back."

We come to appreciate the occasional nature of I-Thou when we go back and forth between I-Thou and I-It. There's a flip-flop, an oscillation, many times in a day, even in a single conversation. And for the times a soul despairs when I-Thou "vanishes," Buber's use of the word "but" reassures us that I-Thou is not gone for good. Be trustful that it will return, Buber reminds us. Keep faith that the curtain will reopen.

D'rash: A Personal Reflection

HOLINESS COMES, GOES, AND RETURNS

A sign in the shop where I service my car says, "Insurance rules prohibit customers from entering the repair area." Despite this "curtain" of sorts that stops me at the door, I have a warm, personal relationship with one of the service advisors, Chris. We bought five cars from this dealership over the years, and, thanks to Chris, each of the last two made it to 250,000 miles. I joke that it's the equivalent of driving one car all the way to the moon and the other back.

When I'm there for service, Chris and I might talk a bit about kids and family before we talk about the car. And when I ask him to look into a squeak or a rattle, an odd smell or a steering wheel shimmy, I know that when he says that my car needs a repair, it really does, that what he says is going on behind the curtain is really there.

In our conversations, no matter how abruptly I-Thou turns to I-It, something of that I-Thou abides. In the midst of discussing a click, thump, or shake, or the times one of us is in a hurry and we don't talk personally at all, I instinctively have faith that something of I-Thou will again be there. I know we care about each other, even as the curtain closes.

The dealer's head office sometimes sends me a postservice survey email, asking me to rate the service department's performance on a scale of 1 (awful) to 5 (great). As I give Chris a 5, I think of Buber's negative reaction to turning a relationship into a number. Yet, I remain mindful of the intermittent in I-Thou, which, thanks to the Eternal Thou, has a lasting impact, despite any earthly impediment.

Kedoshim

Hebrew Humanism

LEVITICUS 19:1–20:27

You shall be holy, for I, your God Adonai, am holy.
—Leviticus 19:2

P'shat: Explanation

At the midpoint of the Torah, Kedoshim offers the Jewish ethical centerpiece known as the "Holiness Code," which repeats the refrain, "You shall be holy, for I, your God Adonai, am holy." We see that we achieve holiness by treating one another ethically.

The commentator Or HaChaim notes that holiness does not come to the people of Israel automatically: God's holiness must be earned. The Torah speaks in the future tense: "You shall become holy." The people "become" holy by working at it, with the mitzvot of the Holiness Code as a guide map.

Turning to the details, the Holiness Code envisions an equitable society. It paraphrases and expands on the Ten Commandments, going on to include such mitzvot as loving one's neighbor, shunning gossip, and respecting the elderly. It also protects those who cannot fully fend for themselves. The weak and the strong, the wealthy and the poor, the worker and the employer are all on the same social level.

Kedoshim speaks as well to the farmer-employers in an agricultural society. It holds the landowner responsible for ensuring that the hungry have what to eat and the poor what to wear—the privilege of owning land demands sharing the benefits with those who have no portion.

Likewise, Kedoshim speaks to the merchant, who is assumed to have the financial wherewithal to run a shop and thereby gains an advantage over a customer. The merchant is to keep accurate weights and measures that ensure the fair treatment of customers, who don't walk around with measuring tools. The prohibition against cursing someone who is deaf or placing a stumbling block before someone who is blind ensures that people who hear or see do not impose on those who cannot. In sum, sustaining a holy community means that those who are privileged in one form or another are responsible for those who are not so well endowed.

By honoring and providing for others who are at a disadvantage, Israel becomes God's partner in advancing holiness.

D'rash: Buber's Insight

I am setting up Hebrew Humanism in opposition to
that Jewish nationalism which regards Israel as a
nation like unto other nations and recognizes no task for
Israel save that of preserving and asserting itself.

In Zionism, Buber saw a historic opportunity for actualizing Jewish social values and culture. He wanted Zionism to seize the moment and literally build a new nation from the ground up under a vision exemplified by Kedoshim.

Buber had a complicated relationship with Jewish ritual and the Jewish community. He received a Jewish education in his youth, but by his teens he turned away. Most likely he had long harbored doubts about ritual practice yet put them aside while living with his grandparents. Starting at age fourteen, when he returned to live with his father, Buber observed few Jewish rituals and avoided Jewish communal involvement (except occasional attendance at liberal Jewish services) until his university days, when he found his place among the Jewish people through the emerging Zionist movement.[12]

Through engagement in Zionism, Buber demanded that the Jewish state be built on Jewish spiritual, social, intellectual, and moral values. He asserted that a nation that focuses solely on the politics of its own survival and little else lacks integrity and a moral compass, and eventually dissolves into meaninglessness. Israel, as the Jewish nation, had to stand for something beyond itself—to draw from Jewish teachings to build a moral character and live by Jewish ethical values. The prevailing Jewish politics of pure survival, "nationalism," was little more than a group "preserving and asserting itself" with no understanding of the reason why.

Buber quickly rose to become editor of the official Zionist publication *Die Welt*. *The World* (its English title) provided a podium to promote his Hebrew Humanism ideal of an Israel filled with Jewish learning, culture, and literature and becoming an international beacon of cross-group collaboration and righteousness. Buber foresaw a binational population of Jews and Arabs working the land, shoulder-to-shoulder, as if an extension of the Torah's Holiness Code.

However, Buber's ideals, outspokenness, and strong personality conflicted with others in the Zionist movement, especially its founder, champion, and leader, Theodor Herzl. As antisemitic violence struck many quarters across Europe and Russia, the urgency of establishing a haven for persecuted European and Russian Jewish refugees led Herzl and most of the other leaders to place political necessity first, and ideals, such as Buber's, second: The Jews, Herzl insisted, needed to create a Jewish safe haven immediately, regardless of that nation's political and moral structure. Strongly disputing this approach, Buber emphasized that, in the long term, Jewish security and safety would only be served by upholding Jewish spiritual values.[13] The Buber-Herzl conflict, a collision between two strong-willed men, grew personal, public, and ugly, eventually leading Buber to drop the newspaper editorship, leave the movement, and withdraw from public life.

As the decades progressed, Buber had similar public disagreements with Israel's elected leaders, especially David Ben-Gurion, the first prime minister. At the First World Zionist Ideological Conference in Jerusalem in 1957, for example, Buber responded with outrage to Ben-Gurion's assertion that Israel would be perfected solely through sovereignty over the Land of Israel and restoration of its language (Hebrew). He denounced Ben-Gurion's political vision as a limited product of "false prophets" who dressed up political impulses as prophesy. While Ben-Gurion responded graciously, their differences remained.[14]

In his later years, Buber spoke of Hebrew Humanism as a vision that begins with Divine Revelation and lives out the mandate to be a light unto the nations. Israel would be the exemplar, leader, and supporter of goodness within and between all nations of the word. The soul and body of Israel would endure on this new land only by honoring universal values and embracing the entire, diverse population—not dividing the people and writing some off.[15]

Buber was pragmatic as well. He recognized the Jews' need for safety and security and understood that no human being, Arab or Israeli, was perfect. At the same time, he demanded that Israel's leaders treat Arabs better and avoid framing their political arguments in "messianic" terms. The Israeli government needed to claim its role in shaping the moral character of the people and the larger direction of the new nation, with Jewish-Arab relations providing a meaningful object lesson.

Buber held his ground and upheld his vision of Israel until his death in Jerusalem in 1965.

D'rash: A Personal Reflection

TOWARD SOCIAL JUSTICE

What do we do with Kedoshim today?

Though our lives are not tied to the land as in the past and our ways of caring for people have changed, we can continue to honor the teachings and spirit of the Holiness Code. One way is through faith advocacy: pointing to religious teachings that support the creation of a quality and sustainable social safety net when engaging with those who have the power to actualize it.

More than once, I've brought our synagogue teens to Washington DC to join with hundreds of their peers from synagogues around the country through the Religious Action Center of Reform Judaism's L'Taken Teen Social Justice Seminar. We take an extended weekend to study, pray, sing, learn about Jewish perspectives on public policy issues, and meet with national policy makers.

It's exciting and important for teens to witness the role religion plays in government these days, and to see how their own life experiences, grounded in a researched Jewish framework, can speak to decision makers — who are interested in what teens think. Over the years, our groups have included one teen who knew survivors of a mass shooting and spoke for increased protection from gun violence. Another teen reflected on her painful experience as a sexual assault survivor when calling for laws that ensure women's access to reproductive care. Another described her sister's daily experience of living with disabilities and the need to ensure that those like her are able to receive needed care and accommodations. Another teen spoke of a sibling with diabetes and the urgency of advancing diabetes medical research. And yet another, who lived in Israel, thanked a member of Congress for her support.

One teen, going into the weekend, said his parents had been dismissive of his planned time in Washington; they thought that no one there would listen to a teen. But the teens saw otherwise for themselves. Their stories and reflections were heard; you could see it in the faces of the legislative staff as they took notes, and, more than once, members of Congress decided to include their names as sponsors of the legislation that our teens promoted.

When it comes to providing for those in need, we did it one way in an agricultural age, and we do it another way in the Information Age. But the call remains: to reach for Buber's vision of Hebrew Humanism and the ideals of the Holiness Code.

'Emor

Magic, Manipulation, and Prayer

LEVITICUS 21:1–24:23

*These are the set times of Adonai that you
shall celebrate as sacred occasions.*
—Leviticus 23:37

P'shat: Explanation

'Emor opens with instructions for celebrating Shabbat, Passover, Shavuot, Sukkot, and other Jewish holidays. Six days of labor culminate in Shabbat: The seventh day is for rest. Passover is to be celebrated with unleavened bread and a cessation of work. An unnamed holiday now known as Shavuot, marked by a grain offering, follows fifty days later. Rosh Hashanah (as we call it today) is to be greeted with "loud blasts" and cessation of labor. The Day of Atonement includes self-denial, expiation through fire offerings, and a release from work. Shortly thereafter, the Feast of Booths, Sukkot, is marked with a ritual sacrifice, as well as a foliage celebration, complete with *lulav* and *etrog*.

These sacred occasions recognize the responsibility to work and the need to rest. They capture our excitement at the rebirth of spring, uplift the value of living free of oppression, and express our gratitude for the harvest and other bounty we enjoy. Fundamentally they acknowledge that Israel lives under a Covenant with God, with holidays, sacrifices, and other customs in honor of that sacred pact.

Judaism has long affirmed ritual sacrifice as a way of approaching God. The Torah's Hebrew word for sacrifice, *korban*, includes same three-letter root as *l'hakriv*, "to draw near," as in entering relation. Rabbinic commentator Sforno, underscores this point when he says the person bringing the offering simultaneously "brings oneself close to God" (on Lev. 1:2). Another commentator, Ḥizkuni, adds that *l'hakriv* is the same as *l'hakdish* (to sanctify). That is, when we get close, we get holy (on Lev. 1:2).

Note that the sacrifice brings us close to God without our trying to impose our own will on the Deity. We do not attempt to manipulate God through religious magic and like endeavors. Deuteronomy offers a sweeping ban: "Let no one be found among you who consigns a son or his daughter to the fire, or who is an augur, a soothsayer, a diviner, a sorcerer, one who casts spells, or who consults ghosts or familiar spirits, or one who inquires of the dead" (18:10–11). The Torah has us approach God through sacrifices instead of relying on magic to bend God's will. Where religious magic seeks to manipulate God, the Hebrew Bible provides festivals that are part of the Covenant.

D'rash: Buber's Insight

Magic desires to obtain its effects without entering into relation.

As the Bible distinguishes between magic and sacrifice, Buber equates magic with political manipulation that seeks an outcome without the sacrifice of entering relations. A great nation rests on personal relationship, not the magic of mass manipulation. There is no shortcut to greatness: The honest, respectful, and spiritually and emotionally demanding process of encounter is the only way.[16] Magic is a manipulative I-It, a cheap means of cajoling a higher authority to serve one's needs, as when rituals become magic that reduce God to a pass-through object to get some self-serving thing.

As World War I began, Buber was initially swept up by a popular vision portraying the international conflict in apocalyptic terms, as if there was a divine impulse for this war that would establish Germany as a strong, great, and admirable standout among nations. Eventually, Buber came to see both the elevation of the sanctity of the German homeland and the demonization of the enemy as mass manipulations. German political leaders had cast a magic spell that led to a world war, and Buber would have no more of it.

Buber retracted his support for the war and went on to refine his belief that relationship—not rhetoric or mass manipulation—properly stands at the foundation of a nation. At the same time, you could say that he grew to condemn as "magic" the process of politics without relationship. Propaganda, the fabrication of appearances through shortcuts that appear to be relational, are tricks of the ear and eye and sleights of hand that evidence a power play.

Buber developed this argument in the fall of 1916 in an open letter to his followers in Prague. To do so, he turned to the local legend of a superhuman golem as imagined by Rabbi Judah Loew in the sixteenth century.

The legend went that Rabbi Loew's Prague Jewish community had suffered vicious antisemitic attacks. To protect his people, Rabbi Loew fashioned a golem, a superhuman figure, from a mass of clay. He inscribed God's name on a piece of paper that he placed under the golem's tongue, and the golem came to life. Thanks to the golem, the Jewish community remained safe and secure, but there was a condition—as long as the paper with God's name was removed from under the tongue before each Shabbat, the golem would not run out of control. One Shabbat, Rabbi Loew accidently left God's sacred name in place, the golem went on a rampage, and everything came undone.

In relating this legend in reference to World War I, Buber urged the Jewish community to oppose the war, which he compared to a golem that appeared to offer protection but was destined to bring on great destruction. It was not yet Shabbat, Buber told the Jews of Prague. There was yet time to remove the holy name from the mouth of the war monster and end the magic spell.[17]

D'rash: A Personal Reflection

WHAT PRAYER CAN ACHIEVE

The Bible distinguishes between sacrifice and magic, Buber differentiates between magic and national integrity, and I have come to see the difference between magic and prayer.

Where the Hebrew Bible sees sacrifice as a form of addressing God, today many of us think of prayer as fulfilling that purpose and then some, as a way of asking God for things like health, material security, comfort, and peace. For me, for instance, as I recite prayers of healing for those who are ill or seeking spiritual strength, as I mention people by name from the pulpit, as I listen to members of our congregational family call out the names of others in need, I imagine God sending healing, directly and immediately, in some magical conduit from the heavens to earth. And, when I say the *Kaddish* prayer for the dead, I remember the legend that for each time we recite *Kaddish* for a loved one, that person gets one step closer to God in the heavens, who hears and acts on those words from the prayer book.

Yet prayer is even more than asking for things with the hope of getting them. Prayer is more than magic, more than meets the eye. My mentor, the late Rabbi Chaim Stern, dealt with these very issues when he considered what prayers from the past can do for us, right now. Chaim (he preferred to be called by his first name) was the editor of *Gates of Prayer, Gates of Repentance*, and other major twentieth-century Reform liturgies.

When it came to using a prayer book, Chaim encouraged us to rely on the traditional words of our siddur, because they "teach us what the people of Israel have collectively decided is worth praying for. The prayer book tells us what the Jewish people, in its age-long wisdom, has felt to be valuable, to be permanent, to be right. Through our honest confrontation with the words, we discover something of what we ought to become, and what sort of world we ought to work for."

Chaim continued:

You will find in our prayer book many expressions of joy and thanksgiving for life and its wonders; and many prayers, too, for peace, and justice, and the well-being of our community and of all the families of humankind. You will find cries of pain and grief, for this, too, is part of our Jewish experience and deserves to be felt and overcome. All in all, if you look closely into its pages, and with insight, you will discover the myriad ways our people have found to be Jewish, to be human, and to be the children and partners of God in the creation and development of this world.

We are taught to respond to life with gratitude: we are reminded that we are members of a community, not isolated individuals, part of a people, a heritage, a species made in the divine image. We are urged to live with hope in the future and commanded to act in such a way as to make that future a better one. For as we affirm that such values as justice, freedom, and peace are God's concerns, we learn to make them our own.[18]

More than magic, prayer can change us by shifting our attitude toward life and the way we live in the world.

Be-har

Intersection of Land and Justice

LEVITICUS 25:1–26:2

*The land must not be sold beyond reclaim, for the land is Mine;
you are but strangers resident with Me. Throughout the land
that you hold, you must provide for the redemption of the land.*
—Leviticus 25:23–24

P'shat: Explanation

Four decades in the Sinai wilderness give the Jewish people time to transition from slavery to desert nomads and, eventually, to become settled farmers in Canaan. Be-har provides special instructions for the approaching time in Canaan. The people are to receive equal portions of land. They are to work that land, donate part of what they grow, eat what they need, and store and sell any additional bounty. This land, like all their possessions, ultimately belongs to God. They are to care for God's possessions according to God's rules.

As time passes, however, what began as an equitable distribution of land became imbalanced, with a smaller segment of the population taking title to a growing share of the property. Be-har seeks to restore that original equality through new rules. First, the land is to remain fallow one year in every seven, in the year known as the "sabbatical year." Nothing is to be planted or harvested that year, and, God reassures them, there will be plenty to eat: abundant harvests of prior years will sustain them. Then, seven cycles of six-year plantings plus one sabbatical year of rest bring them to year 50: the jubilee year. As in a sabbatical year, there will be no planting or harvest during the jubilee. What's more, an economic reset takes the land and the people back in time. Any land that had been sold in the years before the jubilee was to be returned to its original owner. Debts were also cancelled, and indentured servants went free. The sabbatical and jubilee observances restored the parity the Jewish people knew when they first reached Canaan. A small number of people would no longer extract an unfair material share of God's grace.

At heart, the sabbatical and jubilee are theological affirmations that the land is God's possession, not the people's. As Psalms 24:1 says, "The earth belongs to God and all its fullness."

D'rash: Buber's Insight

It was the purpose of the Sabbatical year to lead to a renewal
of the organization of society, in order to start afresh.

Buber echoes the spirit of Be-har to propose a vision of social, cultural, and economic equality—an ideal that also reflects the influence of his father, Carl Buber.

Carl owned and operated a large farm, and employed a staff to run the business, yet he was more than just an owner-boss. He took an active interest in the lives of the people who worked for him—what went on in their homes, how their children progressed in school, the well-being of their older relatives—as he also made sure they were properly compensated for their time and energy.

As a farmer, Carl was very much at home with all that lived and grew on his land. He would stand among a herd of horses and greet each one individually, not with a cursory greeting but with a genuine, personal word. He'd carefully inspect corn and break open an ear to taste the kernels. All these contacts were genuine, responsible, and responsive.[19]

Echoing his father's example, Martin was particularly attracted to the ideals of kibbutz living in Israel. Even though he resided in a city, Jerusalem, he championed the value of caring for the land while caring for those working and living on it. The kibbutz epitomized the opportunity offered by the new nation of Israel to establish a just and equitable social order at the outset: "a renewal of the organization of society, in order to start afresh."[20] Communal eating on an egalitarian kibbutz, for example, provided a structure for creating thriving relationships. Personal sharing of kibbutz responsibilities such as cleaning and childcare demonstrated that each member made a contribution to the larger community and that an individual's job description did not define who that person was; it only encapsulated a portion of that person's wholeness.

More broadly, Buber believed the kibbutz would foster a mutually responsive and responsible community, on the land, in God's presence. Working together invited each member to sanctify the daily routine by living in close relationship with the soil and the people it sustained.[21]

D'rash: A Personal Reflection

GROWING OUR OWN FOOD

There is a miracle in the land, as I witnessed only when I reached adulthood and saw firsthand how a small seed receiving proper care produces a life-sustaining harvest.

Most of us don't work the land like we did in biblical days, or as Carl Buber did or Martin Buber dreamed. We may grow tomatoes in season or ride a horse from time to time, but our lives are not tied to nature the way many once were. As a result, there's a gulf between us and the food that sustains us.

I became more attuned to this estrangement after our family moved to rural Western Massachusetts, when we took up gardening and ate what we grew.

I had lived in apartments for the first thirty or so years of my life, and I was an embarrassingly provincial city kid. A neighbor raised tomatoes in his postage-stamp-size backyard one summer and brought a few bright reds over to share. Until then, I was used to a tomato coming in cellophane, as if that was how a tomato grew. My mom put out some slices from one of those bright reds, and I was literally awestruck by that colorful flavor. So, I was excited to try my hand at gardening when we came to the very first spring in our Western Massachusetts home.

I cleared and measured a plot in the sunniest corner of the backyard. I bought wood and built a gardening frame, ordered a load of topsoil dumped on the driveway, and carted the dirt, wheelbarrow by wheelbarrow, to the growing space. As the winter began to break, I bought seeds and grew seedlings under a grow lamp in the basement, and once it looked like the freezing weather was finally behind us, around Mother's Day, transplanted the seedlings into the garden. I looked in on the growing plants daily, watering, weeding, and eventually marveling at how seedlings sprout buds that transform to fruit that is ready to eat, all beginning with a tiny seed.

It really is a marvel that a small seed—of a tomato, zucchini, cucumber, basil, carrot—receiving proper care has the potential to yield so much. There must be a divine secret behind all this. The land is not ours, but God's, sanctified for our use so the fruits of the earth sustain us.

Be-ḥukkotai

Mountains in Time

LEVITICUS 26:3–27:34

*These are the commandments that Adonai gave
Moses for the Israelite people on Mount Sinai.*
—Leviticus 27:34

P'shat: Explanation

Mountains hold an important place in the Hebrew Bible, as they do in the previous week's portion, Be-har. Be-har literally means "on the mountain," as in Mount Sinai. This portion, Be-ḥukkotai, opens with, "If you follow my laws," and closes with the words, "These are the commandments that Adonai gave Moses for the Israelite people on Mount Sinai."

Referencing the metaphor of mountains, my mentor Rabbi Chaim Stern welcomed Rosh Hashanah many years ago with:

> To stand on a mountaintop, to take in the breathtaking vista of terrain, brings spiritual refreshment that makes a climb or drive up worth the effort. Our ancestors also recognized the spiritual potential at the peak. In fact, some of the most important events in our early history occurred on mountaintops. Rosh Hashanah recalls the binding of Isaac on Mount Moriah, the site destined to be the Great Jerusalem Temple. Shavuot celebrates the Revelation of the Torah atop Mount Sinai. Later on, in the Bible, Moses glimpses at the Promised Land from Mount Nebo and Elijah, the prophet, calls us away from idolatry atop Mount Carmel, where

Haifa is today. And the Psalmist cries out for help with the words, "I lift up my eyes to the mountains" (Psalm 121:1).[22]

Chaim brings our thinking to another level when he writes:

As there are mountains in space, so are there mountains in *time*. There are crucial *moments* in life when we are lifted up; when our vision becomes clearer and our perspective better; *moments* when the haze clears, when life's confusion seems suddenly to show a pattern; it makes sense. There has been revealed to us a glimpse of beauty or an insight into truth we had not possessed or even suspected. There are moments in life which become mountains. . . . Our vision is improved and certain trusts, which we had ignored or only half-sensed, become bold beacons of light. Trivialities are reduced to their proper size: Who cares then about petty annoyances or small desires that only a little while before would have consumed us with anger or longing? And at the same time, the important things we had underestimated or taken for granted now become precious beyond words.

To speak of the Revelation received at those mountains of space and in those mountains of time is also to speak of the Revelation of Torah of long ago at the peak of Mount Sinai, and how Buber labored to make that teaching accessible in current times.

D'rash: Buber's Insight

We wish to break through to the spokenness of the word.

Mountains had special appeal to the Buber family. Martin and his wife, Paula, felt at home on hikes through the Swiss or Italian Alps, or the Austrian Dolomites. For Buber, mountains — in space and time — also spoke of Revelation: the Revelation at Mount Sinai and the revelation of *I-Thou*.

And so it was that Buber, together with Franz Rosenzweig, author of the Jewish classic *The Star of Redemption*, embarked on a new, monumental German translation of the Bible that would recreate the experience of hearing God's voice at the mountainside. Premised on the idea that Jews didn't *read* the Torah at Sinai—they *heard* it, the pair conceived of a unique style of translation, resembling speaking, aimed to "break through to the spokenness of the word."[23] Readers would be led into the immediacy of mountains of time and space becoming one.

And yet, Rosenzweig was then in the advanced stages of a degenerative neurological disease. By 1925, he was incapable of picking up a pencil, handling a typewriter, or even speaking—every word required assistance. Nonetheless, he continued to receive visitors, write, and publish—and, on the spot, agreed to Buber's invitation to co-translate. The two began with Genesis. Buber provided the first drafts for weekly Wednesday meetings—"Buber Days," as Rosenzweig called them. Rosenzweig offered comments or suggested changes, which Buber accepted immediately or took time between meetings to consider: A single word could involve weeks of thought and conversation. Book by book, they sent their work to the publisher: Genesis was published in 1925; Exodus, Leviticus, and Numbers in 1926; Deuteronomy, Joshua, and Judges in 1927; both Samuels in 1928; and both Kings in 1929, the year Rosenzweig's health had declined to the point that he couldn't work any longer, and he died shortly thereafter. Buber finished the translation after moving to Israel; it was published in full in 1961.[24]

For all the impediments of health, political unrest and oppression, and international relocation, Buber and Rosenzweig climbed a spiritual mountain.

D'rash: A Personal Reflection

SELLING AN EXPERIENCE WITH INTEGRITY

It didn't look like I was about to receive a mountainside revelation on my way to the office that morning. But something marvelous happened as I stepped up to that Starbucks counter on an otherwise ordinary day.

I had gotten friendly with a barista, a guy about my age. On this visit, I mentioned I'd noticed that at Starbucks, unlike some of the other coffee places, the baristas are trained to give the customer the cup hand-to-hand—not leave it on the counter—and look the customer in the eye as they do it, and the better baristas are able to communicate a genuineness as they do it, too.

He leaned over the counter and almost put his face in mine as if he knew I was a rabbi and he was confessing something about himself that he had yet to share with any other soul and, in a blunt whisper, said, "That's because Starbucks doesn't sell coffee. Starbucks sells an experience."

Oh, that was a corporate talking point, for sure, the kind of thing they must teach in barista school. But whoever came up with that tagline knows something about mountains in time and space. After all, what goes into a cup of coffee? They pour flavored liquid into a mermaid cup, pop on a cover, and include a straw if the drink is cold or a cardboard sleeve if it's hot. Any store can do that. But if you are setting out to provide an "experience"—a moment that addresses a whole person while presenting a quality product—attentive gestures and a genuine greeting can create a mountain in time.

What's more, the barista was being candid with me, even in "corporate speak," as he unconsciously summoned authenticity through posture and speech and offered a wholehearted response to my taking notice of how he and his behind-the-counter colleagues carry themselves. I peered into his world and intuited something: He responded by bringing me in even deeper, as I followed him, absorbed by what he had to say. We put aside the rush and turned off the noise. We stepped out of our roles of coffee maker and commuter—and talked from the heart. I saw his world from his side of the counter, and he saw mine. And right then, in those precious moments, he was more than an hourly worker who just opens and closes a coffee spigot, and for him I was more than just another sale for the company.

To be sure, there's a world of difference between what happened at Sinai with two million at that mountainside, or the exchanges between Buber and Rosenzweig at the peak of creativity, and the little, though heartfelt, exchange between the barista and me. Yet the enduring memory of these mountainside conversations—the Afterglow—says that each of these encounters gave entry to Eternal Thou.

IV

Numbers (Be-midbar)

Be-midbar

NUMBERS 1:1–4:20

At the breaking of camp, Aaron and his sons
shall go in and take down the screening curtain
and cover the Ark of the Pact with it.
—Numbers 4:5

P'shat: Explanation

The name of the fourth book of the Torah, Be-midbar, literally translates as "in the wilderness," where we find the people of Israel a year after the Exodus. As Be-midbar begins, God instructs Moses to "Take a census of the whole Israelite community," a counting that leads to the English name, "Numbers." After the count, Be-midbar instructs the priests on how to care for the portable desert sanctuary called the Tent of Meeting: the tent itself, sacred utensils, the Ark of the Covenant, and more.

And so, the Israelites trek through the Sinai wilderness, set down for a time, relocate when and where God says, and repitch the Tent of Meeting. Note that they make use of the Tent of Meeting as a portable shrine without a permanent imprint. It sits on holy ground, sanctified only when the Tent is there. Once the Tent moves on, the sanctity travels with it, while the place it once stood returns to being as ordinary as it was before the Tent arrived. The holiness of the holy ground depends on where the Tent sits.

What is the point of all this? *Space* is *holy*, but only for a limited *time*. For the Torah, holiness is less a function of *space* and more a function of *time*.

There is another example when Moses meets God at the burning bush. The bush and the ground beneath it are holy, but only for the time that the fire burns as a sign of God's presence. Again, holiness is less about what occupies a *space* and more about what happens in *time*.[1]

This concept would later be reflected in the work of Martin Buber and his friend and colleague Rabbi Abraham Joshua Heschel.

D'rash: Buber's Insight

*There are moments of silent depth in which you
look on the world-order fully present.*

Buber makes it clear in *I and Thou* that I-Thou is about "moments," not places. I-Thou can happen anywhere, and when it happens, the partners enter a period of time when everything fits perfectly: As Buber says, "the world-order fully present."

Buber's time-sensitive spirituality finds a reflection in Heschel's teachings. The two men lived in the same circles in Europe, to the point that Heschel followed Buber as head of the Frankfurt, Germany, Lehrhaus School of adult study.[2] Heschel described how high his spirits rose when he and Buber would have a conversation that sometimes went on for hours. He remarked that Buber, by being true to himself, was an example of how a person can be even more important than their books.[3] After Buber died, Heschel praised Buber for contributing to the growing good of the world by responding to life challenges and carrying a resilience to renew himself and flourish.[4] Heschel recognized that Jewish life—with Buber's life as a model—is lived out in time.

Heschel's wonderful book *The Sabbath* reflects this essential Jewish emphasis on time over space. He tells us that long before we had holy land, we had the promise of holy time. Long before any human beings even dreamed of Canaan as a holy space, there was Shabbat, a sacred time for God, Adam, and Eve to refrain from labor in the Garden of Eden. Recognizing the sacredness of the time of Shabbat, God chose to assess the newly created things of space—earth, sun, moon, trees, animals—as merely "good" and "very good." God reserved the extra special term, "holy," for Shabbat, that one day in seven that arrives each week as a function of time.[5]

It is tempting for us to think that space takes priority over time, because the things of space seem so much more tangible and real than the things of time. We can touch the things that take up space, see them, enter them, fill them up, build on them, visit and revisit them. We can go back to a space we once occupied, but we cannot go back in time. We can, if we have the means, enlarge our space—a home addition, vacation home—but our days are finite. Where space can expand, the time that remains only contracts—it runs out—making time all the more precious.

Judaism is, foremost, a religion of time. Buber affirmed this holiness of time when he taught that each I-Thou is unique—it happens only once, never to be recaptured. I-Thou is independent of space—it can happen anywhere, and where it happens is unimportant. Given our finite life-times, we need to avail ourselves again and again of those limited opportunities for entering I-Thou and meeting God in Eternal Thou.

Interestingly, though Buber and Heschel agreed about many things regarding holy time, they disagree about Israel's experience at Mount Sinai. In Heschel's understanding of Judaism, the Jewish people's unique experience at Sinai, and the specific teachings of Torah revealed there, are first and foremost. That time, and the Torah laws and practices that come from it, obligate the Jewish people for all time. Buber, in contrast, sees each I-Thou as a Sinai unto itself. Sinai happens again and again and again with each I-Thou. Further, what we say to each other in this moment, here and now, is as revealing and truthful as the moment with God at the mountainside.

D'rash: A Personal Reflection

GOING BACK IN TIME AND SPACE

I took a lesson on time and space some years ago, at the end of a subway ride from our Upper West Side Manhattan apartment to the Brooklyn neighborhood of my childhood. The second I got off the train and set foot on the Saratoga Avenue elevated station, I saw that a poured-concrete platform had replaced the splintery beach boardwalk floor planks that would creak and, in my childhood imagination, threaten to break whenever you stepped on them . . . space yielding to the forces of time.

In two words, everything shrunk—after all this time, space got smaller. The corner supermarket with those long aisles and many cashiers where my mother used to take my brother and me was now a tiny grocery store. The towering synagogue where my dad took me to hear the shofar on Rosh Hashanah and helped me find my place in the siddur whenever I lost the page had morphed into an itty-bitty church. The sprawling playground behind my old school, which seemed to go on forever, now took up about as much space as a postage-stamp backyard. What loomed large in memory turned out smaller in person. And when I finally stood in front of our old home, it felt so underwhelming and flat to be there. What happened to all that excitement—the family dinners, holiday celebrations, all with beloved relatives no longer alive . . . stickball on the street with my cousins (all the times we used a sewer cover as home plate) . . . stoop ball with the neighbor's kids on the brick stairs leading to the front door, then crossing the street for an ice cream cone from the corner candy store, now a laundry.

You can return to a location, but you cannot go back in time.

Naso'

Words That Bless Children

NUMBERS 4:21–7:89

"Adonai bless you and protect you!
Adonai deal kindly and graciously with you!
Adonai bestow divine favor upon you and
grant you peace!"
Thus they shall link My name with the people
of Israel, and I will bless them.
— Numbers 6:24–27

P'shat: Explanation

Naso' includes the three-part poetically and concisely worded Priestly Blessing, *Birkat ha-Kohanim*, which asks God to invoke divine protection upon the community members receiving the blessing. The concluding word, "shalom," offers hope for personal and interpersonal peace under God's sheltering presence.

During biblical times, the priests offered *Birkat ha-Kohanim* while standing on a platform called a *dukhan*, which explains the name the prayer commonly receives today, *dukhening*. A longstanding tradition calls for the congregation to avoid looking at the service leaders during the recitation of the blessing, out of the awe for the Divine Presence the blessing evokes. In some communities, as an extra precaution, the service leaders cover their faces with a tallit while the congregation turns to face the rear of the sanctuary. The Priestly Blessing is also recited at festival services, weddings, b'nai mitzvah, and Confirmation, and when many families bless their children and grandchildren at Shabbat and festival dinners. And I have seen Christian religious leaders also recite the Priestly Blessing during their services.

The Rabbis highlight the blessing's third line, the hope that Adonai will "bestow Divine favor upon you." Some Rabbis translate the word "favor" to connote "light." This "light," to Rabbi Nathan, "refers to the light of the Shechinah, God's Presence," a spiritual grace, as well as the illumination from God's teaching: "the light of Torah" (Midrash Sifre Numbers 41:1).

In another interpretation, Rashi extracts a lesson on mindfulness. He explains that the Priestly Blessing attunes awareness to the here and now. We reach this spiritual state of mind by properly preparing for and speaking the blessing: "You shall not be in a hurry to bless them but bless them with intention and wholeheartedly" (on Num. 6:23). In this mindfulness that leads to being unrushed, thoughtful, and focused, we find a measure of spiritual wholeness.

D'rash: Buber's Insight

No, I really want to know how you are. Tell me in detail.

Buber's grandmother, Adele Buber, modeled the blessing of presence of mind in conversation, and blessed her children simply by being true to herself. They say that when she spoke with someone, she really addressed that person, simply by talking and listening. In how she communicated, Adele demonstrated the potential of words to carry a transformational and divine impact.

Martin's grandparents, Adele and Solomon Buber, owned a large farm, mines, and a corn-distribution business. Adele managed the business along with household and family activities. She also pursued personal studies while Martin's grandfather Solomon devoted his time to deep Jewish scholarship and writing.

Adele demonstrated intellectual intensity, even as a teen. At a time and in a community that discouraged, and even forbade, reading by women, she secretly bought books and magazines and hid them for reading when no one was around. Adele imprinted that intellectual drive into her sons, including Martin's father, Carl, and later to Martin during the years he lived with his grandparents.[6]

Adele was the primary compass and force in Martin's early education. She took charge of his at-home schooling, arranging private tutoring with a focus on languages. Though Martin didn't talk at all until he was three, under her mentoring and direction he eventually learned to speak a remarkable array of languages, including German, Hebrew, Yiddish, Polish, English, French, and Italian; and he read Spanish, Latin, Greek, Dutch, and others.

Even as a child, he harbored a curiosity about the significance of how people communicate, which brought him to compare words across languages. Playing alone, he would ask himself a question in French and respond in German. These bilingual self-conversations brought him to wonder why a word means one thing in one language and something else in another, or why it means the same thing across languages, perhaps with a slight difference of a syllable added or removed. He took these interlingual exercises as a demonstration of the power of the word, and the potential of knowing it in multiple languages: This allowed a person to experience the difference on the other side of a relationship while maintaining awareness of one's own.[7]

As a grandparent himself, Buber spoke to his grandkids with an intensity that resembled his grandmother's. His grandson Emanuel Strauss recalled how Buber insisted the grandchildren be fully attentive and reactive when he spoke to them. When he asked them how they were doing, and, sometimes, like many young people, they tried to brush him off with a few words, he refused to let them get away like that, countering with, "No, I really want to know how you are. Tell me in detail." He taught them to be present by being specific.[8]

D'rash: A Personal Reflection

GRANDPARENTS' BLESSINGS

My early life story resembles Buber's in that when my father died when I was ten, my mother returned to work and my brother and I were gifted to have our grandparents move in and care for us. Just as families bless their kids with the Priestly Blessing, Buber and I were blessed by a loving intergenerational influence in our early years.

My grandfather would meet my brother and me at the bus stop when we came home from school or give us a chocolate bar he'd pick up on the way home from work. He loved to show us things, from tools to old coins, anything he found interesting. And on Shabbat morning he would take me to shul, where he'd banter with the guys after the service over a chunk of challah, a piece of gefilte fish, and an occasional shot of schnapps.

I walk whenever I can, just like my grandmother — this is part of her legacy to me. She did not finish high school but was always reading about psychology and going to continuing adult education classes on mental health. She never said so explicitly, but her curiosity about human feelings and behavior demonstrated to me the potential and power in learning about oneself, how self-reflection and self-insight open the door to more substantial and fulfilled living.

Debbie and I recently became grandparents, and we are prayerful, hopeful, and excited. I know well that grandparents make a significant contribution to the life direction of a growing child. And when people ask me, "How do you feel about becoming a grandfather?" the first thing that comes to mind is to respond to the call to be fully present for the next generation of our family.

Be-ha'alotekha

Eternal Thou

NUMBERS 8:1–12:16

*Miriam and Aaron spoke against Moses because of
the Cushite woman he had taken into his household
as his wife: "He took a Cushite woman."*
—Numbers 12:1

P'shat: Explanation

If leading the people is not enough of a challenge for Moses, things
become even harder when his siblings, Miriam and Aaron, speak
against him, saying, "He married a Cushite woman"—that is, a "Black
woman." It is not easy to discern whether their concern about his
wife, the "Cushite," is a reaction to her race, or to her being a tribal
outsider, or her being an additional wife symbolic of disloyalty to his
first wife, Zipporah.

Moses has long been married to Zipporah, whom he met in Midian
prior to the Exodus from Egypt. As a result, most readers thus assume
that the woman referred to as a Cushite is a new and second wife, but
some, such as the poet, philosopher, and commentator Rabbi Abraham ibn Ezra (Spain, 1089–1167), put aside the accusation of neglect
of Zipporah. Ibn Ezra defends Moses by teaching us that there is no
second wife. He explains (on Num. 12:1) that the Cushite is Zipporah, Moses' first and only wife. Ibn Ezra apparently bases his argument on noting that the only time the Torah mentions Moses' wife
Zipporah by name is in Exodus. She is unnamed in Numbers, so it
is not unreasonable to assume that Zipporah is the Cushite. Others
say that Miriam stood up for Zipporah out of the loyalty of a sister

for a sister-in-law. Regardless, the Torah and God sweep aside these concerns and stand with Moses as far as whom he decides to marry.

Be-ha'alotekha goes on to tell us that Moses does not deserve the backbiting—if anything, Moses merits praise. He is "a very humble leader, more so than any other human being on earth" (Num. 12:3). What is more, Moses has special spiritual standing with God. Where God addresses Israel's other leaders in dreams and visions, God speaks to Moses directly, "mouth to mouth, plainly and not in riddles, and he beholds the likeness of Adonai" (Num. 12:8). God also refers to Moses as God's "servant" (Num 12:7) to underscore Moses' devotion to God and the people.

So, with Moses holding such high stature in God's eyes, God calls Miriam and Aaron to task: "How then did you not shrink from speaking against My servant Moses!" (Num. 12:8). God punishes Miriam with "snow-white scales" of leprosy. Miriam and Aaron judge Moses harshly because his wife is Black; ironically, God turns Miriam sickly white.

Miriam's punishment is physical, whereas the Rabbis point out that Aaron suffers emotionally and spiritually. He is deeply distressed at the sight of a suddenly stricken Miriam and turns to Moses to pray for her healing. Moses prays, Miriam enters quarantine, seven days pass, she returns to camp, and the people resume their journey.

This incident shows how words travel far and quickly. A little backbiting, as Miriam and Aaron discovered, can have tremendous impact on people—and even on God.

D'rash: Buber's Insight

Every particular Thou is a glimpse through the Eternal Thou.

As the Torah describes, Moses possesses unique spiritual acuity. Whereas other prophets hear from God in a "dream" or a "riddle," Moses discerns God's word and presence plainly and in the everyday.[9] But it's not just Moses who can encounter the Divine in the ordinary.

Buber affirms that you and I also possess this remarkable spiritual capacity to witness God's being in the daily routine.

Buber speaks of the Eternal Thou as the ultimate spiritual dwelling, an imaginary place where all positive earthly acts and spoken words abide. A person can forsake that spiritual opportunity through gossip. Or, one can speak like Moses, and Buber, and enter God's presence in the everyday.

To illustrate, Buber retells a story of Rabbi Abraham Ya'akov of Sadagora (Poland, d. 1883) about how we learn something from all created things, whether created by God or people. A disciple challenges Rabbi Ya'akov's proposal that human and divine creation are of similar value, as if the rabbi speaks a blasphemy when equating human creation with the godly. He presses the rabbi to explain what lesson we might learn from the example of something human-made like a train. Rabbi Ya'akov points out that a train leaves on time and waits for no one. In the same vein, it only takes a second for a person to miss out on everything. What then do we learn from a telegraph? Rabbi Ya'akov explains: Each word is counted and billed, whether conveyed through an electric wire or spoken face-to-face. And the telephone? Rabbi Ya'akov answers: What we say in one place is heard somewhere else, be it across town or across the country.[10]

Buber's Hasidic masters often pointed to earthly examples to describe heavenly impact. Here, I suspect that Rabbi Ya'akov is asking us to imagine the cosmic significance of earthly communication. What is heard here on earth also resonates with God above—an illustration of Buber's teaching, "Every particular Thou is a glimpse through the Eternal Thou."[11]

D'rash: A Personal Reflection

"ONE & ONE ARE THREE"

I work as an Intentional Interim Rabbi, having the privilege of supporting a congregation in transition between rabbis, for a year or so, until the new rabbi is chosen and arrives. I find it meaningful and fulfilling to partner with synagogue leaders and staff to prepare the congregation for their next rabbi, who benefits from a smooth transition and a strong start. During an interim year, a congregation will iron out the way they make decisions, reduce conflict, begin new initiatives, and/or close programs and activities that are no longer meaningful, sparing the next rabbi significant administrative and organizational burdens and providing that rabbi with more time to get to know the people and build relationships that will carry forward.

There was no such thing as an Intentional Interim Rabbi back when I was ordained. When there was a need for a rabbi to "fill in," a synagogue often turned to a recently retired rabbi to carry the congregation through. What I do is very recent and new and requires specialized postordination training.

Often, when I am interviewing for a new position, a search committee will ask me, "Why do you enjoy working as an interim rabbi?" Underlying that question is a wanting to know why a rabbi would prefer to go to a new congregation each year rather than settle down. After all, the work of the clergy—rabbi, minister, or any other—means so much to people when there is an ongoing relationship. Yet I find that a rabbi does not have to be with a synagogue forever to have a significant and enduring impact. An intentionally time-limited relationship can still be a meaningful one. Meaning comes from what we do with our time together rather than how long the relationship lasts.

For example, think of that schoolteacher or college professor who, during that year or semester, taught you an important lesson about the world or yourself that still stays with you. For myself, as much as I appreciate a longstanding relationship with a doctor, I remember an emergency room doctor and nurse who saw me briefly and only once, yet were so compassionate and thorough that they helped me then and, by following their advice, I keep myself healthy today.

When it comes to the invisible and enduring, my mentor, the late Rabbi Chaim Stern, wrote poetically:

I swear that one & one are three,
I see it always so
when lovers kiss
& friends embrace.[12]

Chaim loved to play with words. And, to be sure, "one & one are three" sounds like some fuzzy math lesson Chaim might offer as a joke with that grin of his. But he was profoundly serious when he wrote "one & one are three." He was telling us that when two people are together wholeheartedly, a third presence, God, enters the relationship. That is how two of us become three; God is that third presence, with us in our love.

Shelaḥ-Lekha

People Want Proof

NUMBERS 13:1–15:41

You, Adonai, appear in plain sight when Your cloud
rests over them and when You go before them in a pillar
of cloud by day and in a pillar of fire by night.
—Numbers 14:14

P'shat: Explanation

"You can't see God," I find myself telling people, as if repeating one of the very first lessons I received as a Brooklyn yeshiva kid, a lesson that my continuing Jewish education would reiterate and expand. Nevertheless, Shelaḥ-Lekha astoundingly leads a person to think otherwise.

As the portion opens, Moses dispatches scouts to spread out across the Land of Israel and bring back word of what the people will face. The scouts return with greatly differing reports: two are optimistic about the opportunities, but the vast majority provide a negative assessment—and the people, discouraged by word that the land "devours its inhabitants," demand to return to Egypt. God takes the negativity as an indication that the people are not yet capable of living freely on their own in Canaan and sentences this generation—all who came from Egypt—to die off in Sinai. Only those born in the wilderness will enter the land.

Now we near the point where the text talks of the people witnessing God in plain sight. At first, God wants to destroy the unfaithful people and have Moses restart the nation himself, but Moses dissuades the Divine from such harsh retribution, reminding God: "You, Adonai, appear in plain sight when Your cloud rests over them and when You go before them in a pillar of cloud by day and in a pillar of fire by night." According to the text, this so-called invisible God does indeed "appear in plain sight," as our Hebrew literally says, "*ayin b'ayin*," Israel met God "eye with eye" (Num. 14:14).

Now, we might wonder, if we humans cannot "see" God in our day, how did the Israelite people see God in their time, in "plain sight," no less?

Representing the minority opinion among our Rabbis, Sforno (Ovadiah ben Ya'akov Sforno, Italy, fifteenth–sixteenth centuries) says the people really saw God, such was the intensity of their visual experience (on Num. 14:14). Rabbi Ya'akov Tzvi Mecklenburg (Konigsberg, East Prussia, nineteenth century) disagrees as vehemently as would any of the yeshiva rabbis of my childhood. He takes a very tight and literal reading of Shelaḥ-Lekha's Hebrew, which, as he correctly points out, is ambiguous. That is, the object of the Hebrew sentence is nonspecific—the Torah does not really say that *the people* saw God, leaving open the possibility that God appeared to someone or somewhere else. Rabbi Mecklenburg continues, "God forbid, that the Eternal God would literally appear to a person 'eye-to-eye'" (on Num. 14:14, *Haketav Vehakabbalah*).

Similarly, the physician, Jewish legal scholar, and philosopher Maimonides (Rabbi Moses ben Maimon, Spain and Northern Africa, 1138–1204) believes it is impossible for God to be seen. A rigid rationalist, Maimonides recognizes our frustration over the human incapacity to fully appreciate or understand the Divine. Since, he understands, it is easier to say what God is not rather than what God is, he suggests that we best speak of God with "negative attributes": God is not a person or animal, God does not have a body, and God does not need food, for instance. To the point of our verse, the implication that the people saw God "in plain sight" is merely a metaphor for their intense experience.

Many modern interpreters have concluded that we cannot see God, but we can witness God's presence and benefit from God's impact. Consider the incident following the calamity of the golden calf. Moses begs of God, "Oh, let me behold Your Presence!" to which God responds, "A person may not see Me and live," but goes on to provide what could be considered second best, "I will make all My goodness pass before you, and I will proclaim before you the name Adonai and the grace that I grant and the compassion that I show." God is not seen, with the possible allowance for Moses, who is extended a shielded glimpse from the back (Exod. 33:19–20). As for the rest of us, we can, at best, witness the impact of this invisible God in life.

When we come to Buber, we also receive a very nuanced consideration. Just as the Torah hints, God cannot be seen, and yet we can witness God's presence in life, indirectly.

D'rash: Buber's Insight

He cannot directly concern himself with
God, but he can converse with Him.

Buber affirms that we do not see God as we see a person. Rather, we meet God through human encounter.

The proof? We cannot prove anything about God. All we have is faith, even in this possibility of indirectly witnessing God.

Buber's primary translator and interpreter Maurice Friedman points out that for Buber, we do not witness God the way we see a thing; rather, we sense a continuing Divine Presence as our circumstances change from one moment to the next. God, and our perception of God, is always changing, in relation to the moment.[13] Ultimately people are continually called to act in ways that make God real.

Buber cites Rabbi Moshe Leib of Sassov (Ukraine, late eighteenth century), who was well known for his love of human beings, even those who would harm others.[14] When someone asks for help, Rabbi Moshe Leib insists that we must avoid turning that person away with self-serving words that direct them to take their problem to God. Rather, we are to act as if God does not exist, no one else is around, and we are the sole ones who can help. Human beings are God's agents for the good. Lending a hand will bring forward God's presence.[15]

God, Buber teaches, is not seen or addressed directly, but appears as a by-product of our relationships. Sought outright, God is unapproachable. Sought through people, the path is clear, as I-Thou opens to Eternal Thou.

D'rash: A Personal Reflection

"I WANT TO SEE GOD"

"I want to see God," said Michael, one of our religious school students. "Why can't I see God?"

Michael would say this just about every time we ran into each other. Each time, I tried as hard as I could to enter his frustration, and dig deep within myself to find new words to tell him why we cannot see God's face like you see mine and I see yours. All we can do is see God's goodness when people are kind and loving.

But my take on God's "I will make all My goodness pass before you . . . but you cannot see My face" did not do it for Michael. He never accepted these answers from me. He was adamant. He'd think for a moment and say, "But I want to *see* God! Why can't I *see* God?"

Frustration is contagious; here I caught it from an eleven-year-old. He wanted proof, I wanted to give it to him—and we both came up empty.

We all face questions we cannot answer. For all our learning and experience, much of life remains a mystery. Yet I do believe that we see God between us, as I did when Michael asked me those questions and I struggled to do my best in response.

Koraḥ

NUMBERS 16:1–18:32

*You have gone too far! For all the community are holy,
all of them, and Adonai is in their midst. Why then do
you raise yourselves above Adonai's congregation?*
—Numbers 16:3

P'shat: Explanation

When outrage and anger flare up, whether in the Bible's days or ours, whether for political or personal reasons, horrible damage may result—as happens in this portion bearing the name of the Torah's notorious rebel, Koraḥ. Koraḥ gathers a group of the disaffected and self-righteously begins a political campaign accusing Moses and Aaron of usurping leadership.

A heartbroken Moses places the matter in God's hands. God obliterates the rebels, who are either swallowed up by the earth, burned, or struck by plague. The leadership of God, Moses, and Aaron is reaffirmed.

The Torah and the Rabbis are universal in their defense of Moses and condemnation of Koraḥ. They portray Moses as God's humble public servant and the people's selfless leader, working tirelessly under God's direction. The commentator Ibn Ezra, like a modern-day political analyst, opines about Koraḥ's twofold grievance against Moses: that Moses usurped leadership and engaged in political patronage. In Ibn Ezra's description of Koraḥ's accusation, Moses not only grabbed power for himself; he also exploited his position to dole out plum jobs to relatives, especially his brother, Aaron, who became High Priest. Koraḥ, also a Levite and a firstborn, claims that he deserves one of those jobs. Making matters worse, Korah allies with the Reubenites, Datan and Aviram, whose complaints date all the way back to Genesis and Joseph, whom they accuse of undermining Joseph's older brother Reuben, their ancestor. Here, Datan and Aviram act on that smoldering grievance by challenging the appointment of Joshua, of the tribe of Joseph, as Moses' successor, and these three aggrieved tribal leaders approach Moses to settle the score (on Num. 16:1).

Even as the Rabbis criticize Korah, they have no problem with disagreement within Israel per se. In fact, the Rabbis praise the process and content of the arguments between Rabbi Hillel and Rabbi Shammai of later centuries as being "for the sake of Heaven." Here, however, the Rabbis condemn the self-serving grievances of Korah and his followers as "not for the sake of Heaven" (*Pirke Avot* 5:17). Korah brought only damage. We can disagree but must do so respectfully. And heaven forbid that those disagreements turn violent.

D'rash: Buber's Insight

The abyss between man and man is
threatening to become unbridgeable.

Just as the Torah records Korah's rebellion, Buber witnessed violent conflict.

Buber lived through two world wars and then through more than two decades of conflict in Palestine and Israel. In a landmark lecture, "Hope for this Hour," delivered during the Korean War and the rising Cold War at Manhattan's Carnegie Hall on a visit to the United States in 1952, Buber offered uncharacteristic pessimism: "The abyss between man and man is threatening to become unbridgeable."[16] He feared humankind was approaching a catastrophic point of no return.

As an example of the "unbridgeable" also echoing the circumstances surrounding Korah's rebellion, violent political disagreement rocked Germany immediately after World War I, resulting in the brutal murder of Buber's mentor, colleague, and friend of two decades Gustav

Landauer (1870–1919). Landauer's influence on Buber's life direction was second only to that of Paula, Buber's wife. For instance, when Buber was initially swept up in the misguided spirit of German nationalism after the outbreak of World War I, only an intense exchange with Landauer turned Buber's excitement into realism (see 'Emor).

Landauer, a highly visible and outspoken pacifist, anarchist, and activist, was the subject of ongoing German government surveillance and persecution. Where Koraḥ was selfish, Landauer was selfless. Landauer's outspoken commitment to justice and equality, and his larger-than-life persona, led some to see him as like a biblical prophet. German authorities, however, arrested and incarcerated him as a political prisoner for more than a year until, for some unknown reason, they decided to release him.

When World War I ended and a new regime took charge of Germany, Landauer put his anarchism aside to accept a position in the fledgling government, out of a conviction that this administration would finally be the one to advance justice and peace. But a few days later, counterrevolutionaries took office, and Landauer lost his post. Friends urged Landauer to flee Germany for his life, and he made plans to escape, only to change his mind and stay to resist the new regime. The police soon arrested him; he was to be executed. Friends and colleagues argued for a trial, and Landauer received a hearing that very same day. It was said he provided a strong defense, but he was nevertheless convicted of crimes against the state and immediately taken to be beaten and shot. His friends and loved ones were unable to find him or learn of his well-being for days.[17] Buber carried the memory of this "unbridgeable" conflict and the influence of Landauer for the rest of his life.

D'rash: A Personal Reflection

WHEN POLITICS GET MEDICALIZED

When politics take a horrible turn, the research and writings of Dr. Robert Jay Lifton speak to the reasons, consequences, and potential for human resilience.

An American psychiatrist, laureate, and author and editor of twenty-nine books on genocide, violence, and human renewal, Lifton has written about his conversations with people who endured and recovered from awful, life-threatening situations, among them Japanese survivors of the Hiroshima atomic bomb and Vietnam veterans returning to civilian life. Lifton references Buber when he uses the phrase "Imagine the Real" to describe what it is like to fathom life after a nuclear attack. The destruction and heartache of Hiroshima and Nagasaki were real, to be sure, yet the lived experience during that calamity is beyond what any person can possibly imagine. Ultimately, Lifton's writing demonstrates the remarkable human capacity to endure a significant trauma and go on to build and live a meaningful life.

One of Lifton's books, *The Nazi Doctors: Medical Killing and the Psychology of Genocide*, grew from a decade of individual conversations with Nazi doctors and their Holocaust victims, a book I found to be profoundly troubling, and exhausting to read. Lifton examines the central role of doctors and medical arguments in the Nazi genocide of Jews. Beyond the common knowledge of the hideous so-called Nazi experiments on Jewish victims, he demonstrates how the Nazi medical community was at the center of Jewish extermination. Doctors ran the camps, overseeing selection of Jews for death, supervising the genocide, and administering the disposal of human remains.

Lifton sets off to understand how a physician, who is sworn to do no harm and advance human well-being, could be a perpetrator of genocide. He goes on to argue that a perverted process of rationalization enabled these doctors to convince themselves that destroying Jews was the best thing for the health of Nazi Germany. In a pseudoscientific argument, one Nazi doctor compared Jews in Nazi Germany to an infected appendix that, left unattended, would kill a person. Just as a doctor would remove a threat to a patient's body, the Nazis needed to remove the threat of Jews from the body of society, thereby, in this gruesomely distorted logic, honoring their medical calling by protecting the purportedly superior Aryan genetic lines.

I had the opportunity to have dinner with Lifton, and I found him warm, charming, thoughtful, and, as you might imagine, a wonderful listener. And I was deeply affected to think I was sharing an evening of conversation with someone, sitting across from me over a dinner table, who had also sat across from Nazi doctors who had perverted their medical capacities for harm instead of healing.

Ḥukkat

On Jewish Law

NUMBERS 19:1–22:1

That shall be the law for them for all time.
—Numbers 19:21

P'shat: Explanation

The ashes of an unblemished red heifer and a sprinkling of water remove the ritual contamination that follows contact with a corpse. It is a puzzling mitzvah—the Torah offers no rationale, explanation, or motivating value for offering up a "red cow without blemish, in which there is no defect," with "dung included." Unlike any other sacrificial animal, this cow must be one "on which no yoke has been laid." What is more, the Torah offers involved instruction for disposing of the sacrificial ashes, including sprinkling a mixture of ashes in water on days three and seven, postcontact. Finally, unlike most other rituals and moral instruction, the Torah specifically affirms the importance and continuity of this practice: "That shall be the law for them for all time" (Num. 19:21).

The Rabbis are equally perplexed. To be sure, spiritual cleanliness is essential to the Torah and hence to them, but with other mitzvot seeming much more significant and their basis so much clearer, why does the Torah specifically single out the red heifer sacrifice for perpetual observance? Some Rabbis suggest that we receive this mitzvah for the sake of studying and learning from it, and nothing more. Yet one midrash tells us that the rationale for this mitzvah was even beyond the understanding of wise King Solomon, who said, "'All this I considered, and I investigated the situation of the red heifer, I inquired, and I examined in detail. As Ecclesiastes (7:23) says, 'All this I tested with wisdom. I thought I could fathom it, but it eludes me'" (Numbers Rabbah 19:3). It stumped King Solomon and baffles us.

Buber offers guidance on what to do in such a situation.

D'rash: Buber's Insight

Is this particular law addressed to me and rightly so?

When it came to keeping a mitzvah that left a person puzzled or unmoved, Buber had a reputation of indifference, if not hostility. He rejected Jewish rituals that did not speak to him, even more widely kept mitzvot, especially in his earlier years. In one glaring example, Buber was a Shabbat guest at the home of a local rabbi. The rabbi asked Buber to wear a *kippah* for the traditional *Motzi* prayer over bread. Buber, appearing annoyed by the request, declined.[18]

While Buber's behavior was rude and off-putting, his reaction demands a closer look, beginning with a consideration of his deep friendship with his colleague Franz Rosenzweig, with whom he had extensive, respectful, and ongoing dialogue on the role of law in Judaism.

Rosenzweig upheld the experience with God at Mount Sinai as the central Jewish moment. The outcome of that time of Revelation—the Torah and the teachings that flow from it, the Written Law and Oral Law—obligate Israel in perpetuity. In contrast, Buber taught that whatever people learn from each other in I-Thou is as truthful and monumental as what Israel heard at Sinai. Buber summed it all up by telling Rosenzweig that he asked himself of each mitzvah, "Is this particular law addressed to me?"[19] That is, did the current moment of encounter command him to follow this specific Jewish practice? Did he feel obligated to do this right now?

Buber did not accept the entire system of Jewish law, halakhah, as a body of obligation for himself. He did not allow other Jews, past or present, to impose their rules on his life. Rather, he approached each mitzvah individually, considering its personal meaning in that very moment. Some accused him of "cherry-picking," selecting only those mitzvot he liked and disregarding the rest, to the point of undermining Judaism. Some called him lazy for taking "an easy way out" of living a more responsible and fuller Jewish life. In response, Buber held that his religious obligations arose out of a deeply considered personal commitment. He arrived at his conclusion based on a challenging and rigorous process of spiritual self-examination.

Buber expected the same of others. He expected others to bring their life experiences to Jewish learning, to find their own branch on the Jewish Tree of Life, all the while remaining open to heartfelt consideration of other Jewish ways of living.

Buber became more embracing of halakhah as he got older. His family well knew that he expected his grandson to be ritually circumcised.[20] And on one notable occasion, after speaking at a Shabbat dinner in his honor at the Jewish Theological Seminary in Manhattan, Buber needed to return to his hotel over a mile away. It was chilly and raining that night, and the then seventy-three-year-old Buber generally did not mind riding on Shabbat, so it would not have been much of an issue for him to accept an offer of a cab. But he decided to decline the offer and walk thirty blocks down Manhattan's Broadway in foul weather out of respect for his hosts. He got to the hotel soaking wet.[21]

This is who Buber was and what he gives us. He asks each one of us to ask ourselves, "Is this particular law addressed to me?"

D'rash: A Personal Reflection

"HOW LONG IS SHIVAH?"

When it comes to deciding personal religious practice, it is important to start with a Jewish framework. "Rabbi, how long is shivah?" is a question that I and many other rabbis face more than any other. So, here is how the decision-making works.

Shivah is Hebrew for the number "seven," making this a question that answers itself—a relative dies and a Jewish family observes shivah for seven days. When I was a kid, that is what my family did when a relative died. My entire family, both sides, lived within walking distance in the same Brooklyn neighborhood, and a death meant taking a postfuneral shivah week to mourn, all of us together. We stayed the full week on those low benches, with the mirrors covered and the men going unshaven.

But things have changed, for us and for many others. Early Reform Jews shortened the mourning period to three days, and today some people tell me that they are not going to sit at all. As for me, as a rabbi responding in one of those situations, the question is less about "How long will you sit?" and more about *"How will you decide how long you will sit?"*

That is, what we consider to be "Liberal," "Progressive," or "Reform" Judaism emphasizes what has been called "informed will." First, we inform ourselves of the tradition. Then, we exercise a willful consideration based on personal conscience. In sum, the *process* of deciding can be as important as what we eventually decide to do. For me, this self-examination rests on an honest understanding of Buber's approach: "Does this mitzvah speak to me right now?"

There is a world of difference between just doing what I feel like doing without thinking about it and making an informed decision that starts with Jewish teaching and leads to deciding whether this Jewish teaching speaks to me right now. The deliberation is as important as what that consideration leads to doing.

So, when I get asked that question, "Rabbi, how long is shivah?" I open my response with what the Jewish tradition teaches. The rest of the conversation flows from there.

Balak

Quick and Decisive Punishment

NUMBERS 22:2–25:9

Phinehas, son of Eleazar son of Aaron the priest,
has turned back My wrath from the Israelites by
displaying among them his passion for Me, so that I
did not wipe out the Israelite people in My passion.
—Numbers 25:11

P'shat: Explanation

As the portion Balak closes, men of Israel join with Midianite women in idolatrous practices that include forbidden and immoral sex, and God orders the ringleaders to be put to death. In that very moment, a leader of Israel brazenly consorts with a Midianite, sparking Phinehas, the grandson of Aaron the priest, to brutally execute the couple on the spot. Phinehas's quick action immediately ends a killer plague that God inflicted on the people on account of their idolatry. God praises Phinehas's zeal and rewards him with a "Covenant of Peace" that grants priesthood to him and his descendants in perpetuity.

To be sure, Judaism would have us condemn and prevent sexual immorality and idolatry, and safeguard people from plague. And a reader of the story will recognize that Phineas follows God's instructions when putting a sinner to death. Yet many, including the Rabbis are distraught over what appears to be his violent impulsiveness.

Skilled at defending the Torah against accusations of promoting unwarranted and impulsive violence, Ramban stands up for Phinehas's drastic behavior, arguing that Phinehas was a great leader in a very important moment. By taking the law into his own hands,

Phinehas ended the plague and delivered a life-saving intervention on behalf of Moses, whose attention was consumed by caring for the people during a crisis (on Num. 25:5). By killing the sinners, Phineas brought the outbreak to a swift and conclusive end.

The Torah is surely not opposed to capital punishment: It invokes the death penalty for idolatry, Sabbath desecration, blasphemy, defying parents, and other sins. What is more, the Torah sets out methods of execution: stoning, strangulation, burning, and death by sword. Notably, however, later Jewish sources turn away from these brutal practices. The Rabbis of the Mishnah and Talmud impose so many procedural safeguards against a capital conviction that it becomes just about practically impossible to carry out the death penalty.

Viewed in this context, Phinehas is an outlier for taking the law into his own hands and taking a life without due process.

D'rash: Buber's Insight

The death sentence has not diminished crime—on the contrary, all this exasperates the souls of people. . . . Killing awakens killing.

The story of Phinehas, or, in Hebrew, Pinḥas, gives us one chapter in the long evolution of Jewish attitudes toward capital punishment. Martin Buber provides another lesson when openly protesting the execution of Nazi war criminal Adolf Eichmann.

Adolf Eichmann was the only person that modern Israel ever tried for a capital offense and executed. Buber, a well-known figure living in Jerusalem at the time of the conviction, publicly called for reducing Eichmann's death sentence to a life sentence. Buber despised what Eichmann did, and said he was not motivated by pity or compassion. Rather, he believed that the commandment "You shall not murder" (Exod. 20:13) applied equally to the individual and the state, making the execution equivalent to state-sponsored murder.

Buber also argued that capital punishment does not serve as a deterrent. Rather, it makes killing appear acceptable — even encouraged. As he told *Time* magazine in June 1962: "The death sentence has not diminished crime — on the contrary, all this exasperates the souls of people. . . . Killing awakens killing."[22]

Buber also worried that the execution would appear to put all the blame on Eichmann and let Nazis who worked under his command feel exonerated of their own crimes. What is more, no punishment could make up for the magnitude of Eichmann's heinous behavior.

Buber protested directly to Israel's prime minister, David Ben-Gurion. This was not the first or only time Buber brought a grievance to Ben-Gurion — the two had many years of public disagreements behind them, all flowing from their fundamentally different visions for the State of Israel. Where Buber saw Israel's identity in moral and spiritual terms, Ben-Gurion, even as a visionary, was more of a tactical politician. The clashes were reminiscent of the earlier conflict between Buber and Zionist founder Theodor Herzl.

Ben-Gurion did take the time to listen to Buber's concerns, with a generous spirit and deep respect. He went to Buber's home to hear him out. In a conversation lasting two hours, Buber urged life imprisonment for Eichmann — on a kibbutz of all places. Eichmann would have to work the Land of Israel as a tangible demonstration of the Nazis' defeat and Jewish strength, continuity, and triumph.

Buber's opposition to the death penalty drew widespread public criticism and condemnation. He was shaken but held his ground. Eichmann died by hanging on May 31, 1962.[23]

D'rash: A Personal Reflection

EVEN AN HOUR BEHIND BARS

As much as I am opposed to capital punishment, some crimes are so vicious that even the death penalty seems inadequate. Yet, people do not always realize that being in prison is punishment plenty. As testimony, when I get a call to make a pastoral visit to someone inside a prison, I need to prepare myself to enter another world.

Walking into a prison, even as a visitor, means being told to dump my wallet, ID, credit cards, keys, belt, pens, phone, and more into a closet locker—while a guard at the prison entrance holds onto the locker key. I'll walk empty-handed and empty-pocketed through a metal detector and double-locked doors—one door must noisily slam locked before the other door can open—all controlled remotely by a guard I cannot see but must trust is there for me and will let me in and, eventually, out.

I am ushered into a secure, somewhat private area to hear out the story of a person whose eating, sleeping, health care, and relations with others are tightly controlled by prison staff. I hear about fighting, spoiled and dirtied food, drugs, and fear. "You can't imagine how anyone can live like this, Rabbi," this person tells me. And I cannot tell you how unburdening it is to be able to leave, get all my things back, and walk out the front door, a free person heading to my car. I cannot imagine how people survive there. A prison is a place where the human spirit is sentenced to die.

I had a similar feeling years earlier, a block away from Manhattan's Columbus Circle. Often, late on a Saturday evening, I'd walk back to my apartment, passing women and children, predominately Black and Latino, lumbering up the steps of chartered buses under the weight of blankets, stuffed animals, bags, food, and other supplies. I later learned, from newspapers, that they were taking six- or eight-hour overnight bus rides to visit loved ones in upstate New York prisons. Millennia ago, our ancestors left behind Egypt and bondage, staggering under the weight of silver, gold, and clothing that the Torah says they "borrowed" from the Egyptians. Here, folks carrying simple possessions stumbled up the steps of charter buses to visit beloved relatives behind bars.

I question the nature of the criminal justice we impose, which sometimes appears as more than a fair share. In these situations, we are punishing the family, including children, along with the incarcerated. Shouldn't there be a limit? Can we draw a line? How much punishment is too much?

Pinḥas

Evolving Jewish Law

NUMBERS 25:10–30:1

And Adonai said to Moses: "The plea of Zelophehad's daughters is just: you should give them a hereditary holding among their father's kinsmen; transfer their father's share to them."
—Numbers 27:6

P'shat: Explanation

When members of Israel join the Midianites in idolatry, the Torah tells us that a terrible plague of unknown nature strikes the community, and many people die. A census follows. Then Zelophehad's daughters speak up to claim their rights of inheritance.

We generally speak of Israel as a patriarchy, where men inherit. Family title and resources pass from father to son, never to a wife or daughter. In a situation of a levirate marriage, for instance, when a married man dies without leaving behind sons, a brother is to marry his widow and receive his estate; the widow's wishes are secondary, while her late husband's name and possessions continue in that family (Deut. 25:5–6). Though the law fell into disuse, it stood as an example: Women of the Torah do not inherit—until we meet Mahlah, Noah, Hoglah, Milcah, and Tirzah, the five surviving daughters of Zelophehad, who ask for their share.

The daughters approach Moses and the High Priest before all the people, at the entrance to the Tent of Meeting, the official place of communal business. Their honorable father, who died in the wilderness, left no son as heir, and so, they maintain, they are the rightful inheritors of his name and his assets. Moses hears them out and takes their concern to God, who responds immediately: The daughters are to inherit.

Some Rabbis argue against the simple reading of the text. Rashi, for instance, claims that the sisters uncovered an existing law that Moses did not yet know about (on Num. 27:7). But there is much to be said for taking the story of Zelophehad's daughters at face value: as an innovation in inheritance law and an advance of women's rights in their day and going forward.

D'rash: Buber's Insight

She might teach you what it is to be a woman.

We see Buber's respect for women in the case of a young man who approached Buber to question whether to go ahead with an upcoming wedding. The questioner believed that his fiancée was not his intellectual equal and he had little to learn from her. When the young man asked if he should marry her or not, Buber responded sharply in the affirmative: "She might teach you what it is to be a woman."

Buber upheld that there is learning to be gained from every person. That is, there are two kinds of wisdom—book knowledge and people knowledge—and both are worthwhile. We typically learn facts from books, compared to people knowledge, which comes from being aware and responsive in the presence of others. What we learn from sharing our lives with other people brings us a deeper understanding and appreciation of ourselves, our world, and our spiritual calling. In this case, the man could learn from his fiancée by sharing in the reality of her life experience, just as Buber learned from his wife, Paula Winkler Buber.

From the days of their meeting as classmates at the University of Zurich in 1899, Martin and Paula continued in a loving, robust, trusting relationship spanning six decades. Though often overshadowed by her husband's work, Paula's achievements stand on their own. She was an author and essayist whose best-known novel, *Muckensturm*, published under the pseudonym Georg Munk, portrayed the rise of Nazism in a small German town. An exhibition devoted to her work at the Jewish Museum of Augsburg, Germany, in 2017 bore the praising title "Tough, Brilliant and Unobjectionable."[24] She was also a trailblazer: one among a small number of women attending university in her time, and one of the first women to bike the Alps.[25]

Paula grew up in a Catholic home with little opportunity to meet Jews. In early adulthood, she was upset to see Jews, especially Jewish children, singled out for mistreatment, and she eventually involved herself in Jewish causes. She joined Martin as an activist in the early twentieth-century Zionist movement and converted to Judaism.

Martin lovingly supported Paula's writing as she supported and helped with his, as when she advised him on fine points of German words for the Hebrew-to-German Bible translation, or when she wrote for his Hasidic story collections.

Paula was the singular influence on Martin's life. Everything begins with relationship, just as the extended and vast creative period of Buber's life began with his relationship with Paula.

D'rash: A Personal Reflection

WHAT LOVE FEELS LIKE

"This feels just right."

Whenever I'm meeting with a couple to plan a wedding, I ask questions like, "How did you meet?" "What did you initially find interesting in each other?" and "What led to your decision to get married?" That last question—remarkably—always gets the same response: "This feels just right." I often wonder whether or not to keep asking, yet I still do, as if maybe, one time, I will get a different answer. So far, though, that hasn't happened.

There is visible contentment and peace behind that response. It indicates that a deep longing is being fulfilled. The tone of voice communicates that the couple is at home, happy and comfortable with each other. And, almost every time, as the couple and I talk, I think about my relationship with my wife, Debbie.

As far as I can tell, Buber did not envision women as rabbis or cantors in Judaism, or as clergy in other faiths. Yet he calls on us to look beyond superficiality—gender, age, and social background—and speak directly to another person, which leads me to think he would have welcomed and encouraged the ordination of women, and he wouldn't have been terribly shocked to see a marriage of two rabbis, like Debbie and me.

After forty years of marriage, Debbie and I were recently blessed to become grandparents. We took out the old family photo albums and turned to pictures of when we became parents. My body got stiff just from the intensity of the memories I reexperienced. "How did we do it all?" I wondered. We were two rabbis, Rabbi Deborah Zecher and Rabbi Dennis Ross, serving two synagogues and raising three kids under one roof, a sum astronomically greater than the simple total of its parts.

Like Martin and Paula, Debbie and I met in school—in our case in rabbinic school, in the library of the old Hebrew Union College–Jewish Institute of Religion library on Manhattan's West Sixty-Eighth Street. Debbie was and continues to be a trailblazer, among the first generation of women ordained as rabbis, an accomplishment especially visible in our decision, as a two-rabbi household, to pursue two congregational careers. My mentor, Rabbi Chaim Stern, wrote of such relationships, "Blessed are those who are lovers and friends." To be this close in relation, with comfort and candor, honesty and respect, caring and listening and suggesting and supporting, to be able to intuit the needs of a person is, altogether, a great grace.

Mattot

Imagine the Real

NUMBERS 30:2–32:42

Are your brothers to go to war while you stay here?
—Numbers 32:6

P'shat: Explanation

Mattot offers a lesson on the importance of seeing both sides of a situation.

The people arrive at the region outside Canaan assigned to Reuben and Gad for permanent settlement. The two tribal leaders propose that their communities stay right there and not advance. Thus they will be spared the burden of having to cross the Jordan River with the remaining ten tribes and go on to battle the Canaanites.

The request aggravates Moses, who recognizes the depth of the challenges the people will soon confront. He wants everyone together, and he sees selfishness motivating a request that would leave Israel short two tribes in the fight. He calls out Reuben and Gad, pointedly asking, "Are your brothers to go to war while you stay here?" Underscoring another possible negative impact, he accuses them, "Why will you turn the minds of the Israelites from crossing into the land that Adonai has given them?" (Num. 32:7). The Rabbis also imagine Moses castigating the tribal leaders, and that the peeling off will offend God.

Reuben and Gad come around to recognize the validity of Moses' arguments. They realize the need for their wholehearted presence and contributions. As a counteroffer, they propose that in exchange for the privilege of settling their families in place then and there, the men of their tribes will serve in the front lines of the upcoming fight on the other side of the Jordan River, then help establish each tribe where it belongs, and only then return to their new homes. This plan, arising from an understanding of both sides of a situation, satisfies everyone.

D'rash: Buber's Insight

I was compelled to imagine just this killing, but not in an optical way alone, but may say so, just with my body.

Echoing the example of a turnaround by Reuben and Gad, Buber raises the term "Inclusion" to encourage us to see life from the other person's perspective.

First, Inclusion brings aspects of another person's universe into your experience, all while you remain aware of your experience. For a simple example, imagine your hand resting on my arm. Imagine the feeling in your hand and, at the same time, imagine how your hand feels to me—that is the beginning of Inclusion.

To practice Inclusion, a person begins by doing what Buber calls "Imagine the Real." Buber relates how Rabbi Moshe Leib of Sassov received wide deep praise for his ability to empathize with the heartache of others. When asked about his capacity to include himself in someone else's pained experience, Rabbi Leib said that others' angst was his and that he had no option but to endure their pain as his own.[26] Of course, Rabbi Leib could not precisely experience that person's real experience; he was able to "imagine" that real.

Buber gives us another example of how to Imagine the Real during his public conversation with pioneer of mental health and psychotherapy Carl Rogers, in which Buber unburdened himself of heavy memories of the brutal death of his friend, colleague, and mentor Gustav Landauer at the hands of police following the end of World War I. "I was compelled to imagine just this killing," he told Rogers, "but not in an optical way alone, but may say so, just with my body."[27] Buber attempted a visceral reliving of his dear friend's suffering.

To be sure, what Landauer experienced was "real"; Buber, who never witnessed the carnage, could only "imagine" it. Nonetheless, to Imagine the Real is a first step toward Inclusion, where both sides of the conversation see themselves and each other at the same time.

D'rash: A Personal Reflection

WALKING IN ANOTHER'S SHOES

Rising early one dark winter morning, I put on my sweats, a pair of sneakers, hat, and gloves and headed into the freezing air to start the day with a walk. But something was wrong. Within fifteen minutes, both feet began hurting terribly, as if being squeezed from all sides, top and bottom, in a vise. I tried whatever I could to ease my pain. I loosened the laces, walked on just the sides of my feet, and then tried walking on just heels and then toes. Nothing helped. I cut short my walk to free my feet from their agony . . . and when I got back home, in the better light, I realized what had happened: I had taken Debbie's sneakers instead of mine. I literally walked a mile in someone else's shoes, and it hurt something terrible.

Inclusion means seeing both sides. But even in the best of relationships, no matter how well two people know each other, we never really know what it is like to walk in another's shoes, to live that life. We are as different as our shoe sizes and then some. That old, worn-out saying was just a saying to me until I literally put my feet in Debbie's shoes.

Mase‘ei

Interfaith Relations

NUMBERS 33:1–36:13

*When you cross the Jordan into the land of Canaan, you
shall dispossess all the inhabitants of the land; you shall
destroy all their figured objects; you shall destroy all
their molten images, and you shall demolish all their cult
places. And you shall take possession of the land and settle
in it, for I have assigned the land to you to possess.*
—Numbers 33:51–53

P'shat: Explanation

There is something deeply unsettling about God's instructions in
Mase‘ei. God exhorts Moses to tell the people: Israel must evict "all
the inhabitants of the land" of Canaan and obliterate their places and
objects of worship.

The Torah gave us an opposite picture earlier on. As soon as the
Jews leave Egypt, the text drives home the importance of remember-
ing their time in bondage and cultivating an abiding commitment to
love and protect the stranger.

But now here in Mase‘ei the Torah takes an entirely different
approach. The Jews secure the land that God "assigned" to them by dis-
possessing "all" of Canaan's current residents and obliterating all signs
of their idolatrous practices. They are to destroy those who are different.

The Rabbis are troubled by the appearance of merciless intolerance.
Midrash Sifre Numbers (157), for instance, attempts to clear God of

responsibility by placing the onus on Moses for issuing the military orders—an interpretation that contravenes the intent of the Torah's text. To the contrary, God instructs the Jews to do this.

Some of us struggle with this issue at the Passover seder. Yes, the Haggadah elevates the Jewish value of compassion by reiterating the memory of the slave experience as the basis for the moral responsibility to love and protect the stranger. And yes, when it comes to the downfall of those Egyptians who harmed the Hebrews, we are not to celebrate their deaths—rather, we spill drops of wine in tribute to their suffering, even as we recall their hostile behavior. But still, for centuries, traditional Haggadot have emphasized retribution alongside reconciliation. After the seder meal, when we pour the cup of Elijah and open the door to welcome the prophet, those Haggadot have us say the following words from the Hebrew Bible: "Pour out Your fury on the nations who do not know You, upon the kingdoms that do not invoke Your name, for they have devoured Jacob and desolated his home!" (Ps. 79:6–7); "Pour out Your wrath on them; may your blazing anger overtake them" (Ps. 69:25); "Oh, pursue them in wrath and destroy them from under the heavens of Adonai!" (Lam. 3:66). Highly troubled by these words, many editors of contemporary Haggadot have removed them, as did Buber at his family seder.[28]

Reflecting on this intolerant side of the Hebrew Bible and the Haggadah, a reasonable person might ask, "What's so horrible about idolatry?" After all, idol worship seems to be a benign practice, nothing worse than saying a few prayers to a wooden or stone figure. Yet, in some cases, the "figured objects" and "molten images" of Canaan were part of a larger religious system that included ritualized prostitution and perhaps human and child sacrifice.

Nonetheless, I am still troubled by why total eviction and destruction were necessary.

D'rash: Buber's Insight

I have found in Jesus my great brother.

Buber calls on us to retain and cherish our differences. Two do not become one in I-Thou. Rather, our differences provide the substance for honest, open discussion of our relations.

Buber likened those who hold different faiths to siblings, who may resemble one another and have similar character traits—but the commonalities only go so far. By saying, "I have found in Jesus my great brother,"[29] Buber was asserting a shared spiritual lineage, as well as the belief in a historic Jesus, yet rejecting for himself a theological Jesus who had a relationship with God unlike anyone else.

Buber had many close Christian friends and colleagues with whom he discussed sensitive religious issues with candor and respect. Even when he and they differed in their approach, the loving affirmation, *I value you as a person,* came through strongly.

In one example from earlier in his career, almost a decade before *I and Thou* was published, Buber's close attention to religious differences enabled him to discern an important fundamental of his faith in God.

As World War I approached, Buber was visited by an old acquaintance, the Reverend William Hechler. Buber had met Hechler by chance on a train ride years earlier. Their conversation had revealed a shared and deep interest in Zionism and the establishment of Israel, though for very different reasons. Buber saw Israel as a safe haven for Jews and a country governed by Jewish values and enlightened by Jewish culture; Hechler saw Israel's establishment as a requirement for the return of Jesus as Christ. Such was their kinship with differences.

A decade and a half after this first meeting, Hechler visited the Buber home in suburban Berlin to present an extensive and detailed case that the Bible's book of Daniel had predicted an imminent, apocalyptic, and world-consuming war. While Buber apparently believed war was on the horizon, he respectfully disagreed that the conflagration was foreseen by the Bible, to Hechler's apparent disappointment.

At the end of the visit, Buber walked Hechler back to the train station. Meanwhile, Hechler, disturbed by Buber's failure to confirm his "literal" Bible reading, placed his hand on Buber's shoulder and asked Buber if he believed in God, since it appeared to him that Buber was spurning God's word in Scripture. Buber reassured Hechler that there was no reason to worry about his belief in God, and Hechler left.

Yet, Buber came away from the conversation deeply troubled by Hechler's question about God. Just what kind of God, if any, did he uphold? Buber stood still for a while to think through the answer. Finally—and it is not clear whether this happened minutes, hours, or months later—Buber received a bolt of insight: The Jewish God is not a God who plans out the details of human life or even a catastrophic war. For Judaism, neither the Bible nor God do that. Rather, people possess free will and shape their destiny. What is more, when it comes to God, Jews do not speak *about* God, indirectly, as we would talk about a third person—they speak *to* God, directly, as we would talk with a person in real time, as in I-Thou. The revelation we gain from speaking to another person is as truthful as the revelation we get from Scripture. This was a formative experience for Buber, an insight critical to releasing *I and Thou* some nine years later.[30]

While there is no further record of another Buber-Hechler meeting or correspondence, Buber learned something critical about his faith, thanks to a candid question from his spiritual brother.

D'rash: A Personal Reflection

ACROSS RELIGIOUS LINES

I was just ordained, new to my first congregation and synagogue life, when my senior rabbi, Rabbi Chaim Stern, came into my office and asked me to drop everything. He apologized for forgetting to tell me that there was a meeting with the Chappaqua Interfaith Council right then, and he knew I would want to be there.

As we rode over, I could see that Chaim was excited, while I had no idea what to expect. The meetings were not on my job description, and we had rarely discussed community interfaith work when I was in rabbinical school. But looking back on that moment, Chaim's invitation turned out to be one of his greatest gifts to me.

That very day, I began building relationships with the area's Christian clergy. Our working relationships grew into trusting friendships that strengthened our community and continue to bless me today. The Reverend Larry Bethune of the First Baptist Church in Chappaqua, New York, and I held interfaith pulpit exchanges, community education programs on controversial social issues, and more. Later in my career, the Reverend Robert Kyte of the First Congregational Church in Dalton, Massachusetts, and I as the rabbi in a synagogue in neighboring Pittsfield, Massachusetts, co-led an interfaith trip bringing our respective church and synagogue members to Israel. More recently, my work with Planned Parenthood has brought me into relationship with the Reverend Tom Davis, a historian of clergy activism on behalf of access to health care that includes contraception, safe and legal abortion, and sex education for teens, and author of *Sacred Work: Planned Parenthood and Its Clergy Alliances*. Together we raise awareness of the history of religious support for access to women's health care. Together we call for protecting church-state separation in public life, and for the exercise of conscience regarding personal decisions about whom to marry and whether or not to become a parent. Caring and collaborative relationships across religious lines have blessed my work and my life.

V

Deuteronomy (Devarim)

Devarim

Dealing with Anger

DEUTERONOMY 1:1–3:22

Because of you Adonai was incensed with me too.
—Deuteronomy 1:37

P'shat: Explanation

As the first portion in the Torah's fifth and final book, Deuteronomy, opens, Moses reflects on a painful incident in the wilderness (Num. 20:1–13).

The people were without water, their survival at risk. Having so little faith in Moses, they complained they'd be better off dying as slaves in Egypt than dying of thirst with him and Aaron in the wilderness. God told Moses to gather the people, stand beside Aaron, hold his walking staff over a rock and receive water. Well, he basically did that— but unfortunately much more: First, he denounced the community as "rebels," then, he struck the rock twice, and sure enough the water flowed as promised. Afterward, though, God told him and Aaron that they had dishonored God and would not be allowed into Canaan.

Now, the text tells us, Moses blames the people: He cannot enter Canaan "because of you" (Deut. 1:37)!

The Rabbis are troubled by Moses' earlier emotional lapse and, here, his failure to accept responsibility for his angry behavior. However, out of love and respect for Moses, some commentators join him in putting the onus on the Israelites. Their defense of Moses starts with recalling the people's unfaithfulness in worshipping the golden calf idol and, later, their cowardly self-doubt in response to the scouts' reports. Had the people only been more trusting in God earlier on, had they only mustered more faith in themselves and Moses, God would have seen fit to have Moses lead them into Canaan immediately, instead of waiting for the generation from Egypt to die off and a new, fresh, energized nation to rise and face the challenges of Canaan. If only the people had behaved better, this incident would have been avoided. So, these Rabbis join the Torah in saying to the Egypt generation: Moses does not enter Canaan "because of you."

Other Rabbis believe God overreacted. Moses pays too great a price and should have been allowed to enter Canaan. Yet other Rabbis say the punishment is justified as an object lesson on the importance of anger management—and this final point resonates the most in the Bible and later Jewish sources.

Elsewhere, the Bible and the Rabbis emphasize the importance of managing one's emotions. Proverbs 16:32 says, "Patience is better than physical might, and self-control than conquering a city"—a metaphoric claim that exercising restraint can be a greater victory than winning a military campaign. Rabbi ben Zoma answers his own question in Mishnah *Pirke Avot* 4:1: "Who is mighty? One who subdues the passions." Resh Lakish of the Talmud may have had Moses in mind when writing, "Whoever angers, if that person is wise, their wisdom leaves. If they are a prophet, their prophecy leaves" (*Pesaḥim* 66b). And "Rabbi I'lai said: With three things a person is recognized, by their cup, by their wallet, and by their anger. 'The cup'—what brings a person pleasure, the wallet—how a person manages money, and 'anger'—self-control—are defining measures of character" (*Eruvin* 65b). At the end of the day, Judaism upholds the importance of anger management.

D'rash: Buber's Insight

I can no longer take this. I'll get in touch with your father.

Buber could be expected to speak his mind, to the point of appearing to take umbrage. This happened when it came to matters of theology or social justice, for instance. And from time to time, he would also experience anger in his personal life.

As if reenacting Buber's experience growing up with his grandparents, Martin and Paula's grandkids moved into their grandparent's Jerusalem home to attend the local school, which seemed a better option than the school where they lived, at Kibbutz Geva, in Israel's North. Sometimes the kids acted like kids, to the frustration of their elders. Buber's granddaughter, Judith, would later recall rare occasions when he would say something like, "I can no longer take this. I'll get in touch with your father."[1] But it seemed he never did.

Anger is a normal and common human emotion, and Buber accepts the impossibility of flawless self-control. Responding to those who demand perfection of themselves or those around them, Buber retells of Rabbi Moshe of Kobryn. As if taunting those who expect human beings to behave perfectly, Rabbi Moshe turns heavenward to dare the angels to take on the same responsibilities as people, such as providing food for the family, caring for children, and earning a living. Meeting the basic requirements of life is so demanding a responsibility that no angel could live as a human on earth.[2] Just as angels are not people, people are not angels for being called upon to walk that Narrow Ridge.

As much as Buber held himself and others to high behavioral standards, he owned up to his mistakes. In his earlier years, Menachem Gershon, an associate of Buber's in Germany who went on to kibbutz activism in Israel, asked Buber's opinion on whether he should go into psychotherapy for help with emotional problems. Buber dismissively claimed that psychotherapy would turn Gershon's heart into a rock, but Gershon went for counseling anyway. Years later, Gershon confronted Buber, who realized he provided poor guidance and admitted his misjudgment.[3]

D'rash: A Personal Reflection

ANGER WITHOUT LOOKING ANGRY

I took a lesson on expressing anger when Debbie and I saw the Mr. Rogers documentary, *Won't You Be My Neighbor?*

This film was a natural for us. Debbie is from Pittsburgh and came to know the show early on because that is where the educational PBS TV series *Mister Rogers' Neighborhood* began. And I lost track of how many hours we spent with our kids watching Fred Rogers walk into his on-air home, take off his jacket and outdoor shoes, gleefully put on a cardigan and tie his sneakers, and sing and talk directly to kids about the issues of life — family conflict, friendship, truth telling, love, war, racism, anger — all in the soft-spoken voice of a pastor, which, as an ordained minister in the Presbyterian Church, he was.

Rogers's gentleness and calmness brought some folks to wonder about his personality, whether he ever got angry. Some even made fun of his upbeat and positive on-air presence, and I often was left wondering myself. Then I saw the movie *Won't You Be My Neighbor?* and something suddenly made sense.

Though neither he nor anyone else ever said so outright, Fred Rogers would get angry, to the point of outrage, whenever kids were ignored or taken for granted, especially when they faced complicated and emotion-filled situations. He would not fly off the handle, use strong language, or throw a fit. Rather, he thought things through and channeled his angry feelings into a positive lesson for kids, presented in that trademark calm demeanor.

As the movie relates, at one point, the mass media gave racial integration of swimming pools plenty of pitched attention, with stories and photos of anger and fighting. Rogers knew that kids were also watching those televised news reports, and were likely frightened and confused. I think he believed that they deserved a positive and nonconfrontational viewpoint. Rogers set up a splash pool on the TV show set, and joined a Black letter carrier in a warm and friendly conversation while the two cooled their feet in the same water on a very hot day. Here yet again, it seemed, Fred Rogers expressed his anger with his hallmark pastoral demeanor and voice by modeling a thoughtful example, all the while teaching a valuable lesson on the importance of respectful relationships.

Va-'ethannan

Chosenness and Universalism

DEUTERONOMY 3:23–7:11

*For you are a people consecrated to your God
Adonai; of all the peoples on earth your God Adonai
chose you to be God's treasured people.*
— Deuteronomy 7:6

P'shat: Explanation

Va-'ethannan evokes strong and mixed feelings in relaying to the early
Hebrews: "Your God Adonai chose you to be God's treasured people."

To speak of Israel as God's "consecrated" and "treasured" is to
describe the community as God's "Chosen People" under the Covenant—a Covenant that obligates Israel to faithfully keep God's mitzvot so that God, in return, lovingly protects and elevates the people
of Israel above others.

The concept of chosenness upsets many Jews and non-Jews, in
large part because of the self-serving superiority this idea stirs up.
Yet the Torah cautions against rushing to equate chosenness with
superiority. First, chosenness does not arrive automatically—it is
hard earned, dependent on Israel's performing the great responsibilities imposed by the mitzvot. Furthermore, Moses explains that
Israel does not really deserve to be chosen in the first place, saying,
"It is not for any virtue of yours that the Lord your God is giving you
this good land to possess, for you are a stiff-necked people" (Deut.
9:6). Chosenness is not an entitlement, but a grace that comes from
putting personal preferences aside and doing hard spiritual work for
God. The rigorous covenantal obligations make chosenness as much

of a burden as a blessing. Classic Jewish thinking tells us that a chosen people is accountable to God like no other. For any arrogance that God's election of Israel may arouse, the Torah tempers chosenness with responsibility.

Yet even as God favors Israel, the Bible explains, God loves the many nations of the world. The prophet Isaiah, for example, underscores Israel's particular election and universal mission:

> Thus said God the Eternal,
> Who created the heavens and stretched them out,
> Who spread out the earth and what it brings forth,
> Who gave breath to the people upon it
> And life to those who walk thereon:
> "I the Eternal, in My grace, have summoned you,
> And I have grasped you by the hand.
> I created you, and appointed you
> A covenant people, a light of nations—
> Opening eyes deprived of light,
> Rescuing prisoners from confinement,
> From the dungeon those who sit in darkness." (Isa. 42:5–7)

He later says,

> Raise a shout together, O ruins of Jerusalem!
> For the Eternal will comfort God's people,
> Will redeem Jerusalem.
> The Eternal will bare God's holy arm in the sight of all the
>   nations,
> And the very ends of earth shall see the victory of our God.
>   (Isa. 52:9–10)

My Bible instructor at the Hebrew Union College–Jewish Institute of Religion, Professor Harry Orlinsky, often emphasized this biblical message that the God of Israel is, at the same time, the God of the universe and all peoples. After all, God fashioned Adam and Eve in the divine image and blessed all humankind through them (Gen. 1:26–28). God loves everyone, going back to the Creation. We again see God's caring concern for humanity after Noah's flood, when God presents what is commonly called "natural" or "Noahide law," which, when upheld, enables a person of any background to enter God's grace.[4]

Today, many Jews embrace chosenness, others make their peace with it, and still others, pointing to the implied appearance of Jewish superiority, reject it. For his part, Buber sees in chosenness caring for other peoples as Israel's mission.

D'rash: Buber's Insight

Our greatest national treasure for which there is
no substitute is our prophetic universality.

Buber balances chosenness and universalism. Reflecting the prophet's message, Buber teaches that the Covenant between God and Israel insists that the Jewish people are responsible for ensuring that all humanity flourishes. In his 1950 essay for the *Hebrew University Yearbook*, "A New Venture in Adult Education," Buber explained it this way: "Our greatest national treasure for which there is no substitute is our prophetic universality."[5]

Buber's "treasure" of "universality" is deeply rooted in the Hebrew Bible. Were Judaism just about Jews, the Torah would introduce Jews and chosenness in the very first chapter of Genesis—but no, instead, Genesis begins with the Creation and the origins of the universe and all humanity, and takes ten more chapters to get to chosenness (in the story of the first Hebrews, Abraham and Sarah).

Later, the Bible's prophets, a favorite source for Buber, expand on the inclusiveness of Genesis. For example, the prophet Isaiah proclaims: "For God has said: 'It is too little that you should be My servant in that I raise up the tribes of Jacob and restore the survivors of Israel: I will also make you a light of nations, that My salvation may reach the ends of the earth'" (49:6). In his response to this verse, Rashi casts Israel as "a joy to the entire universe." In essence, Israel's election advances all humanity.

So, Buber encourages us to see that chosenness means more than the perfection of the Jewish people — it demands that all God's children be included in Isaiah's vision, so that God's salvation "may reach the ends of the earth."

D'rash: A Personal Reflection

CHOSEN DOES NOT MEAN PERFECTION

I hear echoes of the Torah's concept of "chosenness" in often-used terms like "American Exceptionalism," "Manifest Destiny," and the "Shining City on the Hill." American politicians typically turn to such language to highlight their belief that the United States is a chosen nation, better than any other. President Barack Obama once said, "I believe in American exceptionalism, just as I suspect that the Brits believe in British exceptionalism and the Greeks believe in Greek exceptionalism."[6] For this he took much criticism that he was disloyal to the American ideal. Back in 1861, President Abraham Lincoln described himself as a "humble instrument in the hands of the Almighty," and spoke of the United States of America as, "His almost chosen people."[7]

In my view, the United States, for all its greatness, was not yet that perfect union in 1861 nor is it today — and, as we look around nowadays, we can say similar things about the Jewish people. And yet, when I reflect on the decision of my father, grandparents, and great-grandparents to immigrate to the United States and of my privilege to live here, most days, as both an American and a Jew, I feel like I am "almost chosen," too.

ʿEkev

Spirituality of Eating

A human being does not live by bread alone but . . .
one may live on anything that Adonai decrees.
—Deuteronomy 8:3

P'shat: Explanation

God took loving care of us at Sinai. ʿEkev tells us that we always had good clothing because, thanks to God, "your garments did not wear out" (Deut. 8:4). We never needed to do laundry in Sinai because, as Rashi imagines, "Clouds of God cleaned their clothes and so that they looked new. Not only that, each child's clothing grew along with them, just like a snail's shell grows with it" (Rashi on Deut. 8:4). God provided ample food and drink, and met our spiritual needs, too, leading Moses to say, "A human being does not live by bread alone but . . . one may live on anything that Adonai decrees."

As for "bread," ʿEkev hints that eating becomes an opportunity for spiritual exploration. The Rabbis point out that our *Motzi* prayer, the traditional blessing over bread, praises God who "brings forth bread from the earth," as if fresh loaves literally spring up from the ground. The Midrash goes further, suggesting that a miraculous "bread tree" in the Garden of Eden sprouted loaves for the picking, sparing Adam and Eve all the work of having to plant and harvest grain, grind flour, knead dough, and bake bread—thanks to the One who literally "makes bread spring up from the earth."

Bread tree or not, there is something miraculous in having food to eat, in Sinai or in our own day. As ʿEkev suggests, there's a literal

202

miracle in every bite, even in the mass-baked plastic-wrapped loaf at the supermarket—a wonder that, without a prayer like the *Motzi*, we might otherwise fall into taking for granted.

Buber also brings us into greater appreciation for the grace of food.

D'rash: Buber's Insight

The Hidden Light

Buber named his collection of Hasidic stories *The Hidden Light* (originally in Hebrew, *Or Ha-ganuz*) for the spirituality latent in the mundane busyness of the day. He tells of Rabbi Nachman of Bratslav, who retells his grandfather the Ba'al Shem Tov's observations that the world is filled with tremendous illumination. Tragically, the smallest hand can obscure that great amount of light; and yet, mindfulness while dipping a spoon into a bowl of soup offers an opportunity to recapture that light.[8]

Buber also tells of Rabbi Moshe of Kobryn. At a Shabbat dinner, Rabbi Moshe held up a piece of bread and told his students that a slice of bread sustains human life on two levels, physical and spiritual. The nutritional value of the grains is the first, and obvious, level; the second, veiled, level is evidenced by God's essence contained in the loaf.[9]

I take Rabbi Moshe's words as a summoning of attention to the miracles surrounding our food—a seed's potential to bear fruit; the labor that grows, harvests, transports, and prepares that nourishment for you and me; and the divine spark behind it all.

D'rash: A Personal Reflection

THE MIRACULOUS WITHIN THE OBVIOUS

It really was a miracle, that first slice of warm bread from our first home bread-making machine, that breadbox-sized countertop wonder, a $129 early days economy model that mixed, kneaded, churned, whirred, and filled our home with a wonderful aroma. That is, until the day we left the machine unattended. Vibrations led our first bread maker to hobble to the counter edge and fall to the floor, giving us an irrepairable and inedible mess of glass, aluminum, and dough. This bread machine had miraculously taught itself how to walk! Lesson well learned: Bake bread on the floor!

We're now on our third miraculous model. The miracle starts when you put flour, water, yeast, a little salt, sugar, and olive oil into a metal container with a black tail that plugs into holes in the wall: what we call an electrical outlet. Push a button and—four hours of whirring later—a loaf of bread appears!

I used to take the story of Eden's bread tree as just another religious fantasy, but no longer—not when the bread tree for our day exudes a house-filling aroma that raises anticipation of savoring a crisp crust and a soft, warm inside, topped with a little bit of blueberry jam.

Re'eh

Privilege and Responsibility

DEUTERONOMY 11:26–16:17

There shall be no needy among you—since your God Adonai
will bless you in the land that your God Adonai is giving you.
—Deuteronomy 15:4

P'shat: Explanation

Privilege—which gives a person an economic edge over others—
carries responsibility, as when it comes to those experiencing poverty in Re'eh.

With talk of food in the previous portion, Re'eh promises that no
one in the Land of Israel will ever be hungry because, "There will be
no needy among you." Even with that clear and wishful reassurance,
Re'eh later contradicts itself with, "If, however, there is a needy person among you, one of your kin in any of your settlements in the land
that your God Adonai is giving you, do not harden your heart and shut
your hand against your needy kin" (Deut. 15:7).

Now, the opening word of this verse, "If," has just two letters, yet it
is larger than life for suggesting that poverty, hunger, and need may
well continue. And as we get deeper into Re'eh, the Torah backtracks
further with, "For there will never cease to be needy ones in your land,
which is why I command you: open your hand to the poor and needy
kin in your land" (Deut. 15:11). How, then, should we take the Torah's
initial pledge, "There will be no needy," all the more so alongside the
reality of our world today where so many struggle to eat and to live?

Rashi addresses the discrepancy by saying that the Torah is not
speaking about current social conditions. Rather, it provides a *pre-*

scription for ensuring that "there shall be no needy among you" in the future. That is, when we keep the mitzvot, protecting the less privileged by, for example, upholding the economic safeguard practices of the sabbatical and jubilee years (on Deut. 15:4), only then will poverty be no more, thanks to us. What is more, to "open your hand to the poor and needy kin in your land" includes paying a worker's "wages on the same day, before the sun sets, for he is needy and urgently depends on it; else a cry to Adonai will be issued against you and you will incur guilt" (Deut. 24:15). In other words, "If" Israel is faithful, there will be no poor. "If" Israel is not entirely faithful, then, "There will never cease to be needy." The mitzvot are a hedge against poverty and hunger.

D'rash: Buber's Insight

[My father] took part in the life of all the people who in one or another matter were dependent on [him]. . . . He troubled about the family relationships, about the upbringing of children and schooling, about the sickness and aging of all the people. . . . To sightless charity he was fiercely averse; He understood no other help than from person to persons, and he practiced it.

Buber recognized that privilege carries responsibility, thanks in large part to his father's strong and compassionate spiritual modeling.

Carl Buber demonstrated deep personal concern for the well-being of those who worked for him (see also the commentary to Be-har). He cared for the larger community in his town as well. Rather than offer up what he thought best, he took the time to inform himself by listening to those in need so that he could provide what they deemed useful.[10]

To illustrate the importance of listening to the person you want to help, Buber tells of Rabbi Naphtali of Roptchitz. On Shabbat ha-Gadol, "the Great Shabbat," right before Passover, Rabbi Naphtali returned home from synagogue with his spirit unusually forlorn. He was tired out from preaching about the needs of the poor, he explained to his wife. The Passover holiday was approaching; matzah, wine, and everything else was unusually expensive this year; and the poor had particularly great needs.

His wife asked how the congregation reacted, and Rabbi Naphtali said he accomplished only half of what was needed. He could tell he had convinced people in need to accept charity. (He understood they had their own pride and dignity.) However, as for the rest, those of means, he was uncertain whether he was yet able to convince them to give.[11]

D'rash: A Personal Reflection

THE HELPING HAND STRIKES AGAIN

Generosity can do more harm than good. Someone once spoke of "the helping hand strikes again" to describe the times a potential donor, out of high intentions, imposes on the dignity of another human being. One Shabbat evening, my helping hand struck someone too.

There were plenty of leftovers after a temple Shabbat dinner. As I was about to leave the synagogue for the subway ride back home, I offered to take a tray of food with me and give it to the first person in need I saw. Temple members carefully wrapped and bagged a package with napkins and eating utensils, and, feeling very good about myself, I took it all when I left for home.

When I got to our neighborhood subway station, I finally saw someone sprawled out on the concrete floor, asking for money from riders passing by. I placed the package next to him, wished him a good evening, and continued.

Wasn't I surprised on my way back to the temple the next morning to find the man gone, but the food right where I left it, uneaten and untouched!

I realized that my need to give may well have exceeded his wanting to take, and my self-assumed generosity might have been patronizing and insulting to him. Who was I to presume that he wanted anything to eat?

I took a lesson in not assuming I can help. The particular help I'm offering might be unwanted.

Shofetim

Ends and Means

Justice, justice shall you pursue.
—Deuteronomy 16:20

P'shat: Explanation

The Torah usually says things just once, yet Shofetim says it twice. When instructing judges and officials, Shofetim proclaims, "Justice, justice shall you pursue," bringing the Rabbis to question why the Torah repeats the word "justice."

Commenting on this verse (Deut. 16:20), Rashi sees a motivation for creating a society built on justice and judicial integrity. An honest judiciary keeps the people settled and safe on the land. Such is the impact of a social structure that is secured on a foundation of equity. Ibn Ezra says that the repeated language "speaks to the litigants" as a call to respect the court's decision, win or lose. Another interpretation draws the lesson that a just end is reached only through a just means. That is, the end *does not* justify the means—a just outcome depends on a just process.

While the consistency of a goal and the method of seeking that goal were essential to Buber, he understood that sometimes the means and ends are not in sync.

D'rash: Buber's Insight

*I observed many instances of genuine satyagraha among
Jews, instances of spirit . . . where neither force nor cunning*

was used. Such actions, however, exerted apparently
not the slightest influence on their opponents. All honor
indeed to those who displayed such strength of soul.

As much as Buber affirmed that just and peaceful means are the best way to work toward a just and peaceful end, he also recognized occasions in which force is the only viable option, as illustrated in his open letter to Mahatma Gandhi shortly after the Kristallnacht atrocities.

Kristallnacht, "The Night of Broken Glass," occurred overnight, November 9 to 10, 1938, across Germany and Austria. In this government-supported pogrom, the Nazis ransacked Jewish property, attacked and murdered Jews, and sent Jews to concentration camps. The violence, demonstrating that harming Jews could carry on without internal or international repercussions, marked a major turning point for German Jewry and Jewish communities across Europe.

A few weeks later, Mahatma Gandhi, the Indian champion of nonviolence, offered German Jewry unsolicited advice in an editorial published in the Indian newspaper *Harijan*. Sympathizing with Jews under Nazi persecution (Gandhi noted he'd enjoyed positive relationships with the Jewish community when he lived in South Africa) and acknowledging the depth of antisemitism of previous centuries, Gandhi nonetheless pointed to his success with nonviolence—that is, *satyagraha*, or "soul force"—on behalf of Indians against the British in South Africa. He advised German Jews that they too would have greater success by following his example and responding nonviolently to Nazi attacks: "Let the Jews who claim to be the chosen race prove their title by choosing the way of non-violence for vindicating their position on earth."[12]

Buber, having fled Nazi Germany but a few months earlier, took Gandhi to task in an open rejoinder. He acknowledged the moral preference for pursuing a peaceful end through peaceful action. He also recognized that Indians living in South Africa under the British were deprived and persecuted. But Buber went on to emphasize that any comparison of the Nazi regime and British rule was a false equation.

The British that Gandhi knew and opposed conducted themselves with a measure of decency and forbearance that the Nazis lacked and spurned. Furthermore, Buber continued, many Jews responding nonviolently to Nazi brutality were nevertheless beaten, arrested, and murdered. Peaceful responses to Nazi brutality "exerted not the slightest influence" on the perpetrators, leaving force as the only option for Jews and the larger world.

As much as Buber supported the military effort to defeat the Nazis, he also condemned excessive violence. For instance, when the Israeli military group Irgun bombed the British central government office at the King David Hotel in Jerusalem in 1946, killing eighty people — Jews, Arabs, and British officials — Buber denounced the attack as terrorism and insisted that indiscriminate violence does not advance the struggle for peace, freedom, or wholeness.[13] When Buber received word of the Jewish assassination of Count Folke Bernadotte, president of the Swedish Red Cross who came to Palestine to mediate between Arabs and Jews through the United Nations, he reacted with speechless shock.[14]

D'rash: A Personal Reflection

HOPE MEETS REALITY

Out of a call to responsibility, our son Adam decided to start a new life in Israel, beginning with two years of service in the Israel Defense Forces. Although Debbie and I had always taught our kids that peaceful measures are the best way to pursue a peaceful outcome, this was Adam's decision — and one we also respected, and cherished.

In the winter of 2013, we witnessed Adam's army swearing-in at the Western Wall in Jerusalem. The plaza teemed with a cross-section of Israeli society, with families and guests of the new soldiers speaking Russian, Amharic, French, English, Hebrew, and Arabic. The stirring ceremony, in the chilly air, included an army chaplain's urging the new soldiers to turn to force only as a last resort, because that is what Judaism teaches. And, remarkably and painfully memorable, the ceremony closed with each solider pointing a rifle barrel heavenward with one hand and holding a Hebrew Bible in the other hand—symbols of war and peace, weapon and book in one bundle like *lulav* and *etrog*—for the singing of "Hatikvah," Israel's national anthem. With our son among those new soldiers, we saw that night how Israel is a very complicated place.

In the days that followed, the image of a Bible in one hand and a rifle in the other clung to me, unsettling, even as it made sense. And I remembered the confusion I felt the first time I saw anything like that. I wasn't more than eight or nine when I watched that blockbuster movie *Exodus*, based on Leon Uris's novel on the State of Israel's founding. I didn't understand a lot of what was going on, but several scenes stuck in my memory, including one of a swearing-in for the Haganah, the pre-state Israeli army. In a dark room by candlelight, a recruit placed hands on a Bible and pistol—an image that struck me as discordant even then.

Israel challenges us—the country exudes enmity and love, conflict and unity, all at the same time.

Ki Tetse'

Animal Well-Being

DEUTERONOMY 21:10–25:19

You shall not plow with an ox and an ass together.
—Deuteronomy 22:10

P'shat: Explanation

Judaism has a long and proud history of protecting animals, represented by the term *tza'ar ba'alei hayyim*, or "suffering of living things." While Judaism provides for eating meat and putting animals to work on our behalf, it also places limits on what we can expect animals to do for us, and advances protections for their well-being.

The Torah and, later, the Rabbis often consider an animal to be personal property. Their rules of animal protection are not for the animals' sake, but for their owners'. Yet, taken as a whole, the Jewish tradition values the protection of living things for their own sake. For an example of *tza'ar ba'alei hayyim*, Ḥizkuni provides a rationale for the teaching in Ki Tetse', "You shall not plow with an ox and an ass together." He wants us to know that "God's mercy extends to all God's creatures, and the ass is not as strong as the ox." In other words, it would be cruel to pair the ox and ass under one yoke and leave the weaker ass to be hurt by the physical force of having to work at an ox's more vigorous level. Further on, Ki Tetse' proscribes, "You shall not muzzle an ox while it is threshing" (Deut. 25:4)—it would be mean-spirited to remove a working animal's access to food.

Ki Tetse' also teaches:

If you see your fellow's ox or sheep gone astray, do not ignore it; you must take it back to your fellow. If your fellow does not live near you or you do not know who he is, you shall bring it home and it shall remain with you until your fellow claims it; then you shall give it back to him. You shall do the same with his ass; you shall do the same with his garment; and so too shall you do with anything that your fellow loses and you find: you must not remain indifferent. If you see your fellow's ass or ox fallen on the road, do not ignore it; you must help him raise it (Deut. 22:1–4).

Animal protection is a basic Jewish value.

D'rash: Buber's Insight

*What I experienced in touch with the animal was the Other,
the immense otherness of the Other, . . . which let me draw
near and touch it. When I stroked the mighty mane, sometimes
marvelously smooth-combed, at other times just astonishingly
wild, and felt the life beneath my hand, it was as though the
element of vitality itself bordered on my skin, something that
was not I, was certainly not akin to me, palpably the other, not
just another, really the Other itself: and it let me approach,
confided itself to me, placed itself elementally in the relation
of Thou and Thou with me. The horse, even when I had not
begun by pouring oats for him into the manger, very gently
raised his massive head, ears flicking, then snorted quietly,
as a conspirator gives a signal meant to be recognizable
only by his fellow-conspirator; and I was approved.*

When it comes to *tza'ar ba'alei hayyim*, Buber demonstrated a lifelong affection for animals. As a young child, he rode horses on his grandparents' farm. After dark, he would sneak into the stable to stoke his horse's mane and was taken by the animal's reaction—raising its head, flicking an ear, and snorting as a sign of approval. As Buber would later recall, the horse's "immense otherness" stood Over Against him while deciding whether to let him approach and accept his touch.

As an adult, Buber and his family kept many cats, though in later years in Jerusalem, they were down to "just" three. As the cats spread themselves on the living room couch or hopped in and out of the house through an open window, Buber would speak to them as he would speak to people.[15] He would look them in the eye and wonder whether they recognized him.[16]

Whereas in *I and Thou*, Buber raised the possibility of an I-Thou relationship with animals, as the years went on, he downplayed that potential, believing that the highest spiritual relationship is interhuman. Yet, when Buber lectured, people often still asked about I-Thou with animals, and he rarely responded directly. Rather than explain his updated thinking, he typically turned the question back on the questioner, asking how that individual approached the situation. He engaged in a dialogue instead of offering a lecture. Ultimately, in his opinion, a person's own perception of personal lived experience carries much more weight in their lives.

D'rash: A Personal Reflection

AN UNDERGROUND ENCOUNTER

The half-filled subway car rumbled along, as two women sat next to each other opposite me, one with a large shoulder bag on her lap, the other with a baby in a stroller. Suddenly and unexpectedly, a small dog's head popped out of the shoulder bag, bringing all of us to smile when the dog captured the baby's attention. The dog and baby fixed eyes on each other, oblivious to anything else going on as the train carried on. The women smiled and chatted politely until the next station. The mother got up, the child and the dog broke their gaze, and the women exchanged goodbyes.

By all appearances, that was I-Thou between the two women—a brief conversation about a child and a dog—and an Afterglow evidenced by smiles that lingered after they said goodbye. As for the child and the dog, your guess is as good as mine.

Ki Tavo'

The Fugitives

DEUTERONOMY 26:1–29:8

*My father was a fugitive Aramean. He went down to
Egypt with meager numbers and sojourned there; but
there he became a great and very populous nation. The
Egyptians dealt harshly with us and oppressed us; they
imposed heavy labor upon us. We cried to Adonai, the
God of our ancestors, and Adonai heard our plea and
saw our plight, our misery, and our oppression. Adonai
freed us from Egypt by a mighty hand, by an outstretched
arm and awesome power, and by signs and portents.*

—Deuteronomy 26:5–8

P'shat: Explanation

You can picture the excitement in Ki Tavo', of desert nomads soon to
be farmers anticipating the rewards of settled life. Just imagine, those
first bites of wheat and barley grown on their own land of Canaan!
But Ki Tavo' tells them to put aside that anticipation for a moment
because those fruits are neither theirs nor for their use. The firstlings
go to God, in a biblical thanksgiving ritual that has the farmer travel
to the Temple, stand before the priest, and declare: "My father was
a fugitive Aramean, and he went down to Egypt with meager numbers and sojourned there; but there he became there a great and very
populous nation."

Whenever I see these words, whether in Ki Tavo' or as repeated
in our Passover Haggadah, I've always assumed the Torah is talking

about Jacob and his family leaving their homeland for Canaan as the first steps in the story of the Jewish people's enslavement in Egypt, their numerical growth, and their eventual liberation—but some disagree. Specifically, there's another translation for the Hebrew word *oved* in this sentence, "destroy," that would recast "My father was a fugitive Aramean" into "A fugitive Aramean sought to destroy my ancestor."

For insight, we turn to the writings of the late Nehama Leibowitz, one of the twentieth century's leading Torah teachers, whose work greatly influences my study, teaching, and writing. Her hallmark approach includes a deep exploration of the complicated personalities of the Torah's figures and raises moral and theological issues through close study of the text as interpreted and taught by the Rabbis.

For this verse, Nehama (who preferred to be called by her first name) cites midrash *Sifrei*, which says that the "Aramean" was Laban, and maintains that Laban sought to "destroy" the ancestor of the Jewish people, Jacob. As you may remember, after Jacob fled his brother Esau and their home in Canaan for what he imagined was the safety of Haran, his uncle Laban took advantage of him. In another interpretation, Nehama notes that Rashbam says the fugitives are Abraham and Sarah, who fled famine in Canaan for Egypt, where the watered banks of the Nile River supported the crops. Finally, Nehama points to Ibn Ezra, who maintains that this verse has nothing at all to do with Haran, or Abraham and Sarah. Instead, the declaration reminds us that that Jewish ancestors, Jacob and his clan, traveled to Egypt and (on Deut. 26:5) were freed after nearly being destroyed by Pharaoh.[17]

So, it was Jacob—I guess—that the Torah speaks of, as Jews bring their first fruits to the Temple and present them to the priest. In our time of celebration of plenty, they recall their hard times on the brink of destruction in Egypt and offer up their first fruits in gratitude.

D'rash: Buber's Insight

*They have so radically removed themselves from the
human sphere, so transposed themselves into a sphere of
monstrous inhumanity inaccessible to my conception.*

Buber was a fugitive at age sixty in 1938, when he and his family fled
Nazi Germany for Palestine. The family had little choice other than
to leave, but only after Buber had stood up to the Nazis.

When newly imposed Nazi law prohibited Jews from speaking in
public outside of Jewish settings, Buber continued teaching, even with
the Gestapo in the audience to listen for anti-Nazi speech. Buber cou-
rageously provided it, though he intentionally spoke with such literary
flourish, they could not understand what he was saying. On another
occasion, when the Nazis confiscated Buber's passport, he found the
nerve to go alone to the Gestapo office to reclaim it. Remarkably, they
returned it to him and let him go free.[18]

Buber's work and extensive library caught the Nazis' frequent notice.
On one occasion in 1933, two uniformed Nazi soldiers appeared at the
Buber front door and announced their intention to search the home
and find out what Buber was doing. He told them he was translating
the Bible and pointed to a pile of pages covered with his artful hand-
writing. Seeing how much paperwork was there, the Nazis accused
Buber of translating the Talmud, which was prohibited. Buber denied
the charge and, as proof, pointed to a bookshelf holding previously
published Bible volumes. The Nazis refused to believe him and summoned a Protestant minister, who confirmed that Buber was telling
the truth. That was the end of the incident, though the Nazis subse-
quently returned to the Buber home for more inspections.[19]

D'rash: A Personal Reflection

CONFRONTING A FAMILY LEGEND

I am also descended from Jewish fugitives.

My father, of blessed memory, was born and raised in Havana and, as a teen, came to the United States with his family. My earliest memories of him include he and his Cuban friends bantering in Spanish while working on their cars at curbside or playing dominos at our house. Thanksgiving, Passover, and other holidays and family occasions took on a Cuban flavor, with fried bananas at every meal. And then there was that legend about my father's sister who would have been my aunt—a story of political involvement that led to her murder and burial in the Havana Jewish cemetery, and the family fleeing Cuba to safety in the United States.

My father died when I was young, and the family grew apart, leaving the legend of my aunt, like a plume of cigar smoke, swirling through my soul . . . until a few years ago. My family and I traveled to Cuba to explore the land, see the sights, and meet with members of the Cuban Jewish community. Our trip included a visit to a Havana Jewish cemetery, where we stood Over Against the evidence when, with the help of cemetery workers and a handwritten notebook registry, we found my aunt's grave. My family and I lingered at the graveside, reciting *El Malei Raḥamim* and *Kaddish,* as I marveled at the proof that at least some of this hazy tale was true.

A jagged crack ran down the middle of the oversized headstone, as a cleft in the heart. The stone was inscribed "Sima bat Reb Melech," meaning "Sima, the daughter of Max," my grandfather. The inscription said she had died on the twenty-seventh of the Hebrew month of Elul, in 1946. Also inscribed, in Hebrew, was *eynai zormim d'maot,* "Tears flow from my eyes."

I still struggle to Imagine the Real of those moments, decades earlier, in which my grandparents, father, and other aunt decided to leave behind the grave of their beloved Sima for a new life in the United

States. Perhaps they also did some dreaming about what they imagined would one day be real: that they would tell snippets of this story to the next generation with the hope that their descendants would return to Cuba, seek out the grave, and say a prayer. And perhaps your story, like mine, includes a decision to leave behind a homeland out of a dream that the next generation would live a better life than theirs. For those of us descended from "Arameans" who outran those who would have destroyed us, these fugitive wanderings have shaped the direction and destiny of our lives.

Nitsavim

Equality in Labor

DEUTERONOMY 29:9–30:20

You stand this day, all of you, before your God Adonai—
you tribal heads, you elders and you officials, all the
men of Israel, your children, your wives, even the
stranger within your camp, from woodchopper to water
drawer—to enter into the covenant of your God Adonai.
—Deuteronomy 29:9–11

P'shat: Explanation

Of all the things Moses could underscore at the end of his life, Nitsavim sees him take up the Jewish value of human equality. He challenges the common assumption that a person's job, age, gender, or social background determines that individual's social standing. He insists that each person—tribal head and woodchopper—is of equal worth under the Covenant with God.

In fact, both the Torah and the Talmud emphasize that God values everyone equally. Earlier on, Deuteronomy instructs: "You shall not abuse a needy and destitute laborer, whether a fellow Israelite or a stranger in one of the communities of your land. You must pay out the wages due on the same day, before the sun sets, for the worker is needy and urgently depends on it" (Deut. 24:14–15). In that spirit of honoring the value of labor, the Talmud asks, "Why does a person climb a ladder or hang from a tree and risk death, if not for his wages?" Answering its own question, the Talmud adds, "That person's life depends on it" (*Bava Metzi'a* 112a); work sustains life. So, too, the Sabbath day of rest extends to us, those who work for us, and those we work for (Exod. 20:10). Work is an essential and honored Jewish activity, and rest enables us to return rejuvenated to that work. Everyone who works is on the same high plane.

Buber expands on the value of labor as building a vision of a just society.

D'rash: Buber's Insight

The Jewish farmers have begun to teach their brothers, the Arab farmers, to cultivate the land more intensively; we desire to teach them further; together with them, we want to cultivate the land—to "serve" it, as the Hebrew has it. The more fertile this soil becomes, the more space there will be for us and for them. We have no desire to dispossess them; we want to live with them. We do not want to rule; we want to serve with them.

For Buber, a job is more than a means to make a profit or earn a living—labor opens a portal to social transformation. He praises the social, political, and spiritual benefits of Arab and Jew farming the Land of Israel together.

Buber's vision of spiritual bonding through work comes to the fore in his open letter to Mahatma Gandhi. In the same editorial letter in which Gandhi proposed a nonviolent Jewish response to Nazi aggression (see Shofetim), Gandhi also argued that the British were wrong to impose the Jews on the Arabs, making a case that Palestine belonged solely to the Arabs, and Jews had no right to live there:

Palestine belongs to the Arabs in the same sense that England belongs to the English or France to the French. It is wrong and inhuman to impose the Jews on the Arabs. What is going on in Palestine today cannot be justified by any moral code of conduct. The mandates have no sanction but that of the last war. Surely it would be a crime against humanity to reduce the proud Arabs so that Palestine can be restored to the Jews partly or wholly as their national home. The nobler course would be to insist on a just treatment of the Jews wherever they are born and bred. The Jews born in France are French in precisely the same sense that Christians born in France are French.[20]

Buber rejected Gandhi's argument that Jews were not entitled to their own homeland in Palestine. Instead, in a reflection of the Torah's imperative to love one's neighbor, he called on Jews and Arabs to warmly collaborate in working the Land of Israel and share the bounty (see above).

Buber was also involved with Jewish groups dedicated to a binational state. B'rit Shalom (literally, "a covenant of peace"), established in the mid-1920s, was committed to what they saw as a divine mandate to create a joint nation in which each community would retain its own cultural, social, political, and religious autonomy. Biblical justice demanded nothing less than this kind of collaboration.[21] Later, in the 1940s, Buber was a leader of the political alliance Ichud, which envisioned a vibrant Jewish presence alongside a thriving and robust Palestinian Arab population. While these small groups had limited impact, they demonstrated Buber's commitment to equality built on personal relationships that grew from working the land together.[22]

D'rash: A Personal Reflection

MORE THAN JUST DELIVERING A BILL OF LADING

You don't need to be a farmer to have relationships of equality in the workplace.

My father had a way of speaking with people at work as his equals, whether they worked for him, with him, or around him. As a little kid, I saw it in his "small talk" in the neighborhood with the guy who cut his hair or fixed his car; at his office, when he bantered with the elevator operator or a delivery person; and on his work errands. Dad was in the importing and exporting business, and sometimes he'd take me to the dock or airport cargo area, where he'd drop off something called a "Bill of Lading" with a guy in a small cluttered office, along with a few words that brought a laugh or at least a smile. A Bill of Lading meant more to him than a piece of paper: It offered an opportunity for the personal closeness that comes from sharing words.

Now, I count among my best friends the people I've worked with over the years in synagogues and through social justice advocacy. We've had our share of challenges, achievements, and rewards, including enjoying each other's conversation and company. And I think of Buber's vision when our efforts contribute to social betterment.

Va-yelekh

Wanting More Time

DEUTERONOMY 31:1–30

Adonai said to Moses: "The time is drawing near for you to die. Call Joshua and present yourselves in the Tent of Meeting that I may instruct him."
—Deuteronomy 31:14

P'shat: Explanation

Moses seems at peace with himself as death nears and Joshua steps up to lead, but that wasn't the case at first, according to the Rabbis, who imagine Moses wanted to live long enough to enter Canaan.

In response to God prohibiting Moses from entering the land, the Midrash sees Moses react with distress and defiance. Wrapping himself in sackcloth, he rolls in the dust, praying and protesting. He offers God all kinds of arguments to let him live and finish his work, but God will not yield. He even begs: "If you will not allow me to enter the land of Israel, at least let me as a field animal that eats grass and drinks water" (Deuteronomy Rabbah 11:10). It takes the rise of Joshua, Moses' successor, to get through to Moses that living long enough to at least set foot on Canaan is not to be.

God points out to Moses that as Joshua's standing grows, Moses must enter into decline (*Ha'emek Davar* on Deut. 31:14). Just as the moon shines as the sun sets, so too will Joshua ascend, as Moses' time closes.

Finally, relates the Midrash, God speaks privately to Joshua without saying a word to Moses. Afterward, Moses jealously turns to Joshua and asks, "What did God tell you?" To which Joshua replies, "When God spoke to you, did I know what God said to you?" Realizing the truth in Joshua's words and his envy of Joshua, Moses admits, "I'll die 100 times, but I will never be envious, not even once" (Deuteronomy Rabbah 9:9).

Moses finally accepts the facts. He graciously says to Joshua (in Deut. 31:7): "Be strong and resolute, for it is you who shall go with this people into the land."

D'rash: Buber's Insight

He longs for an extension in time.

It's only natural to want a good thing to last longer than it does. Buber wrote of the person in I-Thou, "He longs for an extension of time." One wishes that I-Thou—like life itself—would stretch on and on. One yearns and fights for life.

Not long before he died, Buber was ill with a high fever when a group of international students was scheduled to visit him at home. His granddaughter, caring for him that day, urged that the meeting be canceled, but Buber was adamant about keeping the appointment, and the guests came.

All told, thirty people from Europe, Africa, and the Far East crowded into his study. They spoke a variety of languages and brought along a multilingual guide to interpret. Nevertheless, Buber, despite his physical condition, was very much himself emotionally and spiritually, took charge, and personally interpreted all the languages. The questions were relatively straightforward, but, given his condition, his responses were intellectually acrobatic, so much so that his neighbors came over to witness the remarkable conversation.[23] With the presence of others raising his spirits, Buber fought to do the most he could within his limits.

Buber's fighting spirit carried on throughout his long and productive life, even as it came to an end.

D'rash: A Personal Reflection

WANTING MORE

"I'm greedy and I want more time."

That's what I heard in my last sit-down conversation with a temple member a few days before his death. He'd been sick for years, and now he was declining fast. He'd called the office and I'd come to the house to talk with him and his wife.

He had notes on what he wanted to tell me. He proceeded to describe each of the things on his "bucket list" that he wouldn't be able to do. But it all came down to one thing: the repeated refrain, "I'm greedy and I want more time."

I offered these words at his funeral, words that have stayed with me through the years that have since passed. I've decided that there's nothing really "greedy" or even self-centered about wanting to live longer. If anything, living longer is also a generous gift to loved ones and friends, when that person continues to be involved in their lives.

And yet, other times, people don't want to go on anymore. They've had enough, especially after a long illness that has drained the family of time, emotion, and resources.

Not long after this man died, another family gathered at a hospital bedside as their loved one faced a medical crisis that no one believed could be overcome. Relatives came from near and very far, including an adult son who traveled to the United States from China and was the last to arrive.

The son went directly from the airport to the hospital, and sat down with his father for a lovely, but brief, conversation. The rest of the family was heading out to lunch, but the son declined the invitation to join them. "No thanks. I just got here, and I want to spend this time with my father." Everyone was fine with that, except for Dad.

"Go!" he ordered.

"But Dad, I just got here, and I don't want you to be alone."

"Go!" he repeated.

"But Dad. . . ."

"GO!"

So, the son went to lunch, and the father died while the family was out.

The son told this remarkable story at the funeral. He said he was convinced his father had chosen this time to die because he'd had enough. He didn't want to live any longer. The time was finally right: He'd just said goodbye to his son. And he didn't want to burden others with watching him as he died.

One person fights for more time while another fights to bring life to an end. Each of us lives out life in our own way.

Ha'azinu

Children in Poetry

DEUTERONOMY 32:1–52

*Like an eagle who rouses its nestlings, gliding
down to its young, so did God spread wings and
take them, bear them along on pinions.*
—Deuteronomy 32:11

P'shat: Explanation

As the people prepare to enter Canaan, Moses turns to poetry to offer a lesson on sacred parenting.

The poem compares the relationship between God and Israel to the relationship between an eagle and its young. Just as newly hatched eagle chicks need a parent eagle's support and protection while learning to fly, the one-time slaves in Egypt, as spiritual fledglings, need God's loving direction while transitioning from dependency to freedom.

The parent eagle teaches the young eagles to fly, then hovers over the nest as the young try it themselves. When the fledglings lose their bearings and start to fall from the sky—which, as they learn, they inevitably do—the adult catches them and bears them to safety, just like God leads and cares for the people of Israel in their vulnerability through the wilderness.

Rashi contributes,

God leads Israel with loving care like this eagle that cares for its young. The eagle does not enter the nest suddenly before it beats and flaps its wings over the young, from tree to tree, from branch to branch, to waken its young that they will summon the strength to receive it. . . . It does not put its weight upon them but hovers over them, touching them and not touching them. . . . When it comes to move them from place to place, it does not pick them up with its claws like other birds. . . . The eagle is only afraid of an arrow so it carries the young on its wings, as if to say, "It is better that the arrow strike me and not strike my young." So, too, the Holy One of blessing, says, "I bore you and brought you to me" (Exod. 19:4) when the Egyptians pursued them and caught up with them at the Sea of Reeds and shot arrows and threw stones at them. (Rashi on Deut. 32:11)

This is Moses' poetic tribute to God's loving protection, which underlies God's call for Israel's fidelity.

D'rash: Buber's Insight

Here we have election, deliverance and education, all in one.

Buber expands on Moses' poetry in his book *Moses*. Just as the parent eagle selects the neediest chick for an extra measure of protective mentoring, God singles out a vulnerable, newly freed Israel for a special destiny. Buber's observation, "Here we have election, deliverance and education, all in one" draws out multiple lessons: on chosenness, redemption, and the importance of teaching the generations that follow.[24]

As a parent, Buber was involved with, but often not attentive to, his children. Paula would joke that when the kids were young, she would never leave them alone with him for fear that he would put them in a desk drawer and forget about them.[25]

Yet Buber was a wonderful grandparent and strong mentor to his students, so much so that, on his eighty-fifth birthday, four hundred Hebrew University students spontaneously paraded from the university up Jerusalem's Ho'vevei Tziyon Street to Buber's front door, carrying torches and singing his praises. He came out on his terrace to receive an honorary student union membership, a first for him, to his delight, as well as a first for anyone in Israel.[26]

D'rash: A Personal Reflection

HOLDING CHILDREN HIGH

Have you ever fallen while carrying your child? If so, as if by instinct, you put the child's safety first.

I tripped twice while carrying children, once on a sidewalk curb with Joshua and once on the ice with Adam. Both times, as I went down, my hands went up, holding my child aloft, taking the force of the fall myself, all without thinking. I got a couple of bruises, but, thankfully, that was it.

Debbie and I have three kids: Joshua, Adam, and Miriam. Their lives take twists and turns, stops and jumps as they move forward with our unwavering support. In the discussion of Shofetim, I told you about Adam. Joshua is a gifted musician—a music director, pianist, arranger, teacher, vocal coach, and more. He is also a Jewish musician with a vocal command of Jewish liturgical music, such that he has led Shabbat and High Holiday services with spirit, animation, and loving grace. His love for music started in primary grades, with piano lessons and participation in the synagogue choir. Small walk-on parts in regional theater later led to his recent Broadway debut. While people are swept up by his performances, the ease he presents hides the reality that this is not an easy field. Nevertheless, Debbie and I have always encouraged and supported him, and we admire his perseverance.

Miriam is an artist and graphic designer who works for a national magazine. As a child, she would draw and paint, and make miniature settings out of clay, such as a set Shabbat table, no more than a few inches high and wide, intricately complete with candles, wine, and challah. Early on, she struggled with art classes that required she follow the teachers' instructions explicitly, so intent was she on creating what *she herself* wanted—until she learned more deeply about shape, texture, color, and light. We encouraged her to follow her teachers' directions, and she learned to experiment with her findings, which she channeled into growing into herself.

It is a gift to see the world through our children's eyes. Still today I often wonder how they got where they did. I only know how important it was, and is, for Debbie and me to stand with them when they fall.

Ve-zo't ha-berakhah

When There Are No Words

DEUTERONOMY 33:1–34:12

*So Moses, the servant of Adonai died there, in the
land of Moab, at the command of Adonai.*
—Deuteronomy 34:5

P'shat: Explanation

In Ve-zo't ha-berakhah, Moses ascends the steppes of Moab to the summit of Pisgah on Mount Nebo, opposite Jericho on the east bank of the Jordan River. As one of his last acts, he takes in the panorama of the land of Canaan, north, south, and west.

The Torah praises Moses' tenacity and strength, even at age 120, saying, "His eyes were undimmed and his vigor unabated" (Deut. 34:7). The Rabbis imaginatively expand on the Torah's description of an older but vibrant Moses. Bekhor Shor points out, "He did not weaken like an ordinary person." Rashi dreams that Moses' physical capacities remained so strong that he could climb all Mount Nebo in one step. Ḥizkuni adds that his eyes radiated light.

An important source of rabbinic thinking surrounding the death of Moses comes from Buber's grandfather, Solomon Buber (1827–1906), a communal leader, scholar, and prolific editor of Jewish literature, including Midrash and medieval Jewish thought. His edition of midrash *Tanhuma*, with its eighth- and ninth-century homilies based on the Torah portion, includes an extended collection of stories about Moses imploring God to allow him to enter Canaan.

In one such story, God refuses Moses' plea to let him live so he can set foot in Canaan, providing an object lesson that whoever lives must die, even Moses. The Rabbis of midrash *Tanhuma* liken his situation to the death of King David: "His breath departs; he returns to the dust; on that day his plans come to nothing" (Ps. 146:4). And *Tanhuma* goes on to say, "Even if a person ascends to the heavens, and makes oneself wings, when that person's end comes, to die, the wings fail, and that person falls before the Angel of Death." Death is final.

D'rash: Buber's Insight

The exalted melancholy of our fate.

As for feelings that accompany the end of life, Buber speaks of "the exalted melancholy of our fate" to describe I-Thou closing. "Fate" speaks to the inevitability, "melancholy" to the sadness, and "exalted" to the holiness that is no more.

When his dear friend and colleague Franz Rosenzweig passed away, Buber recited Psalm 73 at his funeral: "Yet I was always with You, You held my right hand; You guided me by Your counsel and led me toward honor. Whom else have I in heaven? And having you, I want no one on earth."

Buber seems to have been at peace with himself at age eighty-seven, as his own death approached. During what turned out to be his final months, as he sorted through piles of papers and a friend asked what he was doing, he repeated the words of the prophet Isaiah: "Set your affairs in order, for you are going to die; you are not going to get well" (38:1).

Buber died on June 13, 1965, a few months after his eighty-seventh birthday, following a fall and broken hip, which had aggravated a chronic kidney infection. Family members, friends, associates, and dignitaries rushed to his Jerusalem home, among them author S. Y. Agnon, President Zalman Shazar, Prime Minister Levi Eshkol, and former Israeli prime minister David Ben-Gurion, who went on to Israeli national radio to describe Buber's death as a spiritual loss to the entire nation.

The funeral took place the following day at the Hebrew University in Jerusalem. Eulogizing Buber, Hugo Bergmann, his friend for more than six decades, highlighted Buber's life example of approaching Judaism as a struggle to advance a Bible-based vision of justice, truth, and reconciliation, even when it made him unpopular. Bergmann tearfully offered two examples: Buber's acceptance of the German Book Trade Peace Prize, from which he donated the award money to organizations working for peace between Arabs and Jews; and his opposition to the execution of the notorious Nazi Adolf Eichmann, as murder by the state.[27]

D'rash: A Personal Reflection

FINDING WORDS

What do you say to a person when someone this person loved just died?

Clergy are often in this situation, having to decide what to say. And after all these years of being among the "first responders" to news of a death, I have found there is no set formula or "technique." Each person and situation is different. Death may have come suddenly or after a long illness. The deceased may be younger or older. The relationship may have been close or difficult. Each member of the surviving family may take the news of a death differently. These differences make each situation unique and can make my conversation with a survivor feel like the first time I am in this situation.

I've probably come into my own in my responses, as other clergy have, over time. Still, I often notice my hand tightening on the phone receiver when I make or take this kind of call. I always hesitate as I balance on some Narrow Ridge, as I place my whole person on the line each time. After all, how can I be assured that I will respond in a way that helps? How can I possibly know exactly what that person is feeling at that moment? And it is even more complicated when I'm talking with someone I've never met before, which often happens, and over the phone, when I don't have the person's body language to help guide me. So, in this sad and holy moment, this is what I do, and maybe you do this too.

I introduce myself. Then I say, "I am sorry to get this news," because I am. I am sorry for them, I am sorry for their situation, and I am sorry for us having to have this conversation. As much as death is an inevitable and normal part of life, and as fundamental as responding to death is to the clergy calling, I know that practically no one welcomes a death, not even after a long illness.

Next, I stop talking and listen, because people will often have something to say in response. Maybe it is a simple, "Thank you," followed by silence. Sometimes the person wants to tell me how the death happened. Other times, the person jumps right into the funeral details: when and where, and who will speak. Others go on to talk about the deceased, sometimes at length, as they need to do.

In all that listening, after all these years, one common pattern has emerged. Especially with families living all around the country, if not all around the world, assembling family takes some very involved juggling on short notice. Even when there is no travel, the death of a loved one likely upends personal, work, and family plans. So, I often find myself contributing something like, "The time is never right," because it often seems true.

If you struggle to decide what to say in this situation, remember, with all my years of experience, I have similar thoughts. After all, when it comes to someone dying, we are seeing more than any of us can possibly understand.

VI

Holidays

Rosh Hashanah

Where Are You?

In the seventh month, on the first day of the month, you shall observe complete rest, a sacred occasion commemorated with loud blasts. You shall not work at your occupations; and you shall bring an offering by fire to Adonai.
—Leviticus 23:24–25

You are the man who God asks, "Where art Thou?"
—Buber

P'shat: Explanation

The Torah introduces Rosh Hashanah, the Jewish New Year, as an unnamed festival, welcomed with "loud blasts," "complete rest," and "an offering by fire" (Lev. 23:24–25). Today, we sound "loud blasts" of the shofar in synagogue as we pray and reflect in support of *teshuvah*.

Teshuvah often translates as "repentance," as in the *aseret yamei teshuvah*, the Ten Days of "Repentance" between Rosh Hashanah and Yom Kippur. Yet *teshuvah* literally means "return," as reflected in the name Shabbat Shuvah, the Sabbath of Return, falling between Rosh Hashanah and Yom Kippur. The name, Shabbat Shuvah, comes from its haftarah, the book of Hosea: "Return, O Israel, to Adonai, your God" (14:2).

The process of *teshuvah* begins in Elul, on the first day of the last month of the Jewish year, and carries through Rosh Hashanah, Yom Kippur, and the intervening Ten Days of Repentance. It requires introspection that includes reflection on the previous year: what we did and what happened. It means looking back on opportunities squandered or optimized and what the future might bring. It involves identifying what cannot change—sometimes the unwanted needs to be accepted.

On this theme of return and reconciliation with God, Radak points out that "*teshuvah* is important because it reaches the Throne of Heaven" (on Hosea 14:2), reminiscent of Buber's Eternal Thou, where the earthly meets the Divine.

Buber says we return to God by turning to each other. He recalls how God confronted Adam and Eve after they ate from the forbidden Tree of Knowledge of Good and Evil: "Where are you?" (Gen 3:9). To the Rabbis, God's question seemed odd. After all, an omniscient God would know where to find Adam and Eve and not have to ask. The commentator Malbim, Rabbi Meir Leibush ben Yehiel Michel Wisser (Russia, nineteenth century), and colleagues cautioned against taking this questioning literally. Instead of inquiring of their whereabouts, God is really inviting Eve and Adam into spiritual reflection and conversation that leads to repentance. And Buber would add that when it comes to our own shortcomings and failures, we are to have a similar self-evaluation during the High Holiday season.

In his exploration of Hasidism *The Way of Man*, Buber notes that God asked the same question of Cain after he killed his brother Abel: "Where are you?" To Buber, the message is meant, as well, for us: "You are the man who God asks, 'Where art Thou?'"[1] Even though our sins may not be as egregious, the questions are the same: "Where are you? How are you living your life right now?" These questions open self-reflections that can lead to *teshuvah*.

D'rash: A Personal Reflection

WHEN TIME LITERALLY FLIES

For all the times people say that "time flies," I literally witnessed time fly.

I was driving around one late summer afternoon when I noticed someone's loose-leaf appointment book opened on the sidewalk, the book apparently dropped and its pages scattered through the street like fallen leaves in the breeze. No one was scrambling around collecting the pages as far as I could tell, so I figured the owner of the loose-leaf had just given up. Still, I imagined those were my calendar pages going, going, gone with the wind, and in a multitasker's nightmare, imagined myself scurrying around pedestrians and through traffic, pouncing on sheets marred by tires and muddied by puddles, gathering in one day at a time. I'd recover every page but one—and then really panic: *What did I have scheduled on that missing day: a meeting, a class? What if it's someone's wedding?!*

More figuratively, we ingather daily pages into a book of our lives year after year. "Days are scrolls," the twelfth-century Rabbi Bahya ibn Pakuda taught. "Write on them only what you really want remembered" (*Duties of the Heart* 8:90). He thus metaphorically urges us to understand those days' sacredness, and to use them well. When the congregation sings the *Avinu Malkeinu* prayer on Rosh Hashanah and Yom Kippur, which asks God to inscribe us in the Book of Life for a good year, the term "Book of Life" is also a metaphor about the enduring impact of our conduct, even when our earthly pages are scattered by a gentle breeze or the harsh winds of life. In face of life flying away like sheets in a gust, we are to recognize that every day is important, and the responsibility for *teshuvah* is urgent. What we do with our time endures, and our days, like the words on a scroll, will live on.

Yom Kippur

New Thinking

*Mark, the tenth day of this seventh month is the Day
of Atonement. It shall be a sacred occasion for you; you
shall practice self-denial, and you shall bring an offering
by fire to Adonai, you shall do no work throughout that
day. For it is a day of atonement on which expiation
is made on your behalf before your God Adonai.*
—Leviticus 23:27–28

The It of knowledge . . . is composed of ideas.
—Buber

P'shat: Explanation

In days of old, the Torah commands that Jews literally "mark" Yom
Kippur, the Day of Atonement, with "self-denial," an "offering by
fire," and refraining from "work" to promote "expiation." Today Jews
"mark" Yom Kippur by attending synagogue, fasting, abstaining from
sex, and focusing the spirit on *teshuvah*.

In the Torah's description of Yom Kippur, the word "mark," *ach*,
draws attention, as in, "Mark, the tenth day of this seventh month is
the Day of Atonement." *Ach* is rarely used in the Bible.

To Ḥizkuni, *ach* indicates that Yom Kippur is a different kind of
holiday. Where Shabbat and other festivals are spoken of as times
to celebrate with food, wine, and more, somber Yom Kippur is a day
of "self-denial" (on Lev. 23:27), and *ach* calls one to take special note.
Sforno underscores that "self-denial" fosters spiritual attunement by
supporting personal recognition of failure, the seeking of forgiveness,
and making amends (on Lev. 23:27). Overall, the day is meant to bring

a person closer to God, as exemplified by the legendary life story of Buber's collaborator and dear friend, Franz Rosenzweig.

Rosenzweig grew up in a nonobservant Jewish home. In his late twenties, he decided to convert to Christianity, but only after living as a Jew. So he went to synagogue services on Yom Kippur that year—and, to his surprise, was awestruck by the immediacy of a direct, one-to-one encounter with God. He went home, dropped his plan to convert and devoted himself to Jewish learning, practice, writing, and teaching.[2] On the holiest day of the year, he had experienced *teshuvah*, a literal "return to Judaism." He later wrote that on Yom Kippur, a Jew stands, "lonely and naked, straight before the throne of God."[3]

As a German soldier on the World War I battlefront, Rosenzweig wrote most of what would become his classic study of Jewish belief and practice, *The Star of Redemption*, paragraph by paragraph, on postcards mailed home. After the war ended, he edited the cards into the book that would establish him as a significant Jewish thinker and writer.

Among many other attributes, *The Star* elevates what Rosenzweig called "New Thinking." Whereas the "old" thinking dealt only with the mind, the New Thinking speaks to action. Whereas old thinking was about ideals, New Thinking brings us to God's truth through lived human experience, starting with the Jewish experience at Mount Sinai.

Like Rosenzweig, Buber prioritized living over thinking. Buber's observation, "The *It* of knowledge . . . is composed of ideas," was his means of saying that knowledge in and of itself is an inadequate foundation for Jewish spiritual life.[4] While we can learn much from books, we encounter the spiritual through deeds. That is, we don't know God as we know an idea or a fact: we meet God when we meet each other.

D'rash: A Personal Reflection

JEWISH VERSUS SECULAR EDUCATION

"My kid is a 4.0," said a parent, describing her high schooler's perfect grade point average, as if the number determines a person's worth. Yet

I am sure, if questioned, the mother would agree that there is more to a teen than a number on a transcript, and we witness that broader measure in Jewish education.

To be sure, a Jewish education covers the facts when it comes to learning Bible or Jewish history, reading Hebrew and the like. But our synagogues don't rank kids by their test scores; we put them on an equal plane in the classroom and on the pulpit, in youth group and in Confirmation. In contrast to letter grades and number ranking, a religious education affirms the goodness in each human being and our equality in the eyes of God. At the synagogue, we don't measure kids.

I think of the bat mitzvah student with a love for science and biology who was touched by the prayer book's reflection that the body is God's marvel. There was a Confirmation student moved by the prayer for healing and the hope for her brother's return to health. "Why do bad things happen to good people?" another student wanted to know. And yet another, who identifies as Black and Jewish, was drawn to Jewish teachings on social justice. You don't learn all that much about these things in secular education—you need religious education to open a door to the spirit.

Sukkot

The *Holiday*

*Mark, on the fifteenth day of the seventh month, when
you have gathered in the yield of your land, you shall
observe the festival of Adonai to last seven days.*
— Leviticus 23:39

Hold your ground when you meet them.
— Buber

P'shat: Explanation

It surprised me, and maybe you, that the Mishnah calls Sukkot *He-
ḥag*, "the holiday" (*Avot* 5:9), as if every other Jewish holiday is secondary. Yet Sukkot, the harvest festival, celebrates the ingathered fall
produce that sustains the people through the winter into the spring.
Thus Sukkot touches the foundation of life.

The Torah introduces Sukkot with the word *ach*, "mark," in the same
way it introduces Yom Kippur. Where the Rabbis apply *ach* to Yom Kippur as a call to solemnity, the commentary *Da'at Zkenim* (France and
Germany, thirteenth century) teaches that the *ach* of Sukkot reflects
two special joys: the joy of "the harvest" and the joy of "the forgiveness of transgressions" that just happened on Yom Kippur.

The Mishnah (*Sukkah* 5), compiled as the Common Era opened,
describes the joyous Sukkot festivities in the great Jerusalem Temple. Having traveled from all corners of Canaan to Jerusalem, the people enter the Temple court beneath brilliant illumination, before the
gallery-filling assembled multitude, and accompanied by resound-
ing music. Israel's leaders lead a torch dance to hymns and songs of
praise as Levite priests sing Psalms accompanied by flute and harp.

There are libations—liquid offerings of mixed wine and water—and burnt offerings all night long, through sunrise.

Today the Jewish community celebrates Sukkot more quietly and with less flare, by building huts—holiday booths for sitting, eating, praying, and sleeping—and bringing together the four species: etrog or citron, myrtle, willow, and palm branch (Lev. 23:40), and these four species draw a lesson on what goes into a solid relationship (after *Sefer ha-Ḥinnukh*, 324).

The heart-shaped *etrog* represents the heart's compassion. The myrtle leaf resembles the eye, which calls us to be observant, one person of the other. The willow looks like a lip as a caution to be measured in speech. The palm, like a spine, has us stand tall and have a backbone, reflecting Buber's teaching in *I and Thou*: when you meet others, "hold your ground when you meet them."[5] Yet Buber was well aware that a spine, like the palm, will sway in a strong wind—without swaying, it might well snap.

D'rash: A Personal Reflection

ONE'S SENSE OF SELF

I reflected on Buber's advice to "hold your ground" when talking to teens at the Temple during Sukkot. The topic was cheating, and the situation is more complicated and deserves more nuance than just laying down the law about the dangers. Teens are under great pressure to do well. Some think: *I need to ace this test, or my parents will kill me* or *You owe me the answers for the time I helped you*. They may respond to the strain by giving in to the temptation to cheat.

That Sukkot, in the classroom, with the *lulav* as a handheld illustration, I reflected on the importance of having a backbone, standing strong, and holding one's ground. "What is your heart? What do you see with your eye, and speak with your lips, and how do you bring it all together to do what you believe to be right? I won't be with you when you face this situation," I added. "You know what I want you to do, but you have to make up your own mind. You must know who you are and what you are in order to become who you will be."

Shemini Atzeret

Sudden Stop

*On the eighth day you shall observe a sacred occasion
and bring an offering by fire to Adonai; it is a solemn
gathering: you shall not work at your occupations.*
—Leviticus 23:36

I feel the blow too strongly myself.
—Buber

P'shat: Explanation

Seven days and Sukkot, "*the* holiday," ends. The very next day, the
Torah adds one more day of observance, Shemini Atzeret, marked
by another fire offering at the Tabernacle and a cessation of work.

Oddly, the Torah gives us no clue about the deeper significance of
Shemini Atzeret, other than the name: *shemini*, which means "eighth"
(Shemini Atzeret takes place on the eighth day after Sukkot begins),
and *atzeret*, which typically translates as "gathering."

To Rashi (on Lev. 23:36) and others, however, *atzeret* means something else. It speaks to a sudden and abrupt "stop," just as the three-
letter root of *atzeret*—*ayin, tzadi,* and *resh*—means "stop" in modern
Hebrew. Rashi points to an analogy of a monarch who hosts the
royal children for a festival of several days until leave-taking time,
and then tells them, "Please wait one more day. It is hard for me to
part from you." By extension, God feels the same sadness over the
close of Sukkot and seeks one more day with us, Shemini Atzeret,
for celebration.

Many good things in life suddenly come to a close. I am reminded
of how Buber got news of such a stop from his mentee, colleague,

collaborator, and friend, the Nobel Prize–winner Shmuel Yosef Agnon (1888–1970), a central figure in the Israeli literary world.

The longstanding Buber-Agnon friendship began in Germany right before World War I. Both men had a loving and serious interest in Hasidic stories. In time, the two contracted with Haim Nahman Bialik and the Moriah-Dvir Publishing House to release a groundbreaking and comprehensive multivolume work on long-neglected Hasidic practices, beliefs, and values.

The project began in 1922, and within two years Agnon had completed a full draft of the first volume, short of the table of contents, when tragedy suddenly struck. Fire consumed Agnon's home: books, manuscripts, and most of this first draft turned to ash. A profoundly saddened and apologetic Agnon told Buber it would be years, at the earliest, before he would possibly return to the project, if ever. Ultimately, Agnon decided to withdraw from the collaboration and sent what partially readable pages he had to Buber.

Buber was heartbroken about Agnon's ordeal, the loss of the manuscripts, and the likely end of their collaboration. Recognizing that Agnon would not allow himself to be persuaded to rewrite the lost pages, Buber decided not to try to convince him. He wrote his friend the Jewish teacher and thinker Franz Rosenzweig, "I feel the blow too strongly myself."

Buber and Agnon went on to work on Hasidism independently. In 1947, Buber released *Or Ha-ganuz* (The hidden light), which we know as *Tales of the Hasidim*, one of his crowning achievements, credited with rekindling Jewish interest in the Hasidic masters.

After that sudden stop, the grand Buber-Agnon collaboration never came to be, yet their friendship and work carried on.[6]

D'rash: A Personal Reflection

MEANING IN THE FACE OF FINALITY

Bad news comes suddenly, as I witnessed at a hospital bedside.

I was running late at the start of what promised to be a very full day when I stopped at the hospital information desk for the room number of a temple member. The receptionist asked if I had enough time to make a second visit, to another patient I didn't know, who wanted to see a rabbi. Even with all I had to do, I couldn't decline. Soon after, I was in that person's room, and heard: "I was just diagnosed with cancer, Rabbi," said this woman in her fifties. "They said it will kill me within the year, so I asked to see a rabbi because my life is over. Under these circumstances, what meaning can my life possibly have?"

I was still kind of new at this, so I was uncharacteristically quiet for a few moments as I thought about what I was hearing and what I might say. She had received a blunt message that her life would soon come to an abrupt stop. I couldn't begin to Imagine the Real as to how devastating this was for her. And then I remembered my studies of the teachings of a very wise writer, the late psychiatrist Viktor Frankl, and his modern classic book, *Man's Search for Meaning*. Frankl drew from his experience as a concentration camp inmate to teach others how to approach life when time is limited, and things will come to an unexpected end.

This woman looked perfectly healthy in that moment. She seemed to have plenty of life and energy in her and could continue to be able to do for herself and others, at least through the immediate future. So, I struggled to find words, and this is what I said: "Your life has meaning, regardless of how long it lasts. It doesn't become meaningless just because it is coming to a sudden end. That is, if your life is now meaningless, then just adding more time only extends the meaninglessness. In other words, meaning in life isn't about how long you live, but what you do with the time you have. So the question is, 'What will you do with the rest of your limited time to make your it as meaningful as possible?'"

She sort of got it, but wasn't totally accepting, and I couldn't blame her. But I held my ground and finally came up with something convincing: "Listen, I'm finding it a challenge to explain my thinking. So, if you can give me a run for my money, you can do the same for others. Why not use the rest of your time to make a difference to others?

Work with kids. Talk with others who have cancer. I'm sure you can find something that puts who you are to good use."

Something clicked for her. She thanked me and turned to get on the phone. I gave her my business card, offered to talk with her in the future, and I left.

I never heard from her again. And, as something ends, I pray, something else continues.

Simḥat Torah

When You Come to the End

When God began to create . . .
—Genesis 1:1

In the beginning is relation.
—Buber

P'shat: Explanation

The synagogue's Simḥat Torah celebration includes two Torah read-ings: one from the very end of Deuteronomy on the death of Moses, and the other from the start of Genesis, "when God began to create." We honor the tradition of reading the end of the Torah and the begin-ning all in one breath, as a reflection of Ben Bag Bag's words in the Mishnah, "Turn it and turn it because everything is in it. Search in it and search in it since everything is in it. And look in it and grow old and be worn in it. Do not move away from it because there is nothing better than it" (*Pirke Avot* 5:22). That is, hold the Torah close because there is always something to learn, no matter how much you've stud-ied and you know. And for all the times I've ended a year of Torah, I'm excited to start again because, it's true, there is always something to learn in reading the Torah anew.

It takes a measure of humility to sustain a curious mind and keep learning. As encouragement, Buber brings us Rabbi Levi Yitzhak of Berditchev, who was asked why each volume of the Talmud starts with page two instead of page one—that is, with a page number rep-resented by the second Hebrew letter, *bet*, instead of the first letter, *alef*. Rabbi Levi Yitzhak calls us to humility: No matter how much we learn and for all we know, he says, it is as if we never even got to the first page.[7] The most learned are also beginners.

As we begin a new year of Torah reading, Buber offers a nod to the origins of the universe, the story of Creation, when he observes, "In the beginning is relation." He wants us to know that the route to becoming human begins with relationship. A soul grows to fullness and the spirit fulfills its potential through relationships with parents, siblings and family, friends, and community. And as we go through life, there is always something to learn from each encounter.

D'rash: A Personal Reflection

ENDINGS AND BEGINNINGS

I took a lesson on beginnings and endings early on in my career, as a social work intern at a mental health center.

One of my first clients was struggling with alcohol addiction. His drinking hurt his relationships with his wife and children, compromised his ability to work, and contributed to his depression. As our time together went along, month after month, he seemed to be doing better and said he had stopped drinking. But as we approached the end of my internship and our partnership, he confided in me that he had gone back to drink.

Upset at what I took as my failure to prevent his relapse, I shared word of his news, along with my personal feelings, to my supervisor, who wisely offered, "Dennis, you know that whenever you come to the end, you always go back to the beginning." While my supervisor wasn't Jewish, and probably had no idea of the significance of Simḥat Torah, he taught me an important lesson: by anticipating its increased likelihood and recognizing signs of a relapse as my time with a patient comes to an end, I should be less inclined to take the turn personally and be better prepared to try to help this person move forward.

I think about his words in my role as an Intentional Interim Rabbi, in which my work life is all about beginnings and endings. Each year on July 1 I start with a new congregation and leave the following June 30.

Each synagogue is different from the one before. It comes as a surprise to people when I say that congregations are profoundly unique. How they worship, the nature of educational programs through the lifespan, the procedure for making important congregational decisions are so dissimilar that I have to adjust, from one to the other, and keep learning. Walking into an unfamiliar congregation is like walking into a dark theater after the movie started: Everyone else in the room knows who the important people are and what has already happened, all while new things are happening. I have to figure it all out without the background I need. And I welcome the challenge and intensity of the experience.

The year is full and passes quickly. First of all, an interim rabbi is a rabbi, just like any rabbi who teaches, leads services, offers counsel, and partners with the temple's staff and leaders to move the congregation ahead. The particular focus of the interim year flows from the partnership between rabbi, staff, and leaders as we "prepare the congregation for the next rabbi." We identify and work toward a common agenda, be it strengthening teen engagement, rebuilding adult education programs, bolstering staff skills, and more, until time comes to say goodbye. By then, the new rabbi has been chosen and we spend many hours preparing to give the incoming rabbi a strong start and successful tenure.

As the year comes to a close, there are always a few things to squeeze in before I say goodbye, from hiring a religious-school teacher, to caring for someone facing a pastoral need, to making sure an important project receives last-minute attention. And there is always something we wanted to do but didn't get around to completing, or some big problem that jumps out just as my time there ends and winds up in the next rabbi's lap. By June 30, we have said our goodbyes and I head off to my next assignment. And while it may sound overstated and melodramatic, I think of Moses, who brought the people to the Land of Israel but never got to enter.

It is very sad to say goodbye to people I've become close to, especially the temple staff and volunteer leaders. Everyone is working hard, the relationships are intense and very productive, and I am deeply impressed by their commitment and giving above and beyond themselves. Additionally, I develop close relationships with the teens I mentor. Our denominational office requires that my relationships with this community must end there, at least for the immediate future, as the next rabbi settles in and builds relationships. For my sake as well, I too must focus on my next position. But I do think about my former temple as I begin a new year with a new community.

Hanukkah

Because We Never Really Get There

When you enter the land . . .
—Deuteronomy 26:1

Be prepared
For every earthly season!
His hand has ever held thee—
Remain lovingly facing the world
—Buber

P'shat: Explanation

"I've arrived!"

Be the destination a vacation spot, the office, or home after a day of work, getting there says you made it. Time to put up the feet, take in the accomplishment, and relax—it may seem.

Rabbi Nahum of Stepinesht, a sage renowned for his warm and understanding presence, surprised his students by unexpectedly entering the house of study one Hanukkah evening. In keeping with the holiday spirit, the students were playing checkers instead of learning Torah, yet they were deeply embarrassed to have been "caught" in a game when they could have been studying. But Rabbi Nahum's smile put them at ease, and he went on to offer a lesson about checkers and the rules of play. He told them to make only one move at a time, never more than one. He said they are to move forward, never back. And he added that when a marker reaches the last row, a player may move that marker anywhere they want.[8]

It is hard to know exactly what Rabbi Nahum had in mind that night by surprising his students twice—showing up unexpectedly

255

and then offering an on-the-spot teaching on the rules of the game that so absorbed them. Yet an artfully crafted lesson lives within that little sermon.

For all the rushing in life, Rabbi Nahum has us advance a step at a time, only one step. For all of the temptation to dwell on the past, or to try to recreate what was, he walks forward into the future. But when it comes to reaching the last row, I suspect that Rabbi Nahum spoke tongue-in-cheek by suggesting that once people reach a certain destination, they can go wherever they want. I am sure that he well knew that neither he, you, nor I will ever come to a time or place when we have fully "arrived."

The Torah portion Ki Tavo', Hebrew for "when you get there," speaks to the Jewish people's near arrival in the Land of Israel. Indeed, after four hundred years of slavery in Egypt, followed by a forty-year trek through the Sinai wilderness, the Jewish people reach their dream. Yet even though they do achieve the dream, they don't end up living out the hope of doing as they please.

In one example among many, in 168 BCE, the Seleucid Greek soldiers and their leader Antiochus attacked the Land of Israel, ransacked and appropriated the Jerusalem Temple for their use, and outlawed Jewish practice. It took a few years, but the Maccabees fought them off, reclaimed and rededicated the Temple, and gave the people a holiday, Hanukkah. And if you think by then the Jews had arrived, keep in mind that in 70 CE, Roman soldiers sacked Jerusalem and upended Jewish life, and they were forced to reinvent ourselves, yet again. Buber's poem cited above is a call to have faith, stay the course, and continue moving forward.

D'rash: A Personal Reflection

GOING AHEAD

The light and warmth of Hanukkah come to us at the darkest and coldest time of year to offer uplift and hope. We recall the tenacity of Hanukkah's heroes as we kindle the lights, adding one more each night. And then, on the eighth night, we have arrived: The *hanukkiah* is fully aglow. We have reached the last row. And then it ends.

To describe the accompanying loss and sadness, I recall a poem by my mentor, Rabbi Chaim Stern, words beloved by many:

> *It is a fearful thing to love*
> *what death can touch.*
>
> *A fearful thing to love,*
> *hope, dream; to be —*
> *to be, and oh! to lose.*
>
> *A thing for fools this, and*
> *a holy thing,*
> *a holy thing to love.*
>
> *For*
> *your life has lived in me,*
> *your laugh once lifted me,*
> *your word was gift to me.*
>
> *To remember this brings a painful joy.*
> *'Tis a human thing, love,*
> *a holy thing,*
> *to love*
> *what death has touched.*

Purim

A Day Like Yom Kippur

*And these days of Purim shall never cease
among the Jews, and the memory of them shall
never perish among their descendants.*
—Esther 9:28

I can now utter an earnest and joyful yes to my life.
—Buber

P'shat: Explanation

There's plenty in a name, as we see when comparing the Hebrew names of Yom Kippur and Purim. The name "Purim" comes from the Hebrew for the "lots" that Haman cast when picking a date to put an end to the Jews. Yom Kippur, the "Day of Atonement," also goes by the name *Yom Hakippurim*, "Day of Atonements." And isn't it interesting that the name of the Purim holiday is found in the word *Hakippurim*, which can also be translated to mean "like Purim"?

It sure sounds heretical to suggest that somber Yom Kippur resembles raucous Purim. After all, Yom Kippur is for deep self-scrutiny on life-and-death matters, where Purim is for a boisterous megillah reading and a *Purim-spiel*, mockery and ridicule included. On Yom Kippur we fast; on Purim we indulge. To borrow a page from Sigmund Freud, where Yom Kippur is about superego, Purim is all id.

But if we look closer at these two Jewish holidays, the differences are merely superficial. Purim and Yom Kippur merely take different approaches toward the same end.

Both holidays have us remove any masks of self-deception and get a good, honest look at who we really are. We consider our faults seriously on Yom Kippur and with levity on Purim. Each holiday seeks the same change for the better.

So Purim is a day like Yom Kippur. Six months on the calendar between them, dress clothing for one versus costume clothing for the other, yet the degree of self-scrutiny, removal of masks, and hope for change is at the heart of each.

On removing the mask and being true to oneself, Buber tells of Rabbi Zusya of Hanipol, who, imagining himself after death in the heavens, understood that God would not expect him to be a great leader like Moses. Instead, God would call him to account for trying to wear the mask of Moses instead of relying on his own gifts to fulfill the best within him. God would inquire, "Why were you not Zusya?" Why were you not true to yourself?[9]

At times during his young adulthood Buber struggled to remove the mask of expectations placed by others Over Against his own inclinations. Martin's father was dismissive of Hasidic studies and encouraged secular academics, while his grandfather supported a Jewish direction.

Buber sat for his university exams in philosophy and art history, completed his first dissertation on philosophy, and immediately turned to a second dissertation on art history, which would qualify him to teach at a German university. He relocated to Florence, Italy, to better research Renaissance art—but was immediately distracted by the city's natural beauty, local history, and culture. He reflected on the emotional upheaval surrounding his leaving the Zionist movement, studied Italian, and took in a lot of theater. He also worked on his first Hasidic anthology, *The Tales of Rabbi Nachman*, which was under contract and on deadline. Then, as his second thesis neared completion, he abandoned the thesis for the Hasidic work, setting the stage for his life as an independent Jewish scholar and author. In Florence, it appears that Buber removed the mask imposed by others to establish his own life course and destiny.[10]

D'rash: A Personal Reflection

REMOVING MASKS

We were two dozen interfaith clergy and government policy makers sitting around tables arranged in a horseshoe. The topics were daunting—homelessness, affordable housing, people who needed support transitioning from prison to life.

Clergy drew from their real-life experience supporting their members in underserved and underrepresented communities to emphasize the urgency and importance of the needs. Then, a policy maker, seated at the far end of the room, started to speak. Half the group was unable to see her. A minister called out, "Please, can you stand up when you talk? We can't see you. We don't know who you are."

Of all the things to worry about—housing, hunger, the justice system—this minister was upset that he could not look face-to-face at a speaking person. Yet the importance of full facial connection should not be underestimated or ignored. When this minister asked the official to be seen, he conveyed an important message: We can only know who you really are when we can look you in the eye.

Full and honest sight of a conversation partner is so important, especially when feelings run high and nonverbal communication is as crucial as the spoken words. When sight is obstructed by distance, fear, indifference, room layout, or (as I write) COVID, it becomes all the more challenging to be present in I-Thou—for me to know who you are and for you to know me.

Pesach

Education of Character

When, in time to come, your children ask you, "What mean the decrees, laws and rules that our God Adonai has enjoined upon you?" you shall say to your children, "We were slaves to Pharaoh in Egypt and Adonai freed us from Egypt with a mighty hand."
— Deuteronomy 6:20–21

Education worthy of the name is essentially education of character.
— Buber

P'shat: Explanation

We were slaves in Egypt until we became free, thanks to God's compassion, grace, and might. That's the lesson our children are to receive, and we honor this commandment by teaching our children through seder rituals and the Haggadah story.

The Torah assumes our kids will ask about the special Passover observance, and our response can be understood as having two parts. The first part has to do with Passover *facts*: history and rituals such as eating matzah and a seder that includes the Four Questions, Four Children, and Four Cups (or more, when we add one for Miriam and another for Elijah). In the second part of the response, we interpret and impart the *spiritual meaning* of our customs, ceremonies, and collective past, and how those lessons enrich contemporary life.

This second kind of learning starts with the first. After giving kids information, we encourage a compassionate response to the heartache of the stranger, to follow God's example to protect the weak and powerless, just as God took care of us when we were slaves in Egypt. We also teach the importance of expressing gratitude for the grace of freedom, and of maintaining hope during our own dark times.

Buber raised the need for this second kind of teaching in his opening address to the 1939 National Conference of Jewish Teachers in Tel Aviv, saying, "Education worthy of the name is essentially education of character." By "education of character" Buber meant not only teaching behavior and values but also teaching the entire person—the senses and spirit as well as the intellect. Education of character at its best brings us to see who we are as Jews, what we love, what makes for meaningful living, and what makes a person into what we call in Yiddish a mensch, morally strong and solid.[11] Through character education we perpetuate the memory of our history.

D'rash: A Personal Reflection

SETTING THE SPIRITUAL FOUNDATION

Passover set my spiritual foundation.

It began when I was a little kid. As soon as the kosher for Passover foods appeared on the supermarket shelves, my mother took my brother and me shopping, which was a Jewish education in itself when it came to learning which foods were allowed and which were not, and what was special for the occasion—necessities and treats. When the holiday got closer, the kosher-for-Passover dishes came out of the storage cabinet and the house got a good cleaning. And then there were the seders, filled with so much song, energy, prayer, fun—and that food!

There was a chicken farm's worth of eggs—hard-boiled, cut up and eaten in salt water, mashed into egg salad, whipped and baked into cakes or kugels, or mixed with matzah meal and some salt and boiled into matzah balls. And then there was sponge cake: separated eggs—yolks and whites—whipped with the power Sunbeam mixer, then with other ingredients, baked, then cooled on inverted drinking glasses to prevent sagging—which happened anyway but intensified the sweetness and contributed to the texture of, well, a sponge. Both of my grandmothers always had the same disappointing sponge cake outcome, which became a topic of seder conversation, year after year.

Matzah also took on many forms and additions: mixed and fried as *matzah brei* for breakfast, under egg salad for lunch, as kugel casserole for dinner. And the wine, four "cups" — more the size of shot glasses — burned sweetly going down to yield a lightheaded afterglow.

In my home, like so many, we'd take turns reading paragraphs of the Haggadah, and as part assignments went around the table, we'd count down to see who'd get stuck reading the Evil Child of the Four Children. No one wanted to be caught having to read that — until we reached our teens — and then everyone wanted to be "bad." And my thinking changed as I got even older; I grew to appreciate the wisdom of the Simple Child. Especially when facing a difficult situation, a simple question, "What's this?" — instead of a challenge or attack — may well evoke a wise response and teach me something.

Amid all these experiences were "education of character" lessons that continue to shape me today. I was taught to "Imagine the Real" conditions of slavery while recognizing the suffering of those who would harm us (the Egyptians during the plagues, the soldiers who drowned in the Sea of Reeds): in effect, to respect and if possible seek reconciliation with an opponent. The refrain, "You shall love the stranger, you who were strangers in Egypt," speaks to the Jewish people's responsibility to care for those estranged from the social, economic, or political mainstream. The Passover experience set these lessons as my spiritual foundation.

Debbie and I drew from our childhood memories as we readied our home for the holiday. We'd involve our kids in food shopping and decorating the seder table. Family and friends joined us in preparing food, singing, reading, and much laughter. And we added some things, like frog puppets, a fabric look-alike round matzah that got tossed around like a Frisbee, and having our youngest recite the Four Questions while standing on a dining-room chair — a practice that ended once the kids got so tall their heads hit the ceiling.

Yom ha-Shoah

Nuance in Reconciliation

*Remember what Amalek did to you on your journey, after
you left Egypt—how undeterred by fear of God, he surprised
you on the march, when you were famished and weary,
and cut down all the stragglers in your rear. Therefore,
when your God Adonai grants you safety from all your
enemies around you, in the land that your God Adonai is
giving you as a hereditary portion, you shall blot out the
memory of Amalek from under heaven. Do not forget!*
—Deuteronomy 25:17–19

*I see these men very near before me in that especial intimacy
which binds us at times to the dead and to them alone.
Reverence and love for these Germans now fills my heart.*
—Buber

P'shat: Explanation

As the Jewish people's time in Sinai comes to an end, Moses recalls
a painful and tragic incident: the brutal attack the Jews suffered at
the hands of Amalek. Their warriors ambushed the Hebrews and,
in brazen cowardice, instead of attacking their prepared fighters on
the front line, went after the most vulnerable and defenseless from
behind. Ibn Ezra illuminates that Amalek "cut off your tail," attacking "the weak ones in the rear," those who "thirsted for water," and
those "worn by the travel" (on Deut. 25:18).

By instructing the people to "Remember what Amalek did" on the
one hand, and calling upon them to "blot out the memory of Amalek
from under heaven," on the other, Moses presents them with a para-

dox: How do they "blot out" and "remember" at the same time? Bahya captures this mixed message with the instruction, "Do not forget to blot out (the memory)!" (on Deut. 25:19). A person may well forget to remember, but how do you remember to forget?

Buber confronted a similar paradox when he accepted an invitation to receive the German Book Trade's Peace Prize in 1953. As he anticipated, his return to Germany as an honoree would evoke widespread criticism from close friends and Jews worldwide who believed Jews should have nothing to do with anyone or anything from Germany.[12] He would be ahead of his time in taking steps to normalize Jewish relations with Germans and Germany.

At the award ceremony, before an audience that included the president of the West German Republic and other leaders in government and academia, Buber spoke with his typical candor. He underscored his recognition of the magnitude of German atrocities during World War II and made sure his audience knew he did not travel to Germany to forgive. Yet, out of a refusal to judge all German people, he went on to praise those who resisted the Nazis. Of those who stood in defiance, fought back, risked their lives, and paid the greatest price, Buber wrote, "I see these men very near before me in that especial intimacy which binds us at times to the dead and to them alone. Reverence and love for these Germans now fills my heart." He also advanced a vision for a new relationship between Germans and Jews. Upon returning to Israel, he donated the prize of 10,000 German marks to activities to advance Jewish-Arab understanding.[13]

D'rash: A Personal Reflection

YEARS LATER

"Will you take our picture?"

I almost always rub elbows with tourists on my morning walk around Manhattan's Central Park Reservoir. That spot is a visitors' magnet—the panorama of high-rise apartment buildings and skyscrapers form a towering backdrop for the park's trees overlooking the reservoir water. It's easy to spot the tourists, just as they spot me as someone willing to stop in their tracks to take a picture.

"Where are you from?" I'll ask as I fiddle with their camera, as if I didn't already guess the answer to their question from their accent.

"Germany."

Any mention of Germany used to jostle my nerves. Having grown up with family members and yeshiva rabbis who often talked about their experiences in the Holocaust, just hearing a few German words would arouse images of number tattoos on arms, scars, and stories of what the Nazis did. As the years went by, my emotions were amplified by Yom ha-Shoah commemoration services and many more than enough World War II books and movies.

Yet, as in Buber's example to refuse to judge a nation as a whole, I am coming to see that we need to avoid the reification of everything German and instead react with nuance. My wife, Debbie, who recently returned from a rabbis' mission to Germany, reported on the changing attitudes among the German leadership and a revitalizing German-Jewish community.

A public openness to confront the Holocaust was visible in memorials, museums, and her own candid conversations with Germans. Additionally, the prime minister and many early twenty-first-century German leaders have offered sanctuary to refugees from distressed Middle East countries, a welcome that stands out among nations. Even as a German neo-Nazi movement is visible and disconcerting, Germany has turned, and, I pray, continues in that positive direction.

"I am happy to take your picture," I tell the German tourists. "I hope you enjoy your time here." And I mean it.

Yom ha-Atzmaut

A Growing Outcome

Go forth from your native land and from your
father's house to the land that I will show you.
—Genesis 12:1

I owe the urge to this new and more comprehensive
composition to the air of this land. Our sages say that
it makes one wise; to me, it has granted a different
gift: The strength to make a new beginning.
—Buber

P'shat: Explanation

An invisible God bids Abram and Sarai to uproot their lives to start a new people in an unseen place, and the story of the Jewish people on the Land of Israel begins. Rashi looks at the Hebrew, *Lekh lekha*, "Go for yourself!" to teach literally, "For *your* benefit, for *your* good, there I will make you a great nation" (on Gen. 12:1). In other words, God is saying, "Trust me! Face up to the challenge and you and your descendants will be the better!"

Underscoring the emotional and spiritual backdrop, Radak emphasizes how it is hard to leave one's homeland, harder to leave a birthplace, and how much more so to leave family, likely forever. Yet, these first Jews affirm, the spiritual benefits will greatly outweigh the sacrifices.

As if living out the same script four millennia later, Buber, threatened by the rising Nazi regime, left his German homeland for Israel in 1938. Though upon emigrating, he (age sixty) and Paula (sixty-one) were younger than Abram (seventy-five) and Sarai (sixty-five), their situation was deeply complicated.

For financial reasons, Buber needed to work in Israel. And it might come as a surprise that Buber's appointment to the faculty of the Hebrew University in Jerusalem that he helped found came only after a decade of false starts from application to approval, with no shortage of speculation for the reason. It is said that some objected to what they characterized as an undisciplined teaching style, and some were put off by what they took to be his rejection of or indifference to Jewish law. What is more, he didn't have the standard academic teaching credentials; earlier in life, he had chosen not to complete all his doctoral work. When the faculty finally recommended his appointment in 1934, the trustees rejected it, but gave unanimous approval a year later, after his departmental assignment was changed from religion to sociology.[14]

Despite the challenges, Buber thrived in Israel, as did his biblical ancestors. Despite financial, cultural, and language issues—he worried that his spoken Hebrew would be inadequate for college teaching—he nevertheless advanced as a teacher, writer, and mentor of students, showing particular attention to the curiosity and energy that each of his students brought to the classroom. Among his many monumental writings while living in Israel, two stand out: the completion of the final volumes of the Hebrew-to-German Bible translation he began with Franz Rosenzweig, and his Hebrew-language *Or Ha-ganuz* (The hidden light), known to us as the two-volume *Tales of the Hasidim*. In "the air" of Israel, he "made a new beginning," and the benefits outweighed the sacrifices.

D'rash: A Personal Reflection

A VISIT TO ISRAEL

My first visit to Israel, as a college sophomore, was an orientation tour for campus activists. I tried out my Hebrew, the food, and the landscape; took in the variety, wonder, and energy of the Israeli leaders we met; and, when I returned to the United States, found myself excited about visiting again. Next trip was my first rabbinic school year at the Hebrew Union College–Jewish Institute of Religion in Jerusalem, which built my knowledge of Hebrew, gave me a flavor of daily life, and allowed me to travel the land more deeply. I've lost count of the number of times Debbie and I have been to Israel since then. Special visits included leading temple trips, one of my favorites an interfaith trip where we shared Christian and Jewish religious backgrounds, interests, and perspectives.

On our most recent visit, Debbie and I joined a Central Conference of American Rabbis arts and culture tour focusing on film, theater, music, art, and dance. We visited an artists' colony that blossomed across a former industrial neighborhood in South Tel Aviv. The entrance hall of a dim, dreary, bunker-like factory building led to the grimy doors of a freight elevator that creaked open, admitted passengers, and banged shut. The stuffed cab clambered slowly upward and doors thankfully reopened to admit fresh air and light and led us to a selection of brightly lit studios. One offered a video interpretation of the Torah's Creation story. The walls of another bore colorful portraits of women depicted as cats. Another was stuffed with wrought-iron sculptures of immigrants and their suitcases and chests, the metal bars casting full-size human shadows on the bland white studio wall.

The creativity we experienced extended to food. We visited Sindyanna, a one-of-a-kind, not-for-profit business run by Arab and Jewish women in K'far Kana in the Galilee. Sindyanna produces olive oil and other fair-trade items for sale in Israel and abroad, grown on a long-derelict firing range transformed into the country's first Jewish-Arab organic olive grove. Today the generated income enhances Arab-Jewish cooperation and women's economic empowerment. The warm and sweet welcome to Sindyanna was matched by a tasting of the oil—rich and robust. The olive oil soap bars were just the right gift to bring back home—they fit into a tightly packed suitcase and were much appreciated.

Music is central to Judaism and Israel, and Polyphony, in Nazareth, is a music school committed to advancing the arts and pluralism. Polyphony draws Arab and Jewish children for classical music training, group performance—and dialogue. Graduates have gone on to conservatories in Israel and abroad. During a student-led concert for rabbis, with a program of Schubert, Rachmaninoff, and Bach, on piano, wind, and brass, the call to prayer from a nearby minaret beckoned Muslims of that mostly Christian city. The aural blending added another layer of multicultural and interfaith harmony and demonstrated what was for us, until that moment, an unsung success in the bold venture we know as Israel.

Shavuot

Revelation, Then and Now

You, yourselves saw that I spoke to you from the very heavens.
—Exodus 20:19

*The mighty revelations to which the religions appear
are like in being with the quiet revelations that
are to be found everywhere and at all times.*
—Buber

P'shat: Explanation

Shavuot is a double celebration, a rejoicing in the year's first harvest and remembrance of the Revelation of Torah at Sinai. Mentioning the Revelation brings our commentators to question, "What really happened that day on the mountainside?" and their responses provoke animated conversation.

In a wonderful example of interpreting the Torah's sometimes puzzling language, the Rabbis note a peculiarity: Exodus tells us that the people "saw" how God "spoke" at Sinai. Why didn't the Torah say the people "heard" God speak, instead?

Hizkuni, representative of the Rabbis, is convinced that God cannot be seen. His reading—"You did not see my Glory!" (on Exod. 20:19)—disputes any suggestion that God is visible. In other words, to Hizkuni, the Torah doesn't really say the Hebrews "saw" God— even though it does. At the end, Hizkuni, like many commentators, takes the Torah's words as a figure of speech. It reminds me of all the times I hear, "Yes, I spoke with her," when actually the exchange, via text message or email, included no spoken words.

Buber would also agree with Ḥizkuni that no one literally saw God, even though the Torah says the people did. And he would probably also agree with Maimonides that the nature of God and what transpired between God and the Jewish people at Sinai are all beyond our human comprehension and capacity to explain. Going further, Buber might well point to his words in *I and Thou*, "The mighty revelations to which the religions appear are like in being with the quiet revelations that are to be found everywhere and at all times."[15] That is to say, the monumental encounter at Sinai is the spiritual equivalent of a chance meeting of two people exchanging a few, yet heartfelt, words. For an example, Buber points to banter with a railway guard or newspaper vendor or the exchange of smiles with the chimney sweep.[16] We speak of a revelation to describe the grand experience of receiving a major piece of knowledge. Yet in the Revelation of I-Thou, honest words leave an impact. Shavuot falls seven weeks after Passover, celebrates the Revelation at Sinai, and recurs whenever we "hallow the everyday."

D'rash: A Personal Reflection

A QUIET REVELATION

I was making nursing home visits during that extra pocket of time before Shabbat services. On my first visit or two with Joan, I bolted into her room, introduced myself, and expected a quick conversation, as often happens with others—but not Joan, who immediately broke my fast-paced stride. She spoke slowly and thoughtfully and listened carefully, with a presence in conversation that calmed and focused me on things that were more important than what I ordinarily might be thinking about when I'm running around.

That focus was a great gift in those hours approaching Shabbat. I felt grounded, more relaxed, and readier to think about what I wanted to be and do on Shabbat. However harried I was, when I walked through the door into Joan's room, she would take a moment to gather herself and tell me she was happy to see me in a way that brought me into her world on her terms. I slowed down and got calm.

Her husband, Roy, could have retired from work many years earlier, but kept on at the small family business, and he'd visit Joan daily after work. Sometimes I got to see him. He'd listen carefully while Joan and I spoke, and say a few words now and then, not much more. Joan had extended family in the community, yet it was clear that her granddaughter, Kathy, a newly married teacher, was her favorite. I'd occasionally get to talk with Kathy and Joan about our backgrounds, families, and interests.

Some time after the High Holy Days, I officiated at Joan's funeral. The family and I saw each other again at services in the succeeding months, and I left the congregation soon after that.

But what happened between Joan and me stays with me. An aura surrounded us, a magic in dialogue and presence, a spiritual oasis in the middle of a busy and complicated world, as if the *Shekhinah* really lived there, beneath the sheltering Tabernacle of our time together.

We are born with the ability to talk; we never asked for it. This is a gift, the word, the grace of a capacity to communicate with each other and God. From a child's first utterance to a person's last words, we enter God's Presence through the miracle of speech.

Epigraph Source Acknowledgments

I. Genesis

Martin Buber. *Between Man and Man*. New York: MacMillan, 1978, 184.

Martin Buber. *Daniel: Dialogues on Realization*. Syracuse NY: Syracuse University Press, 2018, vii, 52.

Martin Buber. *I and Thou*. New York: Scribner, 2000, 43, 49–50, 77.

Martin Buber. *Meetings: Martin Buber*. Edited by Maurice Friedman. La Salle IL: Open Court, 1973, 45, 68.

"Martin Buber to Robert C. Smith." In *Martin Buber on Psychology and Psychotherapy*, edited by Judith Agassi. Syracuse NY: Syracuse University Press, 1999, 204.

Maurice S. Friedman. *Encounter on the Narrow Ridge: A Life of Martin Buber*. New York: Paragon House, 1991, 246–47.

Maurice S. Friedman. *Martin Buber's Life and Work: The Later Years 1945–1968*. New York: Dutton, 1984, 239.

Paul R. Mendes-Flohr. *Martin Buber: A Life of Faith and Dissent*. New Haven CT: Yale University Press, 2019, 2.

Talia Zax. "Martin Buber Supported MLK in Letter to LBJ." *Jewish Daily Forward*, January 14, 2018.

II. Exodus

Martin Buber. *Eclipse of God: Studies in the Relation between Religion and Philosophy*, Amherst NY: Humanity Books, 1988, 23, 129.

Martin Buber. *I and Thou*. New York: Scribner, 2000, 28, 49, 54, 56, 111.

Martin Buber. "The Love of God and the Idea of Deity: On Hermann Cohen." In *The Writings of Martin Buber*, edited by Will Herberg. New York: Meridian Books, 1956, 103.

Martin Buber. *On Judaism*. New York: Schocken, 1972, 215.

Maurice S. Friedman. *Encounter on the Narrow Ridge: A Life of Martin Buber*. New York: Paragon House, 1991, 164, 438.

Maurice S. Friedman. *My Friendship with Martin Buber*. Syracuse NY: Syracuse University Press, 2013, 77.

III. Leviticus

Martin Buber. "Hebrew Humanism." In *Israel and the World: Essays in a Time of Crisis*. 2nd ed. New York: Schocken, 1963, 248.

Martin Buber. *I and Thou*. New York: Scribner, 2000, 26, 43, 83, 104.

Martin Buber. *Meetings: Martin Buber*. Edited by Maurice Friedman. La Salle IL: Open Court, 1973, 18.

Martin Buber. *Moses: The Revelation and the Covenant*. New York: Harper Torchbooks, 1973, 16, 178–79.

Maurice S. Friedman. *Encounter on the Narrow Ridge: A Life of Martin Buber*. New York: Paragon House, 1991, 168–69.

Rob Anderson and Kenneth N. Cissna. *The Martin Buber-Carl Rogers Dialogue: A New Transcript with Commentary*. Albany: State University of New York Press, 1997, 104.

IV. Numbers

Franz Rosenzweig. *On Jewish Learning*. New York: Schocken, 1966, 114.

Martin Buber. *I and Thou*. New York: Scribner, 2000, 41, 77, 109.

Martin Buber. *Pointing the Way*. Edited by Maurice S. Friedman. New York: Harper and Brothers, 1957, 222.

Martin Buber. *Two Types of Faith*. New York: Harper Torchbooks, 1961, 12.

Maurice S. Friedman. *Martin Buber's Life and Work: The Later Years 1945–1968*. New York: Dutton, 1984, 358, 389.

Rob Anderson and Kenneth N. Cissna. *The Martin Buber-Carl Rogers Dialogue: A New Transcript with Commentary*. Albany: State University of New York Press, 1997, 23.

V. Deuteronomy

Arthur Hertzberg, ed. *The Zionist Idea: A Historical Analysis and Reader*. New York: Atheneum House, 1973, 465.

Haim Gordon, ed. *The Other Martin Buber: Recollections of His Contemporaries*. Athens: Ohio University Press, 1988, 18.

Mahatma Gandhi. "Gandhi & Zionism: 'The Jews.'" *Harijan*, November 26, 1938. Reprinted by the Jewish Virtual Library, https://www.jewishvirtuallibrary.org/lsquo-the-jews-rsquo-by-gandhi.

Martin Buber. *I and Thou*. New York: Scribner, 2000, 30, 107.

Martin Buber. *The Letters of Martin Buber*. Edited by Nahum N. Glatzer and Paul Mendes Flohr. Syracuse NY: Syracuse University Press, 1996, 477–78.

Martin Buber. *Meetings: Martin Buber*. Edited by Maurice Friedman. La Salle IL: Open Court, 1973, 23, 26–27.

Martin Buber. *Moses: The Revelation and the Covenant*. New York: Harper Torchbooks, 1973, 102.

Martin Buber. "A New Venture in Adult Education." In *Martin Buber: The Life of Dialogue*, 4th ed., by Maurice S. Friedman. New York: Routledge, 2002, 116–20.

Martin Buber. *Pointing the Way*. Edited by Maurice S. Friedman. New York: Harper and Brothers, 1957, 232.

VI. Holidays

Dan Laor. "Agnon and Buber: The Story of a Friendship, or: The Rise and Fall of the Corpus Hasidicum." In *Martin Buber: A Contemporary Perspective*, edited by Paul Mendes-Flohr. Syracuse NY; Jerusalem: Syracuse University Press and Israel Academy of Sciences and Humanities, 2002, 68.

Grete Schaeder. *The Hebrew Humanism of Martin Buber*. Detroit MI: Wayne State University Press, 1973, 18.

Martin Buber. *I and Thou*. New York: Scribner, 2000, 38, 43, 50, 110.

Martin Buber. *Tales of the Hasidim: The Early Masters*. New York: Schocken Books, 1975, xii.

Martin Buber. *The Way of Man: According to the Teachings of Hasidism*. Secaucus NJ: Citadel Press, 1966, 11.

Maurice S. Friedman. *Encounter on the Narrow Ridge: A Life of Martin Buber*. New York: Paragon House, 1991, 247, 328.

Paul R. Mendes-Flohr. *Martin Buber: A Life of Faith and Dissent*. New Haven CT: Yale University Press, 2019, 60.

Notes

Introduction

1. Gordon, *The Other Martin Buber*, 6.
2. Buber, *I and Thou*, 11.
3. Buber, *I and Thou*, 47.
4. Friedman, *Encounter on the Narrow Ridge*, 77–78.

I. Genesis

1. Friedman, *Martin Buber's Life and Work: Early Years*, 188–90; Friedman, *Encounter on the Narrow Ridge*, 80–81, 454–55.
2. Slonimsky, "The Philosophy Implicit in the Midrash," 48–51.
3. Buber, *Tales of the Hasidim: Later Masters*, 70.
4. Buber, *Daniel*, vii.
5. "Dag Hammarskjöld, Biographical, the Nobel Peace Prize 1961," from *Nobel Lectures, Peace 1951–1970*, ed. Frederick W. Haberman (Amsterdam: Elsevier Publishing Company, 1972), available at https:// www.nobelprize.org/nobel_prizes/peace/laureates/1961/hammarskjold-bio.html, accessed November 23, 2019.
6. Marin, "Can We Save True Dialogue in an Age of Mistrust?," 4.
7. Henning Melber, "What a Photo Reveals: Dag Hammarskjöld and Dialogue," Dag Hammarskjöld Foundation, March 1, 2016, https:// www.daghammarskjold.se/2341-2, accessed March 17, 2021.
8. Marin, "Can We Save True Dialogue in an Age of Mistrust?," 14–15, 21.
9. Marin, "Can We Save True Dialogue in an Age of Mistrust?," 18–19.
10. Marin, "Can We Save True Dialogue in an Age of Mistrust?," 28.
11. Friedman, *Martin Buber's Life and Work: Later Years*, 310–19; Mendes-Flohr, *Martin Buber*, 313; Marin, "Can We Save True Dialogue in an Age of Mistrust?," 63–66.
12. Buber, *Tales of the Hasidim: Early Masters*, 130.
13. Mendes-Flohr, *Martin Buber*, 95–109.
14. Friedman, *Martin Buber's Life and Work: Early Years*, 33–73.

15. Buber, *Tales of the Hasidim: Later Masters*, 92.

16. Buber, *Tales of the Hasidim: Later Masters*, 44.

17. Buber, *Tales of the Hasidim: Later Masters*, 251.

18. Martin Luther King Jr., "Letter from a Birmingham Jail," April 16, 1963, Center for Africana Studies, University of Pennsylvania, https://www.africa.upenn.edu/Articles_Gen/Letter_Birmingham.html, accessed November 25, 2019.

II. Exodus

1. Buber, *Tales of the Hasidim: The Later Masters*, 134.

2. Friedman, *Encounter on the Narrow Ridge*, 208.

3. Friedman, *Martin Buber's Life and Work: Later Years*, 25–26.

4. Friedman, *Encounter on the Narrow Ridge*, 201–2.

5. Buber, *The Legend of the Baal-Shem*, 41.

6. Friedman, *Encounter on the Narrow Ridge*, 135; Herman, *I and Tao*, 60.

7. Buber, *I and Thou*, 49.

8. Friedman, *Encounter on the Narrow Ridge*, 438.

9. Buber, *Eclipse of God*, 23, 129.

10. Michael Lipka, "10 Facts about Atheists," *Fact Tank*, Pew Research Center, December 6, 2019, http://www.pewresearch.org/fact-tank/2016/06/01/10-facts-about-atheists/.

11. Mendes-Flohr, *Martin Buber*, 8, 154.

12. Gordon, *The Other Martin Buber*, 22.

13. Buber, *Tales of the Hasidim: Early Masters*, 27–28, 226.

14. Friedman, *Encounter on the Narrow Ridge*, 257; Gordon, *The Other Martin Buber*, 25.

15. Buber, *I and Thou*, 56.

16. Buber, *Tales of the Hasidim: Early Masters*, 292.

III. Leviticus

1. Buber, *I and Thou*, 26.

2. See Dennis S. Ross, "What Does Martin Buber Have to Do with 'Will & Grace'?," *ReformJudaism.org* blog, September 26, 2017, https://reformjudaism.org/blog/2017/09/26/what-does-martin-buber-have-do-will-grace, accessed August 28, 2020.

3. Buber, *I and Thou*, 104.

4. Friedman, *My Friendship with Martin Buber*, 35–36.

5. Friedman, *Encounter on the Narrow Ridge*, 334.

6. Mendes-Flohr, *Martin Buber*, 1–7.

7. Friedman, *Encounter on the Narrow Ridge*, 4–5.

8. Friedman, *Martin Buber's Life and Work: Later Years*, 385.

9. See Anderson and Cissna, *The Martin Buber-Carl Rogers Dialogue*.

10. Buber, *Moses*, 16.

11. Buber, *Tales of the Hasidim: Later Masters*, 177.

12. Friedman, *Encounter on the Narrow Ridge*, 22; Mendes-Flohr, *Martin Buber*, 8.

13. Friedman, *Martin Buber's Life and Work: Early Years*, 34–73.

14. Mendes-Flohr, *Martin Buber*, 259–60.

15. Buber, "Hebrew Humanism (1942)," in Hertzberg, *The Zionist Idea*, 457–63.

16. Mendes-Flohr, *Martin Buber*, 109; Friedman, *Martin Buber's Life and Work: Early Years*, 220–21.

17. Mendes-Flohr, *Martin Buber*, 108–9.

18. Chaim Stern, "Prayer," unpublished sermon delivered at Temple Beth El of Northern Westchester on November 11, 1982.

19. Buber, *Meetings*, 22–23.

20. Buber, *Moses: The Revelation and the Covenant*, 178–79.

21. Buber, *Martin Buber's Life and Work: Early Years*, 263–68.

22. Chaim Stern, untitled, unpublished sermon, delivered at Temple Beth El of Northern Westchester, Rosh Hashanah 1972.

23. Friedman, *Encounter on the Narrow Ridge*, 168–69.

24. Glatzer, *Franz Rosenzweig*, 149–57, 367.

IV. Numbers

1. Sarna, *Exploring Exodus: The Heritage of Biblical Israel*, 40–41, 214.

2. Seltzer, *Jewish People, Jewish Thought*, 752–57.

3. Friedman, *My Friendship with Martin Buber*, xvii.

4. Friedman, *Encounter on the Narrow Ridge*, 459.

5. Heschel, *The Sabbath*.

6. Friedman, *Martin Buber's Life and Work: Early Years*, 4, 6, 11.

7. Buber, *Meetings*, 21–22.

8. Friedman, *Encounter on the Narrow Ridge*, 251–52; Gordon, *The Other Martin Buber*, 25, 54.

9. Buber, *Moses*, 156.

10. Buber, *Tales of the Hasidim: Later Masters*, 69.

11. Buber, *I and Thou*, 77.

12. Used with permission. Published in Stern, *Gates of Forgiveness*.

13. Friedman, *Encounter on the Narrow Ridge*, 169–70.

14. Buber, *Tales of the Hasidim: Early Masters*, 22.

15. Buber, *Tales of the Hasidim: Later Masters*, 89.

16. Buber, *Pointing the Way*, 222.

17. Friedman, *Encounter on the Narrow Ridge*, 99–115.

18. Friedman, *Encounter on the Narrow Ridge*, 162.

19. Rosenzweig, *On Jewish Learning*, 114.

20. Friedman, *Encounter on the Narrow Ridge*, 197–98.

21. Friedman, *Encounter on the Narrow Ridge*, 333–34.

22. Friedman, *Martin Buber's Life and Work: Later Years*, 358.

23. Friedman, *Martin Buber's Life and Work: Later Years*, 356–64.

24. "'. . . tough, brilliant, unobjectionable . . . ,' The Writer Paula Buber (1877–1958)," Jewish Museum, Augsburg Swabia, http://www.aejm. org/exhibitions/tough-brilliant-unobjectionable-writer-paula-buber-1877-1958/; "Ausstellungsprojekt Leben und Werk Paula Buber," Augsburg University, https://www.uni-augsburg.de/de/fakultaet/philhist/professuren/germanistik/neuere-deutsche-literaturwissenschaft-2/ausstellugen/ausstellungsprojekt-leben-und-werk-paula-buber/; "Incredibly Clever: Iris Berben Reads Paula Buber," Jewish Museum, Berlin, https://www.jmberlin.de/en/cultural-summer-incredibly-clever, all accessed September 29, 2020.

25. Gordon, *The Other Martin Buber*, 13.

26. Buber, *Tales of the Hasidim: Later Masters*, 86.

27. Anderson and Cissna, *The Martin Buber-Carl Rogers Dialogue*, 23.

28. Gordon, *The Other Martin Buber*, 57.

29. Buber, *Two Types of Faith*, 12.

30. Buber, *Meetings*, 42–44; Friedman, *Martin Buber's Life and Work: Early Years*, 42, 185–87, 300–301.

V. Deuteronomy

1. Gordon, *The Other Martin Buber*, 18.

2. Buber, *Tales of the Hasidim: Later Masters*, 161.

3. Gordon, *The Other Martin Buber*, 101.

4. Orlinsky, "Nationalism-Universalism and Internationalism," 117–43.

5. Buber, "A New Venture in Adult Education," in Friedman, *Martin Buber: The Life of Dialogue*, 116–20.

6. Robert Farley, "Obama and 'American Exceptionalism,'" Fact-Check.org, February 12, 2015, https://www.factcheck.org/2015/02/obama-and-american-exceptionalism/, accessed March 18, 2021.

7. Abraham Lincoln, "Address to the New Jersey State Senate," February 21, 1861, from *The Collected Works of Abraham Lincoln*, edited by Roy P. Basler et al., available at Abraham Lincoln Online, http://www.abrahamlincolnonline.org/lincoln/speeches/trenton1.htm, accessed November 30, 2015.

8. Buber, *Tales of the Hasidim: Early Masters*, 74.

9. Buber, *Tales of the Hasidim: Later Masters*, 163.

10. Friedman, *Encounter on the Narrow Ridge*, 10.

11. Buber, *Tales of the Hasidim: Later Masters*, 197.

12. Mahatma Gandhi, "Gandhi & Zionism: 'The Jews,'" *Harijan*, November 26, 1938, reprinted by the Jewish Virtual Library, https://www.jewishvirtuallibrary.org/lsquo-the-jews-rsquo-by-gandhi, accessed October 31, 2020.

13. Friedman, *Encounter on the Narrow Ridge*, 274–75.

14. Friedman, *Martin Buber's Life and Work: Later Years*, 31; Gandhi, "Gandhi & Zionism: 'The Jews.'"

15. Friedman, *Encounter on the Narrow Ridge*, 242, 437; Gordon, *The Other Martin Buber*, 163.

16. Buber, *I and Thou*, 94.

17. Leibowitz, *Studies in Bereshit*, 317–24.

18. Gordon, *The Other Martin Buber*, 14.

19. Friedman, *Encounter on the Narrow Ridge*, 209–10.

20. Gandhi, "Gandhi & Zionism: 'The Jews.'"

21. Mendes-Flohr, *Martin Buber*, 243.

22. Friedman, *Encounter on the Narrow Ridge*, 269–70.

23. Gordon, *The Other Martin Buber*, 38.

24. Buber, *Moses*, 102.

25. Gordon, *The Other Martin Buber*, 102.

26. Friedman, *Martin Buber's Life and Work: Later Years*, 396.

27. Mendes-Flohr, *Martin Buber*, 322–24.

VI. Holidays

1. Buber, *The Way of Man*, 11.

2. Glatzer, *Franz Rosenzweig*, 24–25.

3. Rosenzweig, *The Star of Redemption*, 327.

4. Buber, *I and Thou*, 38.

5. Buber, *I and Thou*, 43.

6. Laor, "Agnon and Buber," 48–86.

7. Buber, *Tales of the Hasidim: Early Masters*, 232.

8. Buber, *Tales of the Hasidim: Later Masters*, 73.

9. Buber, *Tales of the Hasidim: Early Masters*, 251.

10. Mendes-Flohr, *Martin Buber*, 56–60.

11. Friedman, *Encounter on the Narrow Ridge*, 124.

12. Jewish Telegraphic Agency, "Prof. Buber Presented with 'Hanseatic Goethe Prize' in Germany," June 25, 1953, https://www.jta.org/1953/06/25/archive/prof-buber-presented-with-hanseatic-goethe-prize-in-germany, accessed March 18, 2021.

13. Friedman, *Encounter on the Narrow Ridge*, 327–28.

14. Mendes-Flohr, *Martin Buber*, 202–7.

15. Buber, *I and Thou*, 110.

16. Friedman, *Martin Buber's Life and Work: Middle Years*, 115.

Selected Bibliography

Anderson, Rob, and Kenneth N. Cissna. *The Martin Buber-Carl Rogers Dialogue: A New Transcript with Commentary.* Albany: State University of New York Press, 1997.

Buber, Martin. *Between Man and Man.* New York: MacMillan, 1978.

———. *Daniel: Dialogues on Realization.* Syracuse NY: Syracuse University Press, 2018.

———. *Eclipse of God: Studies in the Relation between Religion and Philosophy.* Amherst NY: Humanity Books, 1988.

———. *I and Thou.* New York: Scribner, 2000.

———. *Israel and the World: Essays in a Time of Crisis.* 2nd ed. New York: Schocken Books, 1963.

———. *The Knowledge of Man: A Philosophy.* Edited by Maurice S. Friedman. New York: Harper, 1965.

———. *The Legend of the Baal-Shem.* New York: Schocken, 1969.

———. *The Letters of Martin Buber.* Edited by Nahum N. Glatzer and Paul Mendes Flohr. Syracuse NY: Syracuse University Press, 1996.

———. *Meetings: Martin Buber.* Edited by Maurice Friedman. La Salle IL: Open Court, 1973.

———. *Moses: The Revelation and the Covenant.* New York: Harper Torchbooks, 1973.

———. "A New Venture in Adult Education." In *Martin Buber: The Life of Dialogue*, edited by Maurice S. Friedman. 4th ed. New York: Routledge, 2002, 116–20.

———. *On Judaism.* New York: Schocken, 1972.

———. *Pointing the Way.* Edited by Maurice S. Friedman. New York: Harper and Brothers, 1957.

———. *Tales of the Hasidim: The Early Masters.* New York: Schocken Books, 1975.

———. *Tales of the Hasidim: The Later Masters.* New York: Schocken Books, 1975.

———. *Two Types of Faith.* New York: Harper Torchbooks, 1961.

———. *The Way of Man: According to the Teachings of Hasidism.* Secaucus NJ: Citadel Press, 1966.

Friedman, Maurice S. *Encounter on the Narrow Ridge: A Life of Martin Buber*. New York: Paragon House, 1991.

———. *Martin Buber: The Life of Dialogue*. 4th ed. New York: Routledge, 2002.

———. *Martin Buber's Life and Work: The Early Years 1878–1923*. New York: Dutton, 1982.

———. *Martin Buber's Life and Work: The Middle Years 1923–1945*. New York: Dutton, 1983.

———. *Martin Buber's Life and Work: The Later Years 1945–1968*. New York: Dutton, 1984.

———. *My Friendship with Martin Buber*. Syracuse NY: Syracuse University Press, 2013.

———. *Pointing the Way*. New York: Harper and Brothers, 1957.

Glatzer, Nahum M., ed. *Franz Rosenzweig: His Life and Thought*. New York: Schocken, 1961.

Gordon, Haim, ed. *The Other Martin Buber: Recollections of His Contemporaries*. Athens: Ohio University Press, 1988.

Herberg, Will, ed. *The Writings of Martin Buber*. New York: Meridian Books, 1956.

Herman, Jonathan R. *I and Tao: Martin Buber's Encounter with Chuang Tzu*. Albany: State University of New York Press, 1996.

Hertzberg, Arthur, ed. *The Zionist Idea: A Historical Analysis and Reader*. New York: Atheneum House, 1973.

Heschel, Abraham Joshua. *The Sabbath*. New York: Farrar, Straus and Giroux, 2005. Originally published 1951.

Laor, Dan. "Agnon and Buber: The Story of a Friendship, or: The Rise and Fall of the Corpus Hasidicum." In *Martin Buber: A Contemporary Perspective*, edited by Paul Mendes-Flohr, 48–86. Syracuse NY; Jerusalem: Syracuse University Press and Israel Academy of Sciences and Humanities, 2002.

Leibowitz, Nehama. *Studies in Bereshit (Genesis) in the Context of Ancient and Modern Jewish Bible Commentary*. Translated by Aryeh Newman. 4th ed. Jerusalem: World Zionist Organization, 1981.

Marin, Lou. "Can We Save True Dialogue in an Age of Mistrust? The Encounter of Dag Hammarskjöld and Martin Buber." *Critical Currents*, no. 8. Uppsala, Sweden: Dag Hammarskjöld Foundation, January 2010.

"Martin Buber to Robert C. Smith." In *Martin Buber on Psychology and Psychotherapy*, edited by Judith Agassi. Syracuse NY: Syracuse University Press, 1999.

Mendes-Flohr, Paul R. *Martin Buber: A Life of Faith and Dissent*. New Haven CT: Yale University Press, 2019.

Oliver, Roy. *The Wanderer and the Way: The Hebrew Tradition in the Writings of Martin Buber.* London: Horovitz, 1968.

Orlinsky, Harry. "Nationalism-Universalism and Internationalism." In *Essays in Biblical Culture and Bible Translation.* New York: KTAV, 1974.

Rosenzweig, Franz. *On Jewish Learning.* New York: Schocken, 1966.

———. *The Star of Redemption.* Boston: Beacon Press, 1971.

Sarna, Nahum M. *Exploring Exodus: The Heritage of Biblical Israel.* New York: Schocken, 1986.

Schaeder, Grete. *The Hebrew Humanism of Martin Buber.* Detroit MI: Wayne State University Press, 1973.

Seltzer, Robert M. *Jewish People, Jewish Thought: The Jewish Experience in History.* New York: Macmillan, 1980.

Slonimsky, Henry. "The Philosophy Implicit in the Midrash." In *Essays,* 48–51. Cincinnati OH: Hebrew Union College Press, 1967.

Stern, Chaim, ed. *Gates of Forgiveness: The Union Selichot Service.* New York: Central Conference of American Rabbis, 1980.

In the JPS Daily Inspiration Series

*A Year with Martin Buber: Wisdom
on the Weekly Torah Portion*
Rabbi Dennis S. Ross

*A Year with the Sages: Wisdom
on the Weekly Torah Portion*
Rabbi Reuven Hammer

*A Year with Mordecai Kaplan:
Wisdom on the Weekly Torah Portion*
Rabbi Steven Carr Reuben
Foreword by Rabbi David A. Teutsch

To order or obtain more information on
these or other Jewish Publication Society
titles, visit jps.org.